Know Your Enemy...
by knowing your God

Learn more about this book and its
author by visiting our web site:

www.overboardministries.com

Cover design by Alicia Munro
Photo credit: Dan and Melissa Clark

This title is available for your favorite eReader. Visit
our web site to choose the format
that's right for you.

All comments or requests for
information should be sent to:
overboard@overboardministries.com

ENDORSEMENTS

Talk about being open and candid about your feelings and struggles! Kori is, and she takes the battles for the mind and spirit seriously as she pushes you to the revealed Word and will of God for peace and winning. Sensitive to God's Spirit–she calls Him "the Commander" in her life–she takes you with her through many emotions and ends up at the cross of our Lord for security and strength.

Knute Larson
Pastoral Coach

* * * * *

I have labored for years helping people all over the world find their identity and freedom in Christ. Then comes Kori, who not only gets it, but shares in the most practical and personal way how every believer can listen to God, and win the battle for their minds over the world, the flesh, and the devil.

Dr. Neil T. Anderson
Founder and President Emeritus of Freedom in Christ Ministries

For Jill

Years ago I jokingly said that I would dedicate my first book to you—never dreaming that I would ever really write one. Thanks for seeing something in me that I didn't see in myself and calling me out. May everyone have a Jill in their lives.

For Craig

If you didn't tell me point-blank, "Kori, you need to write your book now," I never would have had the courage to start.Without you I would still be at the top of the cliff, paralyzed by fear. Thanks for pushing me over the edge.

For Jesus

Thank you for wanting me.

PRAYER OF BLESSING

Heavenly Father,

With hearts full of joy, we honor you as Lord of creation and trust you as Redeemer of our lives. We praise you for destroying the works of the devil and for delivering those who were subject to lifelong slavery (Hebrews 2:14-15). We thank you that through your Son, Jesus, you have rescued us from the dominion of darkness and given us a firm and lasting hope in the resurrection. We bless your holy Name!

Until Christ returns, your Word tells us to "wage the good warfare" and to "fight the good fight of faith" (2 Timothy). To that end, I pray you would use this book as a tool to equip your people for battle. In a day where many people are lovers of evil, I pray that your church will put on the full armor of God and stand firm against all the schemes of the devil.

Our chief prayer, O Lord, is that your Name be glorified. Take this offering and multiply its impact as Christ multiplied the small lunch on the shores of Galilee. We acknowledge your Lordship over all things. For we recognize that "from you, and through you, and to you belong all things. To you be the glory forever" (Romans 11).

Craig Trierweiler
Author's Husband
Pastor, New Hope Community Church

"And though this world, with devils filled, should threaten to undo us, we will not fear, for God hath willed, his truth to triumph through us. The Prince of Darkness grim, we tremble not for him; his rage we can endure, for lo, his doom is sure; one little word shall fell him."
(A Mighty Fortress)

CONTENTS

Dedication   v

Note from the Author   ix

Prayer for the Reader   xi

1   The Commander's Voice   1

2   Spiritual Mind Battles   21

3   Spiritual Weapons   37

4   The Battle Against the World   59

5   Identifying Worldly Mindsets   77

6   Identifying Worldly Cravings   97

7   More Spiritual Weapons   117

8   The Battle Against the Flesh   143

9   Identifying Fleshly Motives   161

10 Identifying Fleshly Attitudes   181

11 Even More Spiritual Weapons   197

12 The Battle Against the Devil   219

13 Identifying Generational Strongholds   243

14 Identifying Territorial Strongholds   263

15 The Battle Plan   281

References   293

Acknowledgements   295

About the Author   301

NOTE FROM THE AUTHOR

Dear Fellow Warriors,

I address you as warriors because you are, whether or not you feel like it. It is my prayer that throughout the pages of this book, you begin to realize who you are and what you are capable of in Christ Jesus. Think of this as an interactive book, where you and I and the Commander God are sitting down with a cup of coffee, having an important meeting. As I tell about my battle stories, failures, victories and lessons learned, listen for the voice of the Holy Spirit speaking directly to you. Our Commander God is able and willing to highlight your own mind battles, struggles, and conquests, revealing truth and setting you free. Then you can write your own book as the Lord gives you an abundance of war stories to fight through, remember and tell others.

My heart is in this book; I don't know any other way to write. There is a **fight** in me to see God's people set free from the ways in which the world, the flesh and the devil have attacked and bound us. But even more than all of that, I want you to know Jesus afresh because when you know Jesus, you have access to everything else that you will ever need! I am praying for you. With all of the strength that God has given me, I am pushing you toward Jesus. He is the One you want. He is the One Who has all that you require to overcome and accomplish MORE than you can even imagine. I have battled in prayer for you, my friends.

Ultimately, this book is an act of obedience to my God. He asked me to write about my relationship with Him and the lessons He has taught me through the years. I am deeply in love with Him and since He has asked me to do this, how can I refuse Him? But it has not been an easy task. In fact, I have fought many fierce battles to write this, but the Lord is my help; He has stayed with me every step of the way and has trained me for war. It has been a great adventure. May Jesus be pleased with my sack-lunch offering. Lord, here are my five loaves and two fish, given to You to do whatever You want with them.

Know that you are deeply loved by God and covered in prayer!

Kori Trierweiler

My prayer for you as you read
Know Your Enemy:

That you would know your God and carry out great exploits. That you will have heroic, daring, bold adventures with Jesus and accomplish great achievements for and with Him. *"But the people that do know their God shall be strong, and do exploits"* (Daniel 11:32).

That as you read this book, you would experience unveiled "Face Time" with Jesus Christ, where you can literally ask Him *anything* and He will reveal it to you. That your face-to-face with Jesus would be deeply satisfying, build your faith, and spill over into every area of your life so that you experience "Face Time" with Jesus wherever you go . . . for the rest of your life. *"The LORD would speak to Moses face to face, as one speaks to a friend"* (Exodus 33:11a).

That as you read this book, God will give you a hunger and a passion to read His book—the Bible. That any negative thoughts, past experiences or demonic influences you have endured would be lifted, so that you are able to read the Bible with passion, understanding, endurance, and excitement. That you would desire the Word of God and prayer more than you desire any other thing in this world. That this book would accelerate your growth in Christ Jesus and propel you to seek hard after God just as David did in Psalm 63.

That you would experience spiritual "Aha Moments" as divine lightbulbs go off in your mind, enabling you to discover lies that you have believed about God, yourself, others or the devil. That the pure light of the Scriptures referenced in *Know Your Enemy* would illuminate your mind so you can clearly see the thoughts that are good/true and the thoughts that are false/destructive. That God would give you the gift of discernment to spiritually see the enemy and all the tactics/lies he has thrown at you throughout your life.

That you would choose to refuse, like Moses chose to refuse, the temporary things of this world in order to gain the eternal delights of the kingdom of heaven.

> *By faith, Moses, when grown, refused the privileges of the Egyptian royal house. He chose a hard life with God's people rather than an opportunistic soft life of sin with the oppressors. He valued suffering in the Messiah's camp far greater than Egyptian wealth because he was looking ahead, anticipating the payoff. By an act of faith, he turned his heel on Egypt, indifferent to the king's blind rage. He had his eye on the One no eye can see, and kept right on going. (Hebrews 11:24-27 MSG)*

That you would love what God loves and hate what He hates. That you would have the discernment to see the discrepancy between what the world promises and what it really delivers: bondage! That God would make the things of this world lose their attraction for you as you see Jesus face-to-face and allow the Source of all beauty, hope, pleasure and delight to meet your every need!

That you would invite God to do MORE in your life through this book than you can think, ask, or even imagine! *"Now to him who is able to do immeasurably more than all we ask or imagine, according to his power that is at work within us"* (Ephesians 3:20). That you will be bold and testify of the excellencies of Him who has called you out of darkness and into His marvelous light! *"But you are a chosen race, a royal priesthood, a holy nation, a people for his own possession, that you may proclaim the excellencies of him who called you out of darkness into his marvelous light"* (1 Peter 2:9).

That you will know beyond a shadow of a doubt that you are a child of God by the saving work of Jesus at the Cross. That as God's child, you believe Him when He says He has made you **amazing and holy** by giving you His heart, His mind, His Spirit, and His nature. *"As obedient children, let yourselves be pulled into a way of life shaped by God's life, a life energetic and blazing with holiness. God said, 'I am holy; you be holy'"* (1 Peter 1:15-16 MSG). May you know and embrace this truth to the core of your being and walk in a God-confidence the devil can't touch and none can rival. May the Lord give you a vision of who you **will be** in your position in heaven so that even now you will believe and grow up into that position, making it a reality for you! May the voices of defeat, discouragement, inferiority and fear be silenced over you and stop paralyzing you from confidently doing all the good works God has called you to do throughout your life.

> *But those who seek and demand my life to ruin and destroy it shall [themselves be destroyed and] go into the lower parts of the earth [into the underworld of the dead]. They shall be given over to the power of the sword; they shall be a prey for foxes and jackals. But the king shall rejoice in God; everyone who swears by Him [that is, who binds himself by God's authority, acknowledging His supremacy, and devoting himself to His glory and service alone; every such one] shall glory, for the mouths of those who speak lies shall be stopped. (Psalm 63:9-11 AMP)*

It's time to live in freedom, friend, because you are needed!

That someday when our battle here is over and we are experiencing the joys of the new heavens and the new earth, may you and I sit down at a banquet table for a feast and tell battle stories! May we marvel together at the greatness of our God, sharing in the plunder and richness of the kingdom of heaven. And at that time, you will *know* me and I will *know* you and I will be honored to know you as one of the great, well-known, famous warriors throughout the heavenlies because of your great faith in God.

And finally, that you would fall madly in love with Jesus and forever increase in your love for Him! I ask this not for you as much as I ask this for HIM! This desire, that His people would know and love Him, is the very heart of our God. When all is said and done, this is what Jesus wants of us. It is why Jesus died and it is why the Father gave us as a gift to His Son. May Jesus have His heart's desire over you!

I pray all of these things in the mighty, limitless, powerful name of Jesus Christ and I ask the Father to seal this prayer with the purifying blood of the Lamb. Amen.

Chapter One
The Commander's Voice

"My sheep hear my voice, and I know them,
and they follow me."
John 10:27

I was in MommyGo mode. It's what I call it when I'm trying to herd all my children toward a goal that no one seems to be aware of but me. It kind of feels like I'm a coach (or sometimes a drill sergeant) randomly shouting out instructions that my kids may or may not follow. We had 20 minutes to get to school and *a lot* to accomplish so the MommyGo mode began: "Darci, what are you doing still in bed? I woke you up 15 minutes ago! Ella, you need to go find your other shoe; I think I saw it in the car. Who hasn't had breakfast yet? Come on, you sleepy-heads, we've got to get moving. Wow, buddy, you *need* your diaper changed! Honey, what do you mean you can't find your backpack; didn't you leave it by the back door? And which do you want in your lunch, a banana or peanut butter crackers?"

With four kids my morning routine can be crazy, but that morning we hit the ground running. Before the madness began, I had crawled out of bed early to meet with the Lord. This particular morning He was teaching me His Word and I really connected with the truth of the passage. My heart was filled with gratitude as I told Him out loud—though not so loud as to wake up sleeping children—that He was an amazing Teacher! I expressed to Him that I loved learning from Him and He was the best Teacher I ever had.

All too soon, the time passed and the kids started to stir. Now, fast-forward to MommyGo mode. In the midst of the rush to get out the door Annika, who was six, found a used sticker while packing her bag for school. I was busy making her lunch when she came up behind me and stuck the sticker on my shirt. "That," she said matter-of-factly, "is from Jesus. My teacher gave it to me and now I am giving it to you." Consumed with the busyness of morning activities, I think I said something like, "That's nice, honey, now go brush your teeth." I was moving right along to the next thing before I really *heard* what she had just told me. My mind replayed her words. *She said her teacher gave it to her. She's giving it to me. It's from Jesus. That's weird. Why would she say that? Why would she say it's from Jesus?*

At that moment I sensed my Father's voice telling me, *Kori, I want you to look at that sticker.* So I put down the jelly knife, quickly yanked on the shoulder of my shirt and took a good look at the sticker. Right there, staring me in the face, it said **Student of the Day!** *Aww!* In a moment, all the crazy activity of the morning ceased. I knew this was no mistake or random thing but rather, it was my very real God responding directly back to my words to Him that morning. Emotions of love and delight washed over me as I soaked in my Father's pleasure for me. Not so much in words but more in a knowing, I could hear my Father tell me, *You think I'm a good Teacher. Well, Kori, I think you're a pretty good student.* I still have that sticker and will always keep it, because that experience was the beginning of a whole new level of learning how to discern the voice of the Father from all the other voices that for years have clouded my mind.

Communication with our Commander

I hope you know this already but if you don't, I should probably break the news to you: We are in a war—a spiritual war. It's an *invisible* war where we see very *visible* side effects. This is why we struggle, this is why life is hard, this is why there is pain, dysfunction and death. We have an enemy. His name is Satan and he is constantly seeking to lie, tempt, accuse, deceive and destroy mankind. He does this by relentlessly bombarding us with thoughts and lies that do not line up with God's truth. We fight daily battles in the arena of our minds, whether or not we recognize them.

In every army there is a line of command. At the highest level there is a commander or king who makes decisions, plans strategies, and disperses assignments. God is over all and interacts with us in many different ways. He is Lord, Father, Creator, Master, Friend, Comforter, and Savior. In this book I want to focus on God's place in our lives as the Ruler and Commander of the armies of the kingdom of heaven.

All of us who have put our trust in Jesus Christ belong to this kingdom and serve God, the Commander. In the battles we face in this spiritual war, we have the privilege to go directly to the top and communicate with the Commander of the armies of the kingdom of heaven at any time. In fact, our only salvation and key to survival is our continued and detailed interaction with our Commander God. We need to hear His voice to receive His comprehensive instructions in a moment, in a split second. In a military unit, each soldier is required to stay in contact with his commanding officer, reporting to and receiving his assignments from his superior. Even when he's out in the field there are times he must have his radio com unit turned on and tuned to the right frequency in order to communicate with his superior. Likewise, we must have our spiritual ears tuned in to the right voice so that we can receive the correct information. But unlike the soldier who is restricted to interact only with his immediate supervisor, our God cut out the middle man and allows us to go straight to the highest authority, for He is Lord and Commander of all. God has the ability to cut through our busy minds and speak to us. This is the way He designed us, but we must train ourselves to be well acquainted with His voice. Our God is willing and able to alert us to danger, direct our path or encourage us to hold on when help is on its way. He is our lifeline as He personally trains and guides us through the many battles we face. But we will not be victorious warriors in the armies of heaven if we do not proactively train to hear the Commander's Voice.

Our God wants to speak to us, but we have to train our ears to hear Him. The place we do this is in the Word of God. We must read it, study it, meditate on it and memorize it. It is life to us and it develops us into spiritual maturity. If we are not reading God's Word we will be, at best, stuck in spiritual infancy or, at worst, completely vulnerable to the enemy's attacks. *"For the word of God is living and active . . . discerning the thoughts and intentions of the heart"* (Hebrews 4:12-13). The Word of God is powerful and it is the only book that is alive. The Lord has chosen His Spirit to hover over and within the words of Scripture. There is treasure in every passage but we have to dig for it. It has been said that it doesn't matter how much of the Word of God you get through, it matters how much of the Word of God gets through you. As we consume the words of the Bible, God will transform us to become more like Christ and equip us for the battles we face every day. *"As newborn babes, desire the pure milk of the word, that you may grow thereby, if indeed you have tasted that the Lord is gracious"* (1 Peter 2:2-3 NKJV).

What we think about a certain situation fuels our behavior, for better or for worse. If I have the wrong perspective about something, that skewed understanding will affect both my approach to the topic and my behavior that follows. So from an early age our enemy, the devil, will surround us with lying voices, seeking to confuse and keep us from the truth about God, ourselves, others and even himself.

As a pastor's kid I was taught early on about the ways of Christianity. One of the things ingrained in me was that we need to read our Bible every day, and this is true. I wanted to be a good Christian, so I would faithfully read my Bible, feel really good about myself, and then check it off my to-do list. What I didn't see then was that my focus was on my own efforts, not on knowing Jesus. Just like the religious leaders in Jesus' day, I read the Bible but didn't really *know* who Jesus was. *"You search the Scriptures because you think that in them you have eternal life; and it is they that bear witness about me [Jesus], yet you refuse to come to me that you may have life"* (John 5:39-40). I didn't understand that reading the Bible is not about duty but is a gift from the Lord, for me to experience a real and personal relationship with an amazingly approachable God. How could I miss this? You guessed it: I had the wrong perspective! I needed the Commander to change the way that I thought about it. I remember when He spoke to my heart and told me He wanted to be in charge of my "devotions." What I know now, but didn't know then, was that He wanted to remove my feelings of obligation, guilt, shame, and self-effort, making my time with Him more of an essential and desired friendship than just an item on my to-do list.

There are many different methods to reading through Scripture, but the Commander did something new in me as He began to lead me in a way I had never before experienced. I would get up in the mornings and quietly ask Him: *Okay, God, where do You want me to start reading in Your Word today?* Then I would just wait for Him to put His thoughts in my mind. Sometimes it was a familiar passage or a fragment of a verse I had to find. Other times He would simply whisper a thought, *Go to John 6.* I would turn directly to that passage and begin reading, waiting for the voice of my Commander to illuminate a portion of Scripture for me. When He stopped me at a verse, I would ask Him questions as if He were sitting next to me. Sometimes I would be led to read the cross-reference verses or go to the topical index in the back of my Bible. The more I followed these particular thoughts, the more I realized they weren't my thoughts as much as they were God's thoughts in my mind prompting me along and teaching me through His Word. I began to identify these thoughts as different from my own—they were somehow distinct. I knew that these were not my own reflections or distractions because each thought led me directly to truth and the Word of God. The more I allowed Him to lead, the more it changed my approach to reading the Bible. I was learning how to identify and trust the distinct voice of God as we traveled through Scripture. One passage would lead to another as a common theme surfaced, which He might connect to a situation I faced only the day before, giving me insight and direction. At first it was like learning how to walk, carefully testing those thoughts, ideas, memories and situations through the Word. As I cautiously stepped out to obey His prompting, He would then meet me on the other side of obedience to confirm it was truly Him. I was in awe of His ability to speak and direct me in the little details of my life as if nothing was beyond His sight, His control, or too trivial for Him.

Since then God has been faithful to lead me one step at a time, building my faith in hearing and obeying that still, small voice. Now I have not only learned how to walk but at times it feels like we are running and even dancing through Scripture, led by the Commander Who is teaching and training me, connecting my thoughts and memories and opening the amazing truths of His Word. The more time I spend with Him in the Word, the more equipped I am to distinguish His thoughts, ideas and directions from all the other thoughts that run through my mind. And believe me, His thoughts are so much more exciting than mine!

God's Distinct Voice

"Hey, aren't you Mike Henry?" People would recognize my dad even though they had never seen him. When I was fourteen, he was the manager and DJ at our local Christian radio station. He hosted the morning show *Coffee with Mike,* and his voice was known to a large listening audience. One day when my mom and dad were enjoying lunch at an out-of-town restaurant, a man overheard my dad's conversation and recognized his voice. Even though this man had never seen my dad, he identified him based solely on the distinctiveness of his voice. Now, I could try to describe my dad's voice to you—it's deep, a bit authoritative sounding, with a hint of dry humor—but you wouldn't be able to recognize it like one of his radio listeners could. Even more than his radio audience, my sisters and I have no problem picking out my dad's voice because we grew up hearing it every day.

The same is true of our Father God. He has a very distinct voice as well, and it is our privilege as His children to hear His voice, know His voice, and obey His voice. The Bible is where He trains us to recognize His voice from all the other voices that come into our minds. When I'm reading a passage of Scripture I usually ask God questions just as I would if a friend was sitting next to me. I invite you to do the same thing. If you don't understand something, ask Him to help you understand it. After you ask your question, you might get the *slightest impression* to look at the footnotes or check the cross-reference passages or turn to another verse, or maybe it's just a gentle nudge to keep reading. Pay attention! Friends, *that* is the voice I'm talking about! When you get that nudge, at that moment you have a choice: to follow that impression or to ignore it. I have been there and, at times, chosen not to follow that voice, but when I do follow it I am never disappointed.

So when you're reading the Bible and a passage speaks about being kind to others, ask Him if there is any area in your life where He would like to see you be more kind. Usually you won't have to wait too long before you will get a thought about a person in your life or a situation where you could have been more gracious. Or maybe He'll put a person you barely know on your mind with an idea of how to bless them. Listen! Once again, *that* is the distinct voice I'm talking about. It must be tested and line up with the truth of the Word, and usually requires obedience. I have learned to act on the things that come to my mind while reading the Word or during a conversation with Him. As we read God's Word we gain understanding into His amazing character by observing God's relationship to His people. We learn how He speaks to us, and the things that He asks of us will always be consistent with His Word, His ways and His character. If you are not sure what you are hearing is

His voice, then ask Him to confirm what He is saying with another Scripture passage or an example in His Word.

Friends, there is nothing like the amazing voice of our God speaking directly to us. He doesn't speak just with words. He speaks with feelings, convictions, memories and impressions. As with any person, the more we get to know God the more we will be able to discern not just the distinctiveness of His voice but the tone of His voice as well. Sometimes we will be able to *hear* the laughter, joy or compassion in His voice. Other times we will be able to *hear* His pain, sorrow or righteous anger toward sin. At times His tone is full of patience and kindness, and other times He is relentlessly firm. Even in times of discipline He is always completely in love with us. I could go on trying to describe to you the Father's unique voice, but it is my prayer that you will experience it for yourself. And if you know exactly what I'm talking about already, then I am asking God to give you even greater knowledge and experience. For this is what the Scriptures say,

> The sheep hear his voice, and he calls his own sheep by name and leads them out. When he has brought out all his own, he goes before them, and the sheep follow him, for they know his voice. A stranger they will not follow, but they will flee from him, for they do not know the voice of strangers. (John 10:4-5)

The Work of the Holy Spirit

Some Christians do not believe that the Commander gives daily counsel and revelation when we seek Him. This makes me sad. They rightly elevate the written Word but fail to acknowledge the work of the Holy Spirit. Friends, it is our right as children of God to have a close and intimate relationship with our Father. One of the many amazing things Jesus did for us was to open the door for us to know God in a personal way, and to pave the way for the Holy Spirit to live in us, revealing to us the things of God. Our minds, no matter how intelligent, are no match for the mind of Christ which is given to every child of God.

The unspiritual self, just as it is by nature, can't receive the gifts of God's Spirit. There's no capacity for them. They seem like so much silliness. Spirit can be known only by spirit — God's Spirit and our spirits in open communion. Spiritually alive, we have access to everything God's Spirit is doing, and can't be judged by unspiritual critics. Isaiah's question, "Is there anyone around who knows God's Spirit, anyone who knows what he is doing?" has been answered: Christ knows, and we have Christ's Spirit. (1 Corinthians 2:14-16 MSG)

We cannot lean on our own understanding in the battles we face —we simply do not have the inside intelligence that we need to be victorious. It would be dangerous for a soldier to go into battle relying solely on his own limited knowledge and assessment of the situation. Great military officers rely heavily on information gathered by their scouts and intelligence officers, using that information to plan their actions. We desperately need to hear the detailed instructions that come from our Commander God. The darkness is not dark to Him and He sees every plot, pit and trap that has been laid out for us.

I love the way in which the prophet Elisha aided God's people in battle simply by listening to God's voice. Elisha obtained step-by-step instructions from God that helped Israel escape the plots and schemes of the enemy army. Every time the enemy king made plans to attack or move positions, the king of Israel seemed to anticipate Syria's next move, escaping the danger. This so frustrated the enemy king that he called a meeting among his men and demanded to know who the traitor was. Which of his own men was giving away their secret battle plans? One of his officers responded, *"None, my lord, O king; but Elisha, the prophet who is in Israel, tells the king of Israel the things that you speak in your bedroom"* (2 Kings 6:12). Because Elisha got his instructions from God, he knew where the enemy camp was located and the full plans spoken in secret by the king of Syria. I cling to the truth of this passage! We too have that same access to God, through the Holy Spirit. We must spend time with our Commander so that we can know the secret, detailed plans the enemy has against us personally. In fact, we will not be victorious in the battle unless we train our spiritual ears to hear and discern the voice of our God.

We *must* listen to our Commander and obey His voice if we are ever going to be mighty warriors in His kingdom. By the power of the Holy Spirit, we are allowed to understand divine things in Scripture that surpass our own intellects. One of Satan's tools is to trick Christians into trusting their human reasoning, afraid to allow the Holy Spirit full access to the thoughts and ideas of their minds. Once again, if we don't think this is possible or if we refuse to believe that the Lord speaks to His children in this way, then we won't rely on this amazing interaction of His Spirit speaking to our spirit. The Scripture declares that we can hear from God in our spirit on a daily, ongoing basis:

> But, as it is written, "What no eye has seen, nor ear heard, nor the heart of man imagined, what God has prepared for those who love him"—these things God has revealed to us through the Spirit. **For the Spirit searches everything, even the depths of God.** For who knows a person's thoughts except the spirit of that person, which is in him? So also no one comprehends the thoughts of God except the spirit of God. Now we have received not the spirit of the world, but the Spirit who is from God, **that we might understand the things freely given by God.** (1 Corinthians 2:9-12, **emphasis** mine)

It is critical that we believe that the Father is able and willing to speak to us, answer our questions, reveal His will, and warn us of what is to come. We must be skilled in hearing His voice so that we are not deceived or led astray in any way.

> But the Comforter (Counselor, Helper, Intercessor, Advocate, Strengthener, Standby) the Holy Spirit, Whom the Father will send in My name (in my place, to represent Me and act on My behalf), He will teach you all things. And He will cause you to

recall (remind you of, bring to remembrance) everything I have told you. (John 14:26 AMP)

The Holy Spirit will teach us all things. He will guide us into truth about the ways and purposes of God, and the truth about any situation or circumstance that we are personally facing. If you need to stop right now to pray and invite the Commander to speak His truth into a certain area of your life, go ahead; I'll wait for you. I invite and encourage you to do this throughout this book. If at any time you sense the voice of the Lord bringing something to your mind that He wants to discuss with you, don't ignore the prompting; simply stop reading and engage in a conversation with the Commander right then and there.

Obedience to His Voice

It is crucial that we not only hear God's voice, but obey it as well. When we hear His voice and obey it, we are training ourselves to hear Him with greater clarity. Likewise, when we hear His voice and ignore Him, it is as if we are walking away from Him, and His voice grows d i s t a n t and faint until we don't hear Him at all. The busyness of life, not spending time with Him, and a preoccupation with our own plans can silence His voice. It is extremely dangerous to simply believe every voice that comes into our minds. There may be many voices bombarding us throughout the day, but only one of them is God's. That is why we must diligently test and train ourselves to truly hear the voice of God. There are Christians who desire God to speak to them but then do not open their Bibles. This is similar to a warrior expecting to conquer in battle without ever unsheathing his sword! *"And no wonder, for even Satan disguises himself as an angel of light" (2 Corinthians 11:14).* This verse is warning us that the devil can masquerade his voice as a messenger of truth—he can mimic things that God would say, but listening to his voice usually produces feelings of fear, doubt, confusion, pride, selfishness or condemnation. For example, I might hear a voice say, *You need to be less selfish and give more of your time.* Now, this could be something that God would say to me or it could be the enemy accusing me of something. Or both. How do I know the difference? Do I listen? Do I take it captive and dismiss it? Ask Jesus for discernment.

One way I've learned to discern is through the emotions that come with the voice. If it is the Lord, then it might come in a firm but gentle way as He convicts me to change. Godly sorrow can be painful for a time but it leads to life and freedom as the Commander's voice draws me in, calling me to confess it as sin and give it to Him. When it is the Lord, it comes with the desire to truly be less selfish and more giving. It is God's Spirit in me energizing and propelling my spirit toward righteousness. But when Satan speaks, his voice comes with shame, accusation, dread, and leaves you feeling worthless. Does the voice come with feelings of belittlement, leaving you feeling an inch tall? Does it make you want to run from a situation or push you into hiding? Does it force you to quickly cover up or deny your issues? There is a difference between God's conviction that we must not rebel against, and Satan's condemnation that we need to reject! We must learn to discern the difference. We will only develop that acute discernment as we read about the character of our God and hear His voice in Scripture.

Ignorance, unbelief, deliberate sin, or refusing to forgive another person can also block my ability to hear God's voice. Check in with the Commander right now. Is there any evidence of those things in your life? There are times when I've come to God with my own agenda, seeking His confirmation of my plans. When I desire something more than I desire the perfect will of God, I can open myself up to deception—hearing what I want to hear, even twisting Scripture to support what I want God to tell me. This approach has left many bewildered, disappointed and stifled in their ability to hear God's voice. Have you ever done that, as I have? Stop and ask the Commander. The voice of the Commander will *never* contradict the written Word—rather, He will confirm it. If you believe that the Lord told you something that goes against the commandments and character of God, then you know it is simply NOT His voice.

So often the Commander uses my everyday life experiences to train me to be sensitive to the leading of His voice. One time He taught me a fabulous lesson about waiting it out when God tells me He is going to do something. I grew up using the New King James and the New International Version of the Bible, and those were the only translations with which I was familiar. Then I started to notice a different version. The first time I recognized this translation was in a teaching book; every time the author quoted Scripture, it was from the Amplified Bible. As I read this translation, I instantly connected with the words because it is similar to the way I think. As I became more acquainted with the Amplified Bible, I felt the familiar prompting of the Commander. I sensed Him saying, *Pay attention here, Kori. I have something I want to show you.* So I asked Him, *Do You want me to buy an Amplified Bible?* I waited. There was a pause and then I thought I heard Him say, *No, Kori, I want to give you one.* That was all He said to me. I didn't really know if I had heard Him correctly so I just kept this to myself and waited to see what would happen.

A week later when I visited a friend, I noticed that she had an Amplified Bible, and I threw out the statement that I was interested in getting one for myself. I thought perhaps she had an old copy of the Amplified Bible to give away and this would be God's provision. But she didn't. *Hmm, was the thought that You are going to give me an Amplified Bible really from You, Lord, or just my imagination?* There was no answer this time. Finally, after a couple more weeks, I concluded that I had not heard the Spirit correctly. Why would I expect God to give me one when I am fully capable of buying it myself? I went online and ordered an Amplified Bible. Within a few days it arrived at my door; I tore open the package and began to read it right away. But God had not forgotten what He told me! Three days later I found a brand-new Amplified Bible on my kitchen counter; somebody had left it on the seat of my husband's car with my name on it. I immediately recognized it as the promised gift from the Lord. I opened the front cover to look for a message. Taped to the inside cover was two hundred dollars. There was no note, no explanation, just the Bible with the bonus cash to make sure I did not miss the fact that God said He was going to give me an Amplified Bible. There was no shame or feeling of failure attached to this lesson, only a confidence that I had truly heard God speak to me in a specific way. Invite the Lord to train you with similar life lessons in the ways of hearing His voice.

Hearing the Commander's Voice in Prayer

God speaks to His children with His Spirit and through Scripture, and He also desires to speak to us through prayer. Too often, we think of prayer as simply talking to God, but forget that the other half is *listening* to Him. Prayer is a conversation, a communication between our Father and His children. It is designed so that we may talk to Him about anything that concerns us and He will answer us. There are times when I am talking with God and I will suddenly get an idea, which may or may not be God's thought. But as I have trained myself to recognize the voice of God in Scripture, I can more readily recognize that same voice as the Commander speaks to me in prayer. As we talk with the Commander, thoughts and ideas can form a plan of action in our minds. With training we can begin to quickly discern the voice of our Father and know His detailed direction for our lives.

Lie Alert:

Are you thinking . . .

- God may talk to other people, but He doesn't or won't talk to me.
- I've messed up so much, I'm not sure if I want the Lord to speak to me.
- Trying to hear from God is really risky; if there is a way to mess this up, I'm sure that I'll find it.
- I'm not sure I want to hear what God has to say to me.
- I don't have time for this; it all seems too hard.
- What if He tells me to do something I don't want to do? Then I will be held accountable.

If any of you lacks wisdom, let him ask God, who gives generously to all without reproach, and it will be given him.

> *But let him ask in faith, with no doubting, for the one who doubts is like a wave of the sea that is driven and tossed by the wind. (James 1:5-6)*

Jesus is our role model and example for listening to and obeying God's voice.

> *In these days, he (Jesus) went out to the mountain to pray, and all night He continued in prayer to God. And when day came, He called His disciples and chose from them twelve, whom He called apostles. (Luke 6:12-13)*

I love what this verse shows us. Jesus was about to start His ministry and choose His disciples, the men who were going to be close to Him as He trained them throughout His ministry. They were going to carry on the works of God and advance His kingdom long after He was gone. Calling the disciples was a critical decision, so Jesus went up the mountain alone to have a conversation with His Father. All night long He talked to God and sought His Father's counsel. God revealed to Jesus the things that He needed to know. I can just imagine the lively and excited conversation they had when the Father gave detailed instructions as to which men would become Jesus' disciples. After receiving His plan of action from God, Jesus went out and immediately chose the twelve. We too have the same privilege to seek counsel from our Father; however, we must be determined in our hearts to obey Him as Jesus did.

Hearing the Commander's Voice Through the Body of Christ

God also speaks to us through the body of Christ. *"For as in one body we have many members, and the members do not all have the same function, so we, though many, are one body in Christ, and individually members one of another"* (Romans 12:4). There are times when the Holy Spirit will choose to speak through a person specifically to us. Do you ever listen to a pastor's message, and the words coming out of his mouth seem as though they are pointed directly at you, as if the message was preached exclusively for you? The pastor may have no idea who you are or what your situation is but you could *swear* he knows your inner thoughts and struggles. It is not the man but the Spirit of God inside of him working to convict you, encourage you, or speak to you about a certain issue in your life. Or have you ever been conversing with a Christian friend when suddenly their words illuminate and confirm the words God had already spoken to you? God talks to us through the body of Christ because we are connected to one another by His Spirit.

We also need one another to keep us all from developing an independent spirit that breeds pride and self-sufficiency. When I sense the Lord speaking to my heart about something that is not explicitly spelled out in Scripture, I will often run my thoughts by a group of spiritually discerning friends. This helps me determine whether I am truly hearing the Father's voice in the matter.

Hearing the Commander's Voice in Our Thoughts

Our God knows everything, and it is His will to impart His thoughts and wisdom into our minds in order to make us more like Christ. He has done this by giving us His mind.

> *"For who has known or understood the mind (the counsels and purposes) of the Lord so as to guide and instruct Him and give Him knowledge? But we have the mind of Christ (the Messiah) and do hold the thoughts (feelings and purposes) of His heart"* (1 Corinthians 2:16 AMP).

God speaks to us in our thoughts by inserting His thoughts into our minds. Sometimes it is in a word, a phrase or even a complete sentence. Other times it feels like four paragraphs of thought that come in a quick ten-second download. These "God thoughts" can dip down and touch our emotions, giving us a greater understanding of what God is communicating to us.

We are complex beings, made in the image of a brilliantly complex God. While teaching us about who He is, He teaches us about who we are. I was reading my Bible one day when I came upon the following verse: *"You have multiplied, O Lord my God, your wondrous deeds and your thoughts toward us; none can compare with you!" (Psalm 40:5).* As I pondered this verse the Holy Spirit highlighted the phrase *"your thoughts toward us"* and I began to wonder, *Does the Lord really think about me personally? And if He does, what does He actually think about me?* This verse says that God not only thinks about me but has multiple thoughts toward me! I wanted to know what they were, so I simply asked Him. *God, if You truly think so many thoughts about me, then could You tell me what some of them are?* It wasn't until later in the day that He spoke into my mind with this sentence, *Kori, you are very similar to My servant, Mary.* God immediately had my attention: *What? I remind You of Your servant Mary? Which Mary?*

He brought to mind the passage in Scripture where the angel of the Lord came to Mary with the news that she would be with child. Even though Mary didn't fully understand, she trusted God and accepted His will. *"And Mary said, 'Behold, I am the servant of the Lord; let it be to me according to your word.' And the angel departed from her" (Luke 1:8).* My Father described how He designed me, giving me a heart like Mary's with a submissive spirit to trust Him even though I don't always understand. I could sense His delight in me. In that moment I began to realize that He loves this quality about me and He made me this way on purpose. He was going to use this characteristic in me to accomplish all that He has planned for me to do. I will never forget how powerfully He spoke to me in that moment. It was like a deep, satisfying drink of the Holy Spirit being poured down into the very core of my being, supernaturally giving me the ability to comprehend His love toward me. *"And hope does not put us to shame, because God's love has been poured into our hearts through the Holy Spirit who has been given to us" (Romans 5:5).*

Hearing the Commander's Voice Through Dreams or Visions

The Word of God is clear that in the last days the people of God will see visions and have dreams of a spiritual nature.

> *And in the last days it shall be, God declares, that I will pour out my Spirit on all flesh, and your sons and daughters shall prophesy, and your young men shall see visions, and your old men will dream dreams; even on my male servants and female servants in those days will I pour out my Spirit, and they shall prophesy. (Acts 2:17-18)*

Paul, Peter, John, Cornelius and Ananias are all examples in Scripture of people who had visions from God. There have been times when the Lord has warned me through a dream of what was to come. When the Lord uses visions and dreams He always confirms what He is speaking through Scripture, the body of Christ, or prayer.

When the Father began to speak to me about writing this book I must admit I battled enormous amounts of fear and doubt that I could even do what He was asking. As I brought my uncertainty and concerns to Him in prayer, a picture of a huge library began to come together in my mind. It was enormous, of beautiful design. Tall windows filled the room with glorious light. Ladders were attached to the bookshelves so that you could climb to the top and reach the books that you wanted. I sensed in my spirit that God was showing me a massive storehouse in heaven filled with books. Some of these books had already been written while others were yet to be written. Then the Lord led me over to a particular shelf and pulled down a book to show me. I couldn't really make out the title but one thing I could see clearly was that the author's name was my own—it read *by Kori Trierweiler!* He proceeded to tell me in my spirit, *Kori, this book has already been written and has been here on the shelf since before time began, waiting for you—for such a time as this. It is time for you to write this book. You do not have to worry about what you will say because I will help you.* With this picture, God spoke His encouragement to me to go ahead and write this book. This is one of those good works I was created to do and it was planned out for me long ago, even before I was born. *"For we are God's workmanship, created in Christ Jesus to do good works, which God prepared in advance for us to do"* (Ephesians 2:10 NIV). So many times the image of that moment in the library has come back to me when I have been discouraged, overwhelmed and ready to give up. I found confidence in the fact that in the heavenlies, this book is already complete.

We can be believers for years and yet be stuck in spiritual infancy because we have not learned to trust and obey the Commander's voice. If this is you, do not be discouraged—there is great hope! God is in the business of growing us to spiritual adulthood. This is not a work that *we* do as much as it is a work that *God* does. No matter how much we have grown in the Lord and learned to trust and obey the Commander's voice, there is always more. We can ask our Father to give us a desire to read His Word, to hear His voice, and to obey His instructions. He is gentle and loving to confirm what He is speaking to us. It is by learning to recognize the Commander's voice that we will be prepared and equipped for the battles we fight in this life.

Prayer:

Dear Father,
I want to know You. I want to hear from You. I want to receive Your instructions so that I may live for You and accomplish all You have for me. I submit to You as my Lord and Commander, and I declare that I will draw near to You and commit myself to be obedient to Your will and commandments. I trust that You will enable me to do so. I need Your help as I submit myself to Your intense training to hear and discern Your voice. Alert me to know when You are training me and help me to follow Your lead. Bring to my mind anything in my life that is holding me back from clearly hearing You, and grant me Your gift of godly repentance. Teach me to discern the tone and

distinction of Your voice from all the other voices in this world. Help me to cling to Your Word all the days of my life and love Your commands. Enable me to know Your voice through Scripture, prayer, the body of Christ, my thoughts, and visions. I trust You and ask that You guard me against any deception in this training process.
In Jesus' name, Amen.

Action Steps: Journal your prayers, answers and all the things the Commander reveals to you.

1. Pray through a passage. Be still before the Lord with an open Bible and ask Him to lead you to a portion of Scripture. Ask Him questions and pay close attention to the thoughts that come to you. Respond to those thoughts and interact with the voice of the Father.

2. When you are with other followers of Christ, ask the Commander to alert you to His voice through them that would confirm a truth that He has already spoken to you.

3. Invite the Spirit to come into your thoughts and give you His. Ask Him to separate them from your own and help you identify the thoughts and ideas that come from the Holy Spirit.

4. Ask the Commander to give you some simple instruction today, something that will require your obedience. Then do it, asking Him to confirm that the direction was from Him.

Chapter Two
Spiritual Mind Battles

You keep him in perfect peace whose mind is stayed on you, because he trusts in you.
Isaiah 26:3

I was enjoying a peaceful day at home before it was time to pick up my older kids from school. I packed my babies in the car, took a quick trip to the store and got to school just in time. While we waited in the carpool line, my three-year-old started pitching a fit and screaming in the backseat. Instantly annoyed, I turned around and scolded her much more harshly than necessary. She stopped her fit immediately and looked at me with shock. When I saw the alarm in her eyes, it awakened me to my present behavior and I realized that I had overreacted. I became aware in that moment that I was not "okay" emotionally.

I asked the Lord, *Why am I so upset right now?* I felt frustrated, irritated and angry, but I didn't know why. As soon as I realized this, I knew I was in some sort of mental battle and needed to take an assessment of the situation. Then an extreme fatigue settled over me as I had thoughts like, *I don't want to deal with this right now . . . I have a right to be angry . . . I'm just tired, that's all . . .*

Taking a deep breath, I asked the Commander to help me sort through this. As I thought back through my day, He brought to mind an incident at the grocery store. *Okay God, what happened at the grocery store that made me lose my peace*? He reminded me of the brief exchange that I'd had with the cashier as I was signing the receipt. I was using one of those automated credit card machines and this particular one malfunctioned. When I asked the cashier about it, her condescending tone implied, "It's not that hard to figure out; just read the directions." As I tried to explain to her that it was the machine that was acting up, it miraculously began to work. I was in a hurry, so I just got my groceries and left instead of standing there defending my honor. This is what happened on the surface, but in my mind something much deeper was going on.

That short interchange with the cashier triggered an old wound. It pushed a button in my mind that said, *"You are a dumb, stupid idiot."* That particular lie has been threaded throughout my life since I was very young. When I get into a situation where I feel belittled or criticized I tend to overreact in a sinful way. At times I believe the lie wholeheartedly, accepting it as truth, which triggers feelings of shame and a desire to hide or retreat. At other times I might become angry and verbally attack the person who offended me. In the situation at the grocery store, I dropped the argument with the cashier when the credit card machine started working, but I was angry about how she treated me. I also had the nagging feeling that I really *was* dumb—so dumb that I couldn't figure out a simple credit card machine and follow basic instructions.

Those feelings, and the emotional pain of previous wounds, were stirring in my head on the drive from the grocery store to the school. I showed no outward sign of this inner turmoil until my little girl began to misbehave—then my angry frustration spewed out all over her. I didn't realize any of this was going on in my mind until the Father helped me dissect my thoughts.

Recognizing the Battle

For years I didn't recognize the subtle attacks taking place in my mind. I didn't pay attention to what I was thinking or ponder why I was having these thoughts. The Word of God says we need to daily examine the things we think to see whether they are true or false, once we come to trust Jesus as our Savior.

> Do not be conformed to this world (this age), [fashioned after and adapted to its external, superficial customs], but be transformed (changed) by the [entire] renewal of your mind [by its new ideas and its new attitude], so that you may prove [for yourselves] what is the good and acceptable and perfect will of God, even the thing which is good and acceptable and perfect [in His sight for you]. (Romans 12:2 AMP)

This testing is a process that will enable us to know God's will for our lives. As we discover the truth of God's Word, we begin to expose the lies that are assaulting us from this world, our sinful flesh and the devil. There are many thoughts or *voices* that play in our minds; we must determine the source.

The Creator fashioned us to be able to hear Him speak to us through our thoughts. He conveys truth so that we may know who He is and experience His love, power and friendship toward us. Satan also speaks to us in this manner, but he uses lies and accusations as he attempts to deceive, condemn and control us. His communications need to be identified and disarmed by the truth.

> For the weapons of our warfare are not of the flesh but have divine power to destroy strongholds. We destroy arguments and every lofty opinion raised against the knowledge of God, and take every thought captive to obey Christ, being ready to punish every disobedience, when your obedience is complete. (2 Corinthians 10:4-6)

God has taught me that there are two parts to this battle. The first is recognizing when we are actually *in* a battle! This should be obvious but so often, it's not. The sneaky little lies of the evil one are stealthy, intended to hit their marks unnoticed by the victim. It takes practice to identify them, and the aid of our Commander to recognize the source of each thought: Is it from

God, the world, my selfish desires, or the evil one? Friends, this is hard work but so very vital to the fight. It is not optional. The Commander instructs us to take every thought captive as a prisoner and determine if it is true or false. The true ones remain, but the false ones must be punished swiftly. I love the language of the above verse as it commands us not to treat these counterfeit thoughts lightly. We are to capture these damaging thoughts and put them to death on the spot.

The second part of the battle is knowing which weapons to use to fight these false thoughts. When we discover the lie or accusation that has tried to set itself up against the knowledge of God, we must know the specific truth from Scripture that will take out that lie and terminate it quickly. The weapon we use is the Word of God, which is the sword of the Spirit. We must make the "lofty opinion raised against the knowledge of God" bow to its knees under the truth of the Word of God, before we behead it. If we do not deal with these negative thoughts the way this passage tells us to, then they will come back to attack us again in greater force and number. This is some serious warfare, friends!

Our Field of Battle

An experienced soldier knows that he needs to be well-acquainted with the landscape of the field of battle. It could be a matter of life or death for him to be familiar with and adapted to the various hills, valleys, swamps, and forests, and especially knowledgeable of the fresh water and food supply. At any moment in this battlefield, he could be attacked by the enemy, becoming wounded, exposed, or isolated. He must know the places of safety and the areas of danger.

Our spiritual war is no different: We need to be well-acquainted with the arenas of our minds. We must understand the types of thoughts that filter through, paying close attention to the ones that can lead us down a path of toxicity. As warriors we need to know our personal areas of strength and vulnerability, because both will be targeted by the enemy. For each of us the terrain is a bit different because of our upbringing, personalities and life experiences. If you are susceptible to the thoughts and temptations of sexual sin, you need to be aware of this and steer clear of any place that would invite the attack of the enemy over your mind. If you are strong in the gifts of praise and worship or prayer, then you need to be aware that the enemy will try to weaken your gift by discouraging you. He may also seek to distract you from your God-given assignment by inflating you with prideful, self-centered thoughts that make you focus on yourself instead of the One Who gave you that gift.

For me, being in a situation where I feel belittled or ignored can throw me down a mudslide of negativity. In my field of battle, there are places of mental quicksand where I can become paralyzed by fear, sinking lower and lower into panic. Because I am now aware of this, I have a few weapons attached to my belt of truth that enable me to avoid this pit of fear. This is not an easy process, but we are not alone; we have a Helper. Our Commander is always with us and He knows everything about us. He knows all of our thoughts and can dissect each of them for us, revealing to us the areas in our field of battle that need our attention. As we listen to His voice, He will show us how to successfully navigate through the battles to attain one victory after another.

Thinking About What We're Thinking About

It has been said that the average person can talk in her mind four to five times faster than she can actually speak aloud. Wow! That's a lot of thoughts to work through. You might say, "Who has time to stop and think about what they're thinking about? Life is so busy. I don't remember what I *said*, let alone what I *thought* today."

Let me tell you, that is exactly where the devil wants you. It is essential that we pay attention to our thoughts. The mind battles we face can be tremendously complex because of our multiple thoughts. For example, at 8:00 a.m. one sneaky lie planted by the enemy can enter your mind. It gets ushered in with all your other thoughts, perhaps with your massive "to do" list. You don't recognize it as a lie but simply accept it. That lie then opens the door for more lies to enter, taking you down a path of negative thoughts and emotions. By evening you have entertained so many lies without realizing it, that you are upset and responding in a sinful way to even the smallest annoyances. Because you didn't recognize the first few lies planted in your mind, you don't even understand why you're upset. In the unseen realm it was an attack of the enemy, complete with a plot and assignment to disarm you, put you in bondage and cause you to sin. If we don't start paying attention to what we're thinking about, Satan will take advantage of us over and over again.

One Sunday morning at church, I passed a woman I barely knew. As I started thinking about this lady, a fictitious scenario played out in my mind. I imagined having a conversation with her where she was responding to me in a mean and offensive way. Getting a little worked up at how she was treating me, I started rehearsing a confrontation with her as if the situation had actually happened. Later that day while running errands, I lost a good thirty minutes replaying this mock disagreement with her and formulating a well-prepared "Christ-like" confrontation to put her in her place. I was totally wrapped up in this mental conversation with her, enjoying myself as I came up with some really great comebacks to her "attitude" toward me. At this point I was entertaining numerous lies and experiencing many negative emotions toward the woman, when in reality I'd never even talked to her! When I finally came out of it, I thought, *Wow, Lord, that was bizarre and random. Why am I even thinking about this lady?*

The very next day I found out that this woman did something very kind for me personally. I was shocked—and then curious—about the timing of my negative thoughts toward her. Where did this fictitious scenario in my mind come from? If I had allowed these thoughts to go unchecked, in the future I might subconsciously think of her with these same negative feelings, never really knowing why I did not like her. If these lies and absurd accusations had not been brought to light by the Holy Spirit I could have easily been used by the enemy to cause offense—holding her at a distance or treating her unkindly, which in turn could cause an *actual* disagreement between us.

We must never forget that we are in a spiritual war. There is an enemy who wants to defeat and kill us. The battlefield is in our minds and we must pay attention to our thoughts. This is simple Basic Training for spiritual warfare, and yet for so many years I was completely unaware of what was happening. As the Lord trained me to go back and think about what I was thinking, I was able to identify the initial lie from Satan and begin to see how believing that lie took me down a road that adversely affected my emotions and behavior. I was then able to put to death anything that did not coincide with the truth of God's Word.

Allowing God to Monitor Our Thoughts

I remember when God began to intensely train me in the area of my thoughts. At times when I was going about my day I would sense His prompting: *Kori, what are you thinking right now?* It was His way of getting my attention. When this happened I would stop and quickly rewind my thoughts, holding them still to examine them. He would then help me identify the ones that I needed to challenge.

For example, on one occasion I was in my car listening to the radio when a "One-Minute Teaching" came on between songs. The woman speaking started the segment by quoting a Bible verse very familiar to me. In fact, I had recently taught on that very passage. Before she went any further, I quickly switched stations—I wasn't aware of a reason for this, I just did it. Then I heard in my thoughts, *Why did you switch the station? What are you thinking right now?* It was the Commander's voice asking me to pay attention to what was going on in the battlefield of my mind. As I stopped to rewind my thought processes, He helped me identify these thoughts: *Oh, I've heard this all before. She's got nothing new to teach me. In fact, I could probably teach her a thing or two about this verse!* As soon as He gently highlighted what I was thinking, I was shocked and immediately convicted by the sin in my heart. I was unwittingly sinking into the quicksand of thoughts bred by a proud and unteachable spirit. Developing an unteachable spirit is no small thing—it opens the door to arrogance, sinful self-sufficiency and, ultimately, rebellion toward God.

I used the weapon of repentance and quickly turned back to the station, willing to be taught. This is one of many times that the Lord has prompted me to examine my thoughts in the moment, cross-examine them with Scripture and immediately destroy the lies with the spiritual weapon of repentance. We do not need to document every little thought as much as we need to be sensitive to the prompting of our Lord. Invite the Commander to do this in your life.

God is with us every step of the way, but like true warriors we must rely heavily on His instructions to take account of our thoughts. Our emotions will also help us identify something going on in our minds that requires our attention. Feelings of sadness, frustration, loneliness, annoyance, and anger are just a few that might indicate that we are in the midst of a mind battle. There may be times when we are so shut down emotionally because of old battle wounds that we cannot define our feelings or thoughts at all. In that case, many thoughts and ideas can run rampant through our minds without any accountability. We must ask the Lord to help us identify the underlying emotions and heal those old wounds with His love. For the believer, this is done by the power of the Holy Spirit. He never leaves us, knows our every thought, knows all the plans of the enemy concerning us, and offers us truth to replace the lies we are most prone to believe.

The Source of Our Battles

Our God has won this war even though the battles are still raging. In the midst of our fight we need to always keep in mind that Satan is defeated and has been stripped of his power by our Savior's work on the Cross and His resurrection. This is an area in which spiritual battles are different from physical battles—in a physical battle, the victor isn't declared until it's over. In a spiritual battle, Satan is technically defeated but still wields power through lies and deception. God has won the war but we are still fighting very real battles in our day-to-day lives. We must stay closely connected to our Commander, never forgetting that because of Him we fight as victors. God has always been and always will be completely in charge. He is the Ruler over everything. *"The Lord has established his throne in the heavens, and his kingdom rules over all" (Psalm 103:19).* We need to believe that every attack of the enemy toward us has been allowed by God, and what the enemy intends for evil, God purposes for our good. *"And we know that for those who love God all things work together for good, for those who are called according to his purpose" (Romans 8:28).*

When we are struggling with something, we often want to know, "Is this an attack from Satan or is this something God is allowing in my life to make me more like Jesus?" The answer to both questions is "yes." The devil may be behind the attack, but he is only permitted to do what God allows. When you read Job 1-2, you will discover that both Satan *and* God had a plan for the battle that Job faced. John 10:10 tells us that with each attack Satan has a desired outcome: to steal, kill and destroy us. But Jesus always has the better plan: He has come so that we may have life to the fullest and highest degree. From the attack in which Satan desires to destroy, God can bring about His desired outcome: freedom and abundant life. The question is, will we listen to the lies of the devil or the truth of God? The stakes are high; they are death or life for us. In the midst of a battle we can waste time and energy begrudging our situation or getting mad at the devil. Or we can set our eyes on our Commander, asking Him to work out His good through us in each battle we face.

In Genesis we read that Joseph was betrayed and falsely accused by his brothers, and as a result he faced many confusing, dark times. God used all of it to build his character, developing every tool he needed to be second-in-command in Egypt and eventually save the lives of the people of Israel. Years later when God fulfilled His purpose in Joseph's life, he said to his brothers, *"As for you, you meant evil against me, but God meant it for good, to bring it about that many people should be kept alive, as they are today" (Genesis 50:20).* We could say the same thing about the attack of the enemy in our lives. Satan means it for evil, but God means it for good. With each attack and battle we fight in this life, our Commander has a purpose—He is training and strengthening us to make us like His Son, Jesus. With each battle, He is training His children to be overcomers! *"For by you I can run against a troop, and by my God I can leap over a wall" (Psalm 18:29).*

Satan's Strategic Attacks

Satan's attacks are neither random nor purposeless. By strategically taking advantage of our weaknesses he attempts to distract us from the work of God. He attacks over and over again in the same fragile, annoying areas so that our focus is on ourselves instead of on God. The devil is not a gentleman and he doesn't fight fair. He will take advantage of times in our lives when we are tired (depleted emotionally or physically), disappointed, lonely, or bored and in need of some excitement. Even times when we celebrate our victories are not considered a no-attack zone for him; he will use any opportunity he can exploit to get our attention off of the Commander and onto our circumstances or ourselves.

At Christmas our church performs an outdoor walkthrough event which presents the gospel story in a powerful way. On our first night participating one year, it took a ridiculously long time to gather our winter gear. Kids were crying. Gloves were missing. Boots were suddenly too small. What had been perfectly fine for school the day before was now inadequate. When it was time to leave I was impatient and we were running dangerously late. *Let's just hurry up and get this night over with!* Battle One.

The second night, right before the performance, my nine-year-old daughter relayed a comment an adult had made to her earlier in the day. It was a complaint directed toward me, and it should have been delivered to me, not her. Instead of preparing to communicate the wonder of the birth of Christ, I immediately plunged into an imaginary battle with this person that was so strong I could hardly focus on what I was supposed to be doing. This mental argument took on a life of its own as I began defending myself and building up a case of wrongs against this person as if I was a prosecuting attorney before a jury. I became so worked up that I didn't have one thought left over to think about the purpose of the evening's event. Battle Two.

The third night of the presentation, my husband had planned to bring dinner home so we could relax before leaving for the performance. However, his work meeting lasted longer than anticipated. I couldn't reach him by phone. The kids were hungry. It was nearing time to leave. Should I feed the kids and meet him there, or should we wait for him and arrive late? I dislike being late and letting people down. More than that, I dislike being forced to make a decision, because I fear that I will make the wrong one. Anxiety and frustration grabbed hold of me. Battle Three.

As I looked back, I realized that each attack was deliberately placed about an hour before our departure, distracting me from the assignment God had given me for the evening. It took me a while to recognize the well-timed attacks and the purpose of the enemy toward me: distraction. He knew just the right buttons to push every time. The devil sought to mar these exciting family evenings with negativity, anxiety and duty, causing me to dread an experience I truly enjoyed. The battlefield is our minds; our weapons are the discernment of the Holy Spirit and the Word of God. We need to capture our thoughts and measure them against God's Word. Then we will be able to thwart the enemy's plans before he gains a foothold into our circumstances.

Satan Targets God's Blessing Toward Us

Satan's aim is not random. The enemy aims his attacks at the gifts and blessings God gives us. The enemy surrounds these good things with his whispering lies of negativity, which then twist our thinking so that we cannot even recognize the gifts we have been given. Some of God's greatest blessings to us include the Bible, prayer, the church, and family, and it is important to consider how these can come under subtle attack.

The Word of God is a gift to every believer, but there is enormous spiritual opposition to reading it. The devil seeks to surround these God-given words with a cloud of negativity. Have you ever had these thoughts about the Bible? *It's so boring. I can't understand it. It's too long and complex or old-fashioned. Is it even relevant to my life? It's just a book of literature, right? I know enough of it already. I can always read it later. It's just a book of "dos" and "don'ts"!* Even though I love the Word of God, there is *still* a battle when it comes time to read it. I have to fight procrastination, apathy and laziness before I even open the book. And then, when I do, there are all kinds of distractions while I am reading. At times, the enemy has me convinced that anything (even a trip to the dentist) would be more fun than reading my Bible. Has this ever happened to you? You are not alone. We must be aware and fight, breaking through these destructive lies surrounding the Scriptures in order to obediently read them and receive the blessings they hold for us. *Lord, come into our struggle here and help us read, study and fall in love with Your words.*

Prayer is a powerful gift from our Lord—in fact, it's even more powerful than we can understand! Satan suffers great loss when God's people pray and stay in close communication with Him, so he tries his hardest to surround our experiences of prayer with negative, confusing, conflicting thoughts. He seeks to overcomplicate it or cause us to treat it as an obligation. He wants to make us think we are not doing it right. He tries to make us feel guilty when we don't pray enough. Or if that doesn't work, he'll try to make us feel guilty that we pray too much, fearing that God doesn't want us bothering Him with every lame detail of our lives. We might have thoughts like: *This is boring . . . Is this even necessary? . . . What a waste of time . . . I've got so much to do . . . I'll pray later.* He also seeks to flood our minds with bad experiences when it comes to prayer. Have you ever been forced to pray out loud and felt like you blundered your way through it? Do you experience fear, dread or feelings of failure surrounding the area of prayer in your life? Are you deathly afraid of having to pray out loud, and do you avoid any situation that might require it? Where do you think that comes from? We have an enemy, and even if we don't know how important prayer is, he does. He will continually set up mental roadblocks to keep us from it. But there is hope and victory to be had if we simply allow the Commander to help us sort out all those negative thoughts about prayer, replacing them with His truth. Tell the Commander how you feel. Be honest with the Lord and ask Him to bring you truth. Then ask Him to teach you how to pray just like the first disciples asked.

The church, which Scripture describes as the body of Christ, is an amazing gift from the Lord. Satan loves to target the church, the gathering together of believers, by making it a place of dread and disunity, or convincing us that it is too tense, demanding, or dull to attend. He tries everything in his power to make this blessing a bad experience for us. I love to go to church but that does not exempt me from mind battles on a Sunday morning. Inevitably some sort of thoughts or emotions surface that make me want to stay home and, in the moment of the battle, these emotions can be very convincing. It could be as trivial as not being able to find the right outfit to wear, or just feeling too tired to go. Satan's lies are often very sympathetic to our emotions, and he suggests all kinds of alternatives in order to keep us isolated from the blessing and safety of the body of Christ. Beware of his tactics and be on your guard when the urge to stay home is stronger than ever. I have found that the times I pushed through those negative thoughts were some of the most important, authentic and deep times I have had with other believers. In fact, I almost skipped church the night the Lord used a small group lesson to convince me it was time to write this book. I'm sure glad I went.

Family is one of the greatest blessings God has given to us. I have a friend who was overjoyed to discover she and her husband were expecting their sixth child. But her joy was somewhat dampened by the realization that she had to tell their friends and family about it. Their last three pregnancy announcements were met with raised eyebrows and hurtful, discouraging comments, suggesting they were a bit crazy or even irresponsible to have so many kids. Even though she desired and welcomed these babies, the unhelpful thoughts and comments from others came back to her mind repeatedly, trying to rob her of the joy and blessing of the new life inside her. *Maybe I am crazy! What was I thinking? I can't even handle the kids I have; what is one more going to do to me? How are we going to make it? What will this do to us financially?* By pelting her with these negative thoughts, the enemy wanted her to think these were her own thoughts and emotions regarding her sixth child, though they were not. This was her mind battle and she needed to fight it with the truth. What does the Lord say about children? *"Behold, children are a heritage from the Lord, the fruit of the womb a reward. Like arrows in the hand of a warrior are the children of one's youth"* (Psalm 127:3-4).

We must learn how to fight defensively, identifying the lies that enter our minds, before we can learn how to fight offensively. The devil's goal is to keep us operating in our old sinful natures instead of becoming the new creations God has made us to be. He seeks to deceive us by tripping us up with constant accusations. He wants to paralyze us with feelings of condemnation, anxiety and fear, rendering us useless in advancing the kingdom of heaven.

Even though Satan has a plan to harm us with every attack, let's not forget that God is completely in charge and His plan is always for our good. As we train ourselves to think about what we are thinking about, my prayer is that we will move past simply enduring the attacks of the enemy and develop a "victory upon victory" mindset—pushing back the gates of hell and reflecting the image of our God in all we say and do.

Prayer:

Dear Father,
I invite You into every area of my mind, heart, soul, body and spirit. I freely admit that I need Your help with each battle I face—to recognize it and then to know the truth that refutes the lie. I am aware that numerous thoughts go through my mind in a day that are contrary to Your Truth. Bring to light the ones You want me to see. I am asking You to alert me, get my attention and enable me to recognize the battles raging there. I also ask for Your help in identifying the source and reason for the thoughts going through my mind. Grant me discernment this day and the wisdom to walk into victory in the mind battles I face.
In the powerful name of Jesus, Amen.

Action Steps: Journal your prayers, answers and all the things the Commander reveals to you.

1. Ask the Commander to stop you today anytime you are in a mind battle, struggling between truth and lies. When you hear Him say in your spirit, "What are you thinking about right now?" Stop. Think about what you're thinking about. In that moment, invite Him to help you sort through the thoughts running through your mind, alerting you to the ones that are not true.

2. At the end of the day, get alone with the Father and ask Him to help you process your day. Ask Him to remind you of your emotions throughout the day. Did you feel happy? Sad? Angry? Annoyed? What caused you to feel that way? Ask God to show you why, and a Scriptural truth that applies to the source of your thoughts.

3. Get in the habit of identifying when you are in a battle. There will be times you can't stop that moment and take the time necessary to sort through all the thoughts. Ask the Lord to remind you of this battle and to then bring the situation back up when the time is right to process it. Trust Him; He has been training warriors for years.

Chapter Three
Spiritual Weapons

Finally, be strong in the Lord and in the strength of his might. Put on the whole armor of God, that you may be able to stand against the schemes of the devil. For we do not wrestle against flesh and blood, but against the rulers, against the authorities, against the cosmic powers over this present darkness, against the spiritual forces of evil in the heavenly places. Therefore take up the whole armor of God, that you may be able to withstand in the evil day, and having done all, to stand firm. Stand therefore, having fastened on the belt of truth, and having put on the breastplate of righteousness, and, as shoes for your feet, having put on the readiness given by the gospel of peace. In all circumstances take up the shield of faith, with which you can extinguish all the flaming darts of the evil one; and take the helmet of salvation, and the sword of the Spirit, which is the word of God, praying at all times in the Spirit, with all prayer and supplication.
Ephesians 6:10-18

Once upon a time, there was an army commander who sent his troops out to battle. No sooner had he dispatched them than one of his men came running back to him in a panic. Wondering what could possibly have gone wrong so quickly, the commander started mentally running through the worst-case scenarios. Then the private shouted in disbelief, "Sir, it's *dangerous* out there! Those guys have weapons and they're *shooting* at us! Bullets were flying right past my head, and one of them almost hit me!" Wide-eyed and scared out of his wits, he grabbed the commander's shoulders and said, "You're not going to believe this, sir, but I think they're trying to *kill* me!" The commander snapped, "What are you talking about? Of course they're trying to kill you! They're the enemy. This is WAR! What exactly did you expect?"

I tell this simple story because, well, it's a bit ridiculous. How in the world could this soldier make it to the battlefield and still be so clueless about the fundamentals of war? This situation would never happen in a well-trained military unit, and yet this is exactly what happened to me. We are all born into a spiritual war, but I was well into my adult years before I realized this. I was just as shocked and unprepared as that soldier. *Wait, what? I'm in a war? I didn't ask for this! What did I ever do to get into a war?*

Even growing up in church I somehow missed the fact that I have an enemy who hates me, and that he *really* is out to destroy me. I walked around in a spiritual fog with no weapons to defend myself, completely oblivious to the personal attacks of the devil. For years I thought I had a right to peace and happiness, and I became super-annoyed when struggles came instead. I was confused and bewildered when I took a hit, I got miffed when others wounded me, and I wasn't above pitching a mild fit when life got hard. I desperately needed this missing awareness: **I have an enemy, and as long as I live on this earth I will have to fight the world, the flesh and the devil, whether I want to or not.** I learned that at any time I can be attacked by the enemy, simply because I live in a hostile, sinful world! Retreat is not one of our options. We must train for this battle or live in defeat. We must fight!

First I had to learn how to identify these attacks when they came. Once I could recognize the battles, I had to learn how to defend myself with the weapons provided by my Commander. This spiritual war is hard and, unfortunately, unavoidable. The good news is that because of Jesus' victory over sin at the Cross, I fight as a victor as I continually abide in Christ! He has paved the way for me to be an overcomer. Prior to the Cross, that was impossible. God has given His children His great and amazing promises along with numerous spiritual weapons to defeat our enemies.

> *For the weapons of our warfare are not of the flesh but have divine power to destroy strongholds. We destroy arguments and every lofty opinion raised against the knowledge of God, and take every thought captive to obey Christ, being ready to punish every disobedience, when your obedience is complete. (2 Corinthians 10:4-6)*

Our Spiritual Weapons of Warfare

Before we can go on the offense, we must first learn how to defend ourselves. I want to explore some of the different spiritual weapons that the Commander has provided for us. We are instructed in Ephesians 6 to daily "put on" our spiritual armor to fight against the enemy: Belt of Truth, Breastplate of Righteousness, Shoes of Peace, Shield of Faith, Helmet of Salvation, and the Sword of the Spirit. For years I had a textbook knowledge of how these pieces of armor function, and I could even visualize myself putting them on, but there was a block over my mind on exactly how they work in real life. I could list the different pieces of armor by heart, but I wasn't using them. In the heat of the battle I forgot everything and just wanted to run for my life! Spiritual armor and the weapons provided for believers were no more than an afterthought until the Commander prompted me to become aware of the attacks in my mind. He then started showing me how to apply the Belt of

Truth or the Helmet of Salvation in my struggle against sin. Once I learned how to identify the battle, He began to train me in the spiritual weapons needed for each conflict.

The pieces of armor and the weapons listed throughout this book are the tactics, strategies, and calls for backup which are at our disposal in the midst of a powerful mind battle. When we maintain constant communication with the Commander, He will train us how and when to use these weapons. When He instructs us to take up a specific weapon in the darkness of an intense battle, we need to be skilled with that weapon, ready to obey Him at a moment's notice. As with physical weapons, we can have a textbook knowledge of their use, but it's not until we handle the weapons in a real, live battle that we actually understand and experience their power. It is essential that we are actively training ourselves *outside* the battle to familiarize ourselves with each weapon, so that the moment a particular weapon is required *in* the battle, we will be able to swiftly wield it against the lies of the enemy.

Train Well and You Will Fight Well

In a physical war, every combatant knows that his very life will depend on the quality and accuracy of his tools. What is a warrior without his weapons? The best soldiers actively train themselves with the most effective weapons available. Ideally they are well equipped with the tools that best match their skill set. They take responsibility for obtaining, owning, sharpening and maintaining those weapons so that they will not fail in the heat of the battle. The highly skilled fighter knows he can't rely upon others to properly clean, sort and store his weapons. They need to be so familiar to him that they're like an extension of himself. He needs to know where they are at all times, their condition and how they handle, so that he is always prepared even for a surprise attack. Likewise, in the battlefield of our minds we must have our armories well-stocked with highly effective spiritual weapons. It is my prayer that we will grow in our understanding and skill with these weapons, finding out how each weapon handles in a fight. It is only through constant drilling that we will be transformed into highly skilled, advanced warriors in the army of God.

Like me, you will probably find some of these weapons to be your favorites. With each fight and each skillful use of our arsenal, we discover more and more about the Commander Who is our prize. He is a good God and has seen fit to give us many powerful weapons in order for us to be more than conquerors. Besides the main spiritual weapons listed in Ephesians 6, there are several weapons found buried in Scripture that we can use in a given struggle. This chapter will introduce a few of these strategies by discussing key Scriptures that mention them, and then walk you through some of my personal battles where I was instructed to use them. We will revisit these concepts and continue to discover more spiritual weapons as we advance through this book.

> **WARNING**: It is only fair to notify you that as we go through this book, the battles in your life will most likely intensify. It's part of our training! We must resist the urge to whine about it (okay, maybe just a little) and gear up for the fight instead. Our God is able to take anything the enemy throws at us and turn it around, redeeming it so that the attacks backfire on Satan. God will help us to gain spiritual ground instead of lose it. Freedom is coming. May that be so in our lives! Amen!

Weapon of Prayer

And pray in the Spirit on all occasions with all kinds of prayers and requests. With this in mind, be alert and always keep on praying for all the saints. (Ephesians 6:18)

Is anyone among you suffering? Let him pray. (James 5:13a)

Elijah was a man just like us. He prayed earnestly that it would not rain, and it did not rain on the land for three and a

> *half years. Again he prayed, and the heavens gave rain, and the earth produced its crops. (James 5:17-18)*

When we are under attack the *first thing* we must do as warriors is make immediate contact with our Commander. This seems so simple and obvious, yet I *often* fail to do this! Sometimes, it takes so long to recover from the surprise shock of the attack that I'm not thinking clearly enough to ask the Lord for help. As the Commander changes my way of thinking to expect these attacks, the lag time between the attack and my call for help is growing shorter. This weapon of prayer is essential for us to understand our Commander's instructions, His perspective and His plan of action. Unlike a military commander, the Lord never leaves us. Our Commander doesn't say, "Go do this, then come back and tell me when it's done." He is with us *always*, especially in the midst of our most confusing mind battles, and He will personally walk us through each stage of the battle we are facing. When we suffer through trials, God is not surprised, nor does He need a moment to recover. He is fully aware and completely trustworthy to oversee all areas of battle in this spiritual war.

The Bible tells us to pray without ceasing, and this is especially true in the midst of the battle. I must humble myself and cry out for help, asking for the ability to discern His voice from all the other battle noises. This takes practice. Too often when I delay or forget to come to Him first, I end up fighting the battle in my own strength and ignorance. Yet I have access to unlimited resources with clear, detailed instruction at the time I need it most, when I stay connected to the Commander through the direct line of the Spirit. It is the one weapon we must never lay aside, because our two-way communication with the Commander will alert us to our next move in the fight.

When my girls were younger they went through a stage where two of them were constantly fighting. This not only grieved me as a mother, but dealing with sibling rivalry day in and day out was downright annoying. Finally, it dawned on me that I could ask the Commander for help in this relentless, energy-draining fight. *Lord, I've tried everything I can think of. What should I do here?* The answer didn't come immediately, so like the "persistent widow" I just kept asking. Then this crazy idea started to develop in my mind. *Maybe I should make them share a room.* My strategy up to this point had been to keep them as far away from one another as possible! The idea to put them *in the same room* seemed counterintuitive, but the thought persisted and I realized that this might be God's instruction for me. After talking to my husband about it, I informed the kids that they were switching rooms. To my surprise, they were all excited about the idea and the transition went smoothly.

Kyle, their baby brother, was still taking afternoon naps at the time, and I had instituted an afternoon rest time where everyone in the family went to their rooms for a little R & R. That meant that the sisters would spend several hours a week alone together in their shared room. You can imagine I was a little nervous about how *that* would turn out! But the Lord knew what He was doing because my girls

> **"If any of you lacks wisdom, let him ask God, who gives generously to all without reproach, and it will be given him."**
> **James 1:5**

miraculously learned how to get along. When they had a disagreement during quiet time, they were required to work it out on their own instead of facing the *terrible* consequences of being forced to take a nap themselves! I could hear them in their room whispering loudly to each other: "Shhh, be quiet!" or "Fine, you can have my Barbie, but . . ." To my great joy, they were learning how to work together. In fact, after a few months, these two would disappear to their room even when it wasn't quiet time and I'd find them lost in the fun of their make-believe games. God had the best solution for my struggle with the girls' conflict; all I had to do was ask. Do you need to ask the Lord for wisdom in a struggle you are facing? Go ahead and lay it out for Him, seeking His advice and asking Him questions.

Weapon of the Word of God

For the word of God is living and active, sharper than any two-edged sword, piercing to the division of soul and of spirit, of joints and of marrow, and discerning the thoughts and intentions of the heart. And no creature is hidden from his sight, but all are naked and exposed to the eyes of him to whom we must give account. (Hebrews 4:12-13)

Every word of God proves true; he is a shield to those who take refuge in him. (Proverbs 30:5)

Jesus said to the Jews who had believed in him, "If you abide in my word, you are truly my disciples, and you will know the truth, and the truth will set you free." (John 8:31-32)

Do not let this Book of the Law depart from your mouth; meditate on it day and night, so that you may be careful to do everything written in it. Then you will be prosperous and successful. Have I not commanded you? Be strong and courageous. Do not be terrified; do not be discouraged, for the Lord your God will be with you wherever you go. (Joshua 1:8-9 NIV)

This weapon cannot be overemphasized. We simply will not be victorious without the truth of God's promises. We desperately need tangible, concrete truth to hold on to while we plod through the swamps of oppression and darkness in the fight against our opponent. The Word of God illuminates our path and gives us an eternal perspective in the midst of our circumstances. To be prepared for the recurring assaults on our minds, we must stock our arsenal by knowing and memorizing specific Bible verses. This is NOT optional for us as warriors in the army of God!

I try to teach my kids the value of memorizing Scripture, but they're young and they can't yet see the full benefit of it. So in order to encourage them to store God's Word in their minds, I challenge them to a memorizing contest with a reward they'll want to work for—*Pizza Party!* You might call this bribery, but I see it as an investment into their spiritual futures. Right now Darci and I are trying to memorize John 15, a well-known passage about abiding in Christ. In the past week we've recited this particular phrase numerous times: *"I am the true vine and my Father is the Gardener. He cuts off every branch in me that bears no fruit, while every branch in me that does bear fruit He prunes so that it will be even more fruitful"* (v. 1-2). Just this morning I found myself in a fierce fight with fear that left me dazed and confused. As I talked to the Commander about it, the phrase *"every branch in me that does bear fruit He prunes so that it will be even more fruitful"* kept running through my mind. I stopped and listened for the Father's voice. I felt Him telling me, *Hold still, Kori, this struggle is about pruning. I am doing something here that you can't understand. I want to take this area of fear and bring you freedom. It's painful now, but I will bring you through this process. I am doing a new thing! The old way was sufficient for a time, but now I want to do even more through you in this area. Wait on Me, and you will see the harvest to come.* This knowledge from the promise of the Scripture we were learning led me through the battle with clarity and a hope for the future.

To be honest, I had mentally separated our Scripture memorization from my everyday life until the Lord connected them for me. I didn't know I was going to be engaged in a battle this morning, but my God did. It was as if, days before the battle, the Commander gave me just the right weapon and instructed me to start sharpening it, even if I didn't yet know why. Then, right when I needed it, the Sword of the Spirit was in my hand and ready. When we proactively learn Scripture before an attack hits, we are building a storehouse of powerful battle verses that are sharpened and ready at a moment's notice.

But for me, more often than not, using the weapon of the Word is hindsight. One day I was talking with a close friend about a topic very important to me, when all of a sudden, out of the blue —*whack!* She delivered a verbal SLAM at me that hit the target— my heart! It was incredibly hurtful to me, a direct hit to an old wound, and I was left blindsided. The mind battle that followed her comment completely knocked me off my feet. I instinctively knew I needed the truth of the Word to hang on to until this emotional earthquake was over. Knowing the mind battle was just going to go from bad to worse by replaying our conversation, I went home, grabbed my Bible and opened it. The Lord gave me a short phrase from a passage that I was able to say over and over again to myself until He brought me safely through that painful battle. Slowly but surely, God's Word stabilized me as I began to regain my spiritual footing and mental perspective. My Commander knew this battle was coming and He was ready and waiting to meet me with the weapon of His Word. Friends, it's powerful!

Weapon of Praise and Worship

Let the high praises of God be in their throats and two-edged swords in their hands. (Psalm 149:6)

Through him then let us continually offer up a sacrifice of praise to God, that is, the fruit of lips that acknowledge his name. (Hebrews 13:15)

But thou art holy, O thou that inhabitest the praises of Israel. (Psalm 22:3 KJV)

Did you know that praise and celebration go hand in hand with faith and victory? Praise and worship are among our most powerful weapons against the devil. When we worship God in the midst of the battle, it shifts our focus from ourselves and our struggles to Someone much more worthy of our thoughts. There are times in worship that our God manifests His presence in a powerful way and it feels like He comes extremely close to us. Worship can lift us above the battle as if we are soaring over it, even as we are walking through it. Because the devil so desires to be worshiped, he can't stand to be around the true, heartfelt worship of God, and he'll do anything in his power to oppose it.

Worship makes the enemy hold his hands over his ears, fleeing for his life and taking all his whispering lies with him. Satan's downfall was his desire to be like God, sitting on His throne and having God worship him. Our worship of God not only lifts us up to the throne of God but also reminds the devil of what he will never have.

Sometimes we just have to stop in our tracks and seize this weapon! In fact, even as I write this book, I take a break at times to put this into practice. When I hit writer's block or a moment of confusion, I stop typing, go into another room, crank up the worship music, lift up my God with my whole heart for a few minutes, and then come back again to write the next section. Hold on a second . . .

. . . Okay, I'm back. Even though worship can be an amazing "holy of holies" experience, that's not always the case. Many times I don't feel like worshiping, and even after I choose to praise God, it brings no "warm fuzzies" to my spirit. When praising God doesn't even come close to reaching my emotions, it's important to do it anyway because worship is ultimately not about me, it's about God! Regardless of my circumstances, struggles or feelings, God is worthy of my praise. When I make the determined choice to wield this spiritual weapon, it is a declaration that Jesus is Lord over all—over me and over this corrupt world, my sinful flesh and the deceptive evil spirits attacking me in that moment. I wonder sometimes if this type of determined worship could be the purest form of all because it's not about me and what I want God to do for me or how I want to feel; instead it's all for the praise of the King!

If we ask God, He is faithful to train us in giving Him praise. We can sharpen this weapon by worshiping God with other believers. In corporate worship on a Sunday morning, the genuine adoration of my brothers and sisters in Christ accelerates and intensifies my own worship experience. The Commander often uses the songs to speak to me about an area of sin in my life, to teach me truth, to encourage me with His love, to direct me to pray for someone in my line of sight, or to give me some type of assignment for later. In the midst of Sunday worship, it is as if I am standing before the throne of God as He openly shares His heart with me. *"One thing have I desired of the Lord, that will I seek after, that I may dwell in the house of the Lord all the days of my life, to behold the beauty of the Lord, and to enquire in His temple" (Psalm 27:4 KJV).*

Weapon of the Name of Jesus

Therefore God has highly exalted him and bestowed on him the name that is above every name, so that at the name of Jesus every knee should bow, in heaven and on earth and under the earth, and every tongue confess that Jesus Christ is Lord, to the glory of God the Father. (Philippians 2:9-11)

Paul, having become greatly annoyed, turned and said to the spirit, "I command you in the name of Jesus Christ to come out of her." And it came out that very hour. (Acts 16:18)

And whatever you do, in word or deed, do everything in the name of the Lord Jesus, giving thanks to God the Father through him. (Colossians 3:17)

When Jesus was preparing to leave this earth and return to His Father in heaven, He gave the gift of His name, the name of Jesus, to His disciples.

And when that time comes, you will ask nothing of Me [you will need to ask Me no questions]. I assure you, most solemnly I tell you, that My Father will grant you whatever you ask in My Name [as presenting all that I AM]. Up to this time you have not asked a [single] thing in My Name [as presenting all that I AM]; but now ask and keep on asking and you will receive, so that your joy (gladness, delight) may be full and complete. (John 16:23-24 AMP)

This is how I understand this verse. Jesus walked with His disciples, showing them His ways, character and ministry. They were the ones who would continue the work He had started here on earth. It was as if Jesus was telling them: If you need anything, anything at all to help you continue My work, use My name. With My name, you can ask the Father for whatever you need. Up until now you have never used My name because I have been right here with you, but now you need to ask and keep on asking. The same is true for us. When we use the name of Jesus, it is just as powerful as if He were right here with us asking the Father on our behalf. His name is more powerful than we can even imagine, it is higher than any other name and it trumps all other authorities. We need to use it wisely, yes, but we must use it often, because we will need it to accomplish all that the Commander has for us to do.

For years, I was a little leery of this weapon. I didn't feel like I knew enough about the powerful name of Jesus, so I never used it—that was a big mistake on my part! I know now that this was the devil's strategy all along. Satan and his demons are subject to the name of Jesus and must flee when they hear it spoken in the faith and authority of Christ's ambassadors. This spiritual weapon is extremely powerful and may seem a bit intimidating to handle. You might think, *How do I use this weapon? What if I do it wrong? What if I ask for something in Jesus' name and nothing happens?* You may have seen others mishandle it, asking (or even demanding) crazy things from God based on the promise of this verse. This makes it easy to unconsciously dismiss the benefit of one of the most powerful weapons we have in the fight. It is our responsibility to study what Scripture says about the name of Jesus and pick up this weapon fearlessly, entrusting the Commander to train us appropriately. Please don't avoid this weapon simply because of confusion. Remember, we are in training, and that means constant practice. We may not always get it right, but we can't just throw up our hands in defeat—we must persevere. When you use His name, it represents His power and authority and is a weapon for us to use against the devil.

Therefore God has highly exalted him and bestowed on him the name that is above every name, so that at the name of Jesus every knee should bow, in heaven and on earth and under the earth, and every tongue confess that Jesus Christ is Lord, to the glory of God the Father. (Philippians 2:9-11)

I am very familiar with dread as a personal enemy. It is an emotion that I used to experience often. In fact, it was so familiar to me I thought it was a normal way of life—that is, until Jesus set me free. Do you want to know how? He instructed me to use the gift of His name! Before that, the feelings of dread were always in the back of my mind. Consistently there was something on my calendar that would stir up these feelings of dread, irrational scenarios, and dark "what if" possibilities. The panicky thought of an upcoming event or situation would dart into my mind and disturb me. The degree of this emotion would vary from *slightly* dreading it, to *sick to my stomach* dreading it. At times I lost hours or days pondering the dreadful event ahead. I might be having a great day and then out of the blue the "attack of dread" would hit like a storm cloud, promising a foreboding doom that was sure to come. At any given time the enemy could launch these thoughts of dread in my mind and I fell victim to them over and over again.

One of those times as I was in the midst of battling dread, the Lord brought a passage to mind. In Acts 16 the apostle Paul was on his way to the place of prayer to preach the gospel message. This was his calling as well as his regular custom. Before he got there he was interrupted by a slave girl who had a demonic spirit. The Bible says that it was a spirit of divination and the owners of the slave girl used her to make money by having her tell people's fortunes. This girl not only interrupted Paul and Silas but she followed them around for days, proclaiming loudly, *"These men are servants of the Most High God, who proclaim to you the way of salvation" (v. 17).* Now, you may think that she was providing a little free advertising, so what's the big deal? But this hounding lasted for days and her actions were a huge distraction from Paul's message. No doubt she constantly interrupted them from the work of God, stealing the spotlight, harassing Paul and Silas day after day, wearing them out with her disturbing presence. It says that Paul became so greatly annoyed that he turned to the spirit and said, *"I command you in the name of Jesus Christ to come out of her"* (v. 18). The passage concludes with the fact that the spirit left within the hour. When I read that passage, the Commander connected it to my current struggle and I knew that I too was being hounded by a relentless, annoying spirit that often distracted me from the work the Lord had called me to do. When that realization hit, the Lord instructed me to use the weapon of His name just like Paul did and command this demonic spirit to leave me alone. So that is exactly what I began to do. Every time I became aware of the feelings and thoughts of dread, I would pull out the weapon of the name of Jesus and tell the harassing spirit out loud to leave me alone, not by my power but by the authority and power of the One Who sits on the throne with everything underneath His feet. Now I rarely battle with dread; it hardly shows up in my life anymore but on the occasion that it does, I know exactly how to fight it. Freedom tastes good! *"Through the resurrection of Jesus Christ, who has gone into heaven and is at the right hand of God, with angels, authorities, and powers having been subjected to him"* (1 Peter 3:21-22).

We can practice using this weapon simply by speaking the name of Jesus out loud throughout the day. I find it to be similar to a spiritual alignment that keeps me focused on Jesus and moving on the straight and narrow path set before me. As we awaken in the morning, it can be the first word on our lips, and when our heads hit the pillow at night may it be the last whispered word before we drift off to sleep. When we speak the name of Jesus, we consciously and purposely focus our hearts and minds upon who Jesus is and all that He represents. Don't think you have to completely understand this weapon before you use it; quite the opposite is true because, as you call on the name of Jesus more and more, the Commander will show you how to more accurately operate such a powerful weapon against the enemy. It is a gift to us. He promises to supply us with His limitless resources when we ask for whatever we need to accomplish His will with the name of Jesus. I had to wade through the muck of doubt, skepticism and disappointment the enemy wanted me to get stuck in before I started aiming this weapon of the name of Jesus right at the heart of the enemy's plans. His name is POWERFUL!

Weapon of the Body of Christ

Be sober-minded; be watchful. Your adversary the devil prowls around like a roaring lion, seeking someone to devour. Resist him, firm in your faith, knowing that the same kinds of suffering are being experienced by your brotherhood throughout the world. And after you have suffered a little while, the God of all grace, who has called you to his eternal glory in Christ, will himself restore, confirm, strengthen, and establish you. (1 Peter 5:8-10)

Pray also for me, that whenever I open my mouth, words may be given me so that I will fearlessly make known the mystery of the gospel, for which I am an ambassador in chains. Pray that I may declare it fearlessly, as I should. (Ephesians 6:19-20)

No warrior fights alone. There are times when I have to call for support and reinforcement from the body of Christ in my battles. I just won't make it without help from other warriors who are alert and experienced in battle. When Paul fought discouragement and fear in prison he pulled out this weapon, pleading for others to pray for him to have the words and the boldness for the task ahead. Sometimes we need prayer coverage, and we need it now! One morning everything seemed to be going wrong, from cranky kids, to getting stuck in a snow bank, to receiving some bad news, to you-name-it, including a looming dark cloud of sadness. I just couldn't shake the battle and I sensed that it was only going to get worse, so I called for backup.

I texted my Bible study ladies a short message of what was going on and asked them to be praying. These friends are well aware of spiritual battles and they were all over this prayer request. Picture a highly trained Special Ops team moving toward you at extraordinary speed, spiritually encircling you with their shields of faith, picking you up when you've got nothing left to give and rushing you out of the heat of battle toward safety. Within minutes of my text for help, there was a lifting of the oppression that just moments before wouldn't budge. Now my day that was doomed to be a *terrible day* was completely redeemed, as the Lord turned EVERY bad thing that had happened that morning into something good. We all NEED fellow warriors who "have our backs" when we are vulnerable. And we need to be aware enough to provide that same prayer support for others. If you don't have this type of support, ask the Commander to build a team around you. Then keep your spiritual eyes open to whom He puts in your path!

There are prayer warriors all over the world who have been trained by the Commander to pray. They may not know the details of whom, where, and why they need to pray, but they are disciplined to obey the urgent promptings of the Holy Spirit. They have taken this verse seriously: *"And pray in the Spirit on all occasions with all kinds of prayers and requests. With this in mind, be alert and always keep on praying for all the saints" (Ephesians 6:18).* We have the privilege to ask the Commander to alert and activate those prayer warriors to intercede for us as we fight the battle at that very moment. Likewise, our brothers and sisters all over the world are facing battles every day. We must never forget that we are not alone in this war, but rather connected to a spiritual and global body of Christ.

One morning as I was vacuuming, my meandering thoughts began to focus on a woman I hadn't thought about in years. I had worked with her and knew her fairly well in college but hadn't seen or spoken to her in ten years. That morning however, without warning, the Lord urged me to pray for her. The urging was so strong that I stopped what I was doing and took some time to pray exclusively for her. While praying, I sensed in my spirit that she was at a crossroads in her life and was going to be making a tough decision very soon, maybe even that very morning. In my emotions, I began to feel the struggle that she could possibly be feeling—even though I didn't know any of the details of the situation. As I experienced and felt her burden, I started praying specifically for peace and clarity over her mind and the boldness to do the right thing regardless of what others may expect of her. It was about 15 minutes of intense prayerful battle before the urgency began to subside. Afterward, I finished my vacuuming. I will probably never know, this side of heaven, exactly what that was all about. Honestly, the experience left more questions than answers but I have learned to be okay with that. I am just so grateful that God used me to pray for one of my sisters-in-Christ who was engaged in rough battle.

Weapon of Thankfulness

Rejoice always, pray without ceasing, give thanks in all circumstances; for this is the will of God in Christ Jesus for you. Do not quench the Spirit. (1 Thessalonians 5:16-19)

Let us come into his presence with thanksgiving; let us make a joyful noise to him with songs of praise! (Psalm 95:2)

And be thankful. Let the word of Christ dwell in you richly, teaching and admonishing one another in all wisdom, singing psalms and hymns and spiritual songs, with thankfulness in your hearts to God. And whatever you do, in word or deed, do everything in the name of the Lord Jesus, giving thanks to God the Father through him. (Colossians 3:16-17)

The weapon of thankfulness is one of our best defenses against negative thoughts, covetousness, selfishness, and the depressing lies of the enemy. Our Commander has instructed us to rejoice always for a reason and we must listen and obey if we are going to be overcomers. Sometimes this is the last thing we want to do in battle! However, thankfulness is a dangerous and deadly weapon against our enemy. It redirects our attention from ourselves and our circumstances to things God has *already* done for us by highlighting the many ways He has blessed us. The weapon of gratitude opens the door to praise, which inevitably leads to JOY. The Word says that the joy of the Lord is our strength! So ultimately, thankfulness leads to renewed strength.

It can be difficult to pick up this weapon and start swinging it in the middle of a battle—especially when I can't seem to nail down one single positive thought! My thoughts can be so toxic that

"Every good and perfect gift is from above, coming down from the Father of lights with whom there is no variation or shadow due to change."

James 1:17

thankfulness seems impossible. When I am in that state of mind, I must be quick, intentional and forceful before I drown in negativity. I simply begin by thanking God for whatever is in my line of sight. If I happen to be in my kitchen, I may begin to thank God for my appliances, forcing myself to be thankful and even exaggerating my enthusiasm a bit to get the thankfulness rolling. "Thank You, God, for my microwave. Wow, I bet I use that microwave 15 times a day . . . I love the 30 second button, it's one of my favorite features . . . and the light underneath that helps me see when I cook. Lord, I am so glad that it works properly. My husband gave this to me as a gift and I am so thankful for it. I didn't even have to pay someone to install it because he did it for me. Thank You for that man. Wow, every good gift comes from You!" Then I move on to my dishwasher and follow this line of thinking wherever it takes me. (You DO NOT even want me to get started on how much I appreciate my dishwasher! I could go into great detail of all the many ways I am so very thankful for that particular appliance.) I will spare you the details, but I must not spare myself. I have to remind myself in times of distress the multiple ways in which the Lord has blessed me, thanking Him for every tiny little detail—even if I have to start with what is right in front of my face.

You see, it doesn't take long to redirect your thoughts. Sometimes the hardest part is getting started, but once we *do* pick up this weapon, it can open the floodgates of thankfulness. One thankful thought leads to another and then another, until we are cruising down the road of gratitude. This can become a habit for us as we sharpen our weapon by daily use. Tell God, out loud, several things that you are thankful for today. Be intentional about increasing your skill in wielding this weapon. It has more benefits than you can even imagine. Who knows? Perhaps it could even save your life one day.

Prayer:

Dear Father,
Thank You for all the weapons that You have given me so that I may be ready and skilled in the battles I face on a daily basis. Teach me about every one of them and help me grow in my understanding of them. At just the right time, bring to mind the spiritual weapons You want me to use and show me how they work in the fight. I trust You to guide me into truth and victory.
In Jesus' name, Amen.

Action Steps: Journal your prayers, answers and all the things the Commander reveals to you.

1. Choose a spiritual weapon from this chapter. Research it by looking up all the verses in Scripture you can find about it. Ask the Commander to reveal the spiritual "features" of this weapon and how it could work in the midst of a mind battle. If the Lord gives you any instructions on how to practice this weapon then be obedient, asking Him to prompt you when and how throughout your day.

2. Choose another spiritual weapon and repeat the above instructions.

3. The next time you recognize that you are in a mind battle, pray! Ask the Lord to help you use one or more of these weapons: Word of God, Praise and Worship, Name of Jesus, Body of Christ, or Thankfulness.

Chapter Four
The Battle Against the World

But far be it from me to boast except in the cross of our Lord Jesus Christ, by which the world has been crucified to me, and I to the world.
Galatians 6:14

Our whole family loves to hang out at Grandma's house. We go there often just to get some downtime from our busy lives. Grandma is one of those hospitable ladies who loves to take good care of her family and, to be honest, we love being taken care of! At her house there is always an abundance of yummy food, laughter, card games, cozy blankets and family time. When my girls were younger, one of their favorite pastimes there was the video game called *Just Dance*. Often, after a huge home-cooked meal, we would all move into the living room, snuggle up with the fire going, and watch the girls display their crazy dance moves. It was fun for the whole family to watch each of my kids' personalities come to life as they felt the freedom to *express themselves* unhindered!

On this video game, there was one particular song with a "get stuck in your head" tune. At first I thought the song was about friendships, but later I realized it was about a girl trying to steal another girl's boyfriend. Even though I didn't play the game, I found myself singing the words to that song over and over for the next few days. I tried to stop it, but the song kept popping back in my mind. (Even now as I write this, the song is *stuck* in my head!)

As I pondered the words of this song, "Girlfriend," by Avril Lavigne, I could sense a familiar prompting from the Commander as He instructed me to pay attention to what was playing out in my mind and the minds of others who might be listening to it. It seemed innocent enough with its catchy beat, but it had a hidden agenda that targeted the minds of young girls. After some research, I discovered that the song promoted jealousy, competition, and a bold, conquering attitude. Whoa! This song was telling young ladies that if they like a guy but he already has a girlfriend, it's okay to seduce him, hate his girlfriend, bash her character and take her down in order to steal her boyfriend. I was obliged to sit down with my girls and point out the worldly ideas in this song. When we talked about it, the girls admitted to knowing the words by heart but not truly understanding what they meant, at least not fully. But like a seed that gets planted in the ground, this song was already committed to memory by my three girls. We had a good discussion dissecting its message and examining how it lined up —or didn't line up!—with the truth in God's Word. I'm glad the Commander alerted me to this but I am sure it won't be the last time it happens. Has this ever happened to you? A song gets stuck in your head, and while it's otherwise a really good song it seems there's always that *one bad word* or that *one phrase* they could have done without. Why is it always the bad part and not the good that replays in our minds? And is it really that big a deal?

Music has a way of penetrating our souls. As we rehearse a song over and over again in our minds, its values and ideas can become ingrained in our belief systems. This fallen world is constantly speaking to us. Are we paying attention to what it is saying? A song strategically placed in a kids' game is just one example of how the enemy uses the things of this world to spread his lies, blurring the boundary lines of God's commandments. We do not need proof that this world is corrupt; most of us can see that already. What we need is God's discernment to understand how this world is influencing us personally, so that we can effectively fight against it.

The Start of This World's Corruption

The "world" we are talking about is not the physical earth, but rather the interactions, mindsets, and cultural structures that define how the human world operates. In order to understand why God's children are in a battle against the fallen, broken aspects of this world and its systems, we need to appreciate how God originally created it and what led to its corruption. Why is it such a hostile environment for us when it was originally created to be a paradise? The spirit-being initially behind the decay of this world was the fallen angel, Lucifer, as he introduced and marketed sin to our first parents, Adam and Eve. Lucifer was one of the most beautiful and powerful angels that God created, and his assignment was to guard the throne of God. Becoming inflated with pride, he decided that he would rather sit and rule on God's throne than guard it. *"Your heart was proud because of your beauty; you corrupted your wisdom for the sake of your splendor. I cast you to the ground"* (Ezekiel 28:17). He was arrogant enough to believe that he could fight God, usurp His authority and gain His throne. But the

"How you are fallen from heaven, O Lucifer, son of the morning! How you are cut down to the ground, You who weakened the nations! For you have said in your heart: 'I will ascend into heaven, I will exalt my throne above the stars of God; I will also sit on the mount of the congregation on the farthest sides of the north; I will ascend above the heights of the clouds, I will be like the Most High.' Yet you shall be brought down to Sheol, to the lowest depths of the Pit."

Isaiah 14:12-15 NKJV

Creator God said, "No!" and threw him down from Heaven like lightning.

When Satan was hurled from Heaven, not only did he lose his fight for the throne of God but he also forfeited his heavenly position and authority. He was utterly defeated, with no place to call his home. The Scriptures don't tell us exactly when this occurred, but we do know that Satan was already in his wicked and fallen state when he approached Eve in the Garden of Eden. His eye looked covetously at this world as the only alternative to set up a throne and build a kingdom for himself. However, there was one problem: God had already given mankind the authority to rule this world. It must have been a burr in Satan's side to see humanity, far inferior to himself in beauty and intelligence, being given the entire domain of this world while he was banished from Heaven and left with nothing.

The Beginning of the Kingdom of Darkness

God set up mankind to rule this world and take dominion over it. Everything that God made, He gave to Adam and Eve to govern. It was a high calling, a huge responsibility and a gift to them to be overseers of the world and all that was in it. The devil knew that as long as Adam and Eve obeyed God, they would stay underneath the covering and protection of God's sovereignty. And so the plot to deceive and to swindle mankind out of his God-given authority over the earth was put in play. Eve was the first to take the bait and believe the same lie that Satan himself had believed: *God is holding out on me and if I take matters into my own hands, then I can be like God.* Adam followed. Once the sin was committed, God's holiness could not come into contact with their fallen nature without destroying them. They were sent out from the Garden of Eden, away from paradise and away from the tree of life. They died spiritually that day and were banished from the garden.

Because of their disobedience, Adam and Eve walked right out from God's authority and protection and gave Satan the place that God had held in their lives by listening to and obeying his lies instead of God's truth. Now that they were separated from God by their sin, the devil easily usurped their authority to rule this world and set up his kingdom of darkness here on earth. *". . . and the whole world lies in the power of the evil one"* (1 John 5:19b). Adam and Eve became slaves of Satan's kingdom of darkness, along with all of their offspring.

God's Solution for This Fallen World

Even though mankind scorned God's original plan for this world, our God provided a way of escape for mankind through His Son, Jesus. God's solution is to transfer all who trust in Jesus from the kingdom of darkness into the eternal kingdom of His Son. For those of us who have surrendered our lives to Jesus, His kingdom —not this world—is our true home. We have embraced the work that God has done for us in liberating us from the grip of the enemy. This is a work that only God can do. Spiritually

> **"But our citizenship is in heaven, and from it we await a Savior, the Lord Jesus Christ, who will transform our lowly body to be like his glorious body, by the power that enables him even to subject all things to himself."**
>
> **Philippians 3:20-21**

speaking, God the Father rescued us from the destruction of this world and has literally enveloped us safely inside the strength, righteousness and personality of His Son. Jesus has overcome this world and we too are overcomers because we are in Christ. We are hidden in Him, abiding and thriving inside of Jesus. This position gives us all the benefits of sons and daughters of God, so that we will not perish with the destruction of this corrupt world. *"He has delivered us from the domain of darkness and transferred us to the kingdom of his beloved Son, in whom we have redemption, the forgiveness of sins"* (Colossians 1:13-14).

The choice to believe in Jesus is a decision every individual must make. We either call upon the one and only Savior Jesus Christ to rescue us from the destruction to come, or we reject God's Son and suffer the consequences of our sin. Those of us who belong to the everlasting kingdom of our God will get to experience the new heaven and the new earth as we dwell in close relationship with God once again. This is the restoration of what was lost to our first parents, Adam and Eve, in the Garden of Eden.

> *Then I saw a new heaven and a new earth, for the first heaven and the first earth had passed away, and the sea was no more. And I saw the holy city, new Jerusalem, coming down out of heaven from God, prepared as a bride adorned for her husband. And I heard a loud voice from the throne saying, "Behold, the dwelling place of God is with man. He will dwell with them, and they will be his people, and God himself will be with them as their God. He will wipe away every tear from their eyes, and death shall be no more, neither shall there be mourning nor crying nor pain anymore, for the former things have passed away." (Revelation 21:1-4)*

By God's word, this corrupt world will one day come to an end. The timeline of the kingdom of darkness and the destruction of this current world are intertwined and culminate at the Judgment Day. *"But by the same word the heavens and earth that now exist are stored up for fire, being kept until the day of judgment and destruction of the ungodly"* (2 Peter 3:7). Even now the physical earth has been affected by sin and darkness and is being held back from all it once was. The Scripture says it is currently longing for the time when God will make all things new.

> *The creation waits in eager expectation for the sons of God to be revealed. For the creation was subjected to frustration, not by its own choice, but by the will of the one who subjected it, in hope that the creation itself will be liberated from its bondage to decay and brought into the glorious freedom of the children of God. We know that the whole creation has been groaning as*

in the pains of childbirth right up to the present time. Not only so, but we ourselves, who have the first fruits of the Spirit, groan inwardly as we wait eagerly for our adoption as sons, the redemption of our bodies. (Romans 8:19-23 NIV)

This is why, if we are honest, even on the best days here on earth we still long for more. Even though we can't quite explain it, we know we were made for more than this world can offer us. We have God's own Spirit living inside of us, giving us a taste of what is to come. *"But, as it is written, 'What no eye has seen, nor ear heard, nor the heart of man imagined, what God has prepared for those who love him'—these things God has revealed to us through the Spirit" (1 Corinthians 2:9-10).* Can you think of a time when you have longed for more? Has the Spirit of God ever given you a taste or glimpse of what will be someday? Invite Him to show you.

We know that this world is passing away. Therefore we are instructed to cling tightly to our new home by identifying and obeying our Commander's decrees and rejecting the systems of this sinful world. Our antidote for this fallen world is the kingdom of heaven.

> *Do not love the world or the things in the world. If anyone loves the world, the love of the Father is not in him. For all that is in the world—the desires of the flesh and the desires of the eyes and pride in possessions—is not from the Father but is from the world. And the world is passing away along with its desires, but whoever does the will of God abides forever. (1 John 2:15-17)*

The degree to which we love this world, embrace its concepts and seek after its pleasures is the degree to which it has a hold on us. The apostle Paul boasted in the Cross of Jesus Christ and claimed that by the Cross the world had been crucified to him, and he to the world. Wow! That means that the world had no hold on Paul and he had no hold on the world. Ideally, that is where all the children of God should be; the world and its glamour has no allure and holds no enticement for us compared to Jesus and our new citizenship in heaven. That might sound a bit foreign to us. Could we really be so enthralled with our Creator and fit so perfectly in the kingdom of heaven that this world truly has nothing for us? This would be a great time to stop and ask the Commander do this very thing in our lives.

World Systems

This fallen world's philosophies, beliefs and world systems have been designed and established by Satan and his kingdom of darkness. He is the mastermind behind the thoughts, ideas and agendas of many of the world's governmental and cultural systems. They affect every nation and ethnic group with written and unwritten rules that can change from generation to generation. Some of these systems are blatantly evil, like the world-wide abortion industry or the pornography and human trafficking industries. Others are more subtle. There are many political, religious, educational, and social systems in place that are helpful, bring order and promote good; yet we cannot ignore the forces of evil *behind* these systems which breed deception and can lead us astray.

An example is the public school system. The school that my kids attend promotes positive character traits such as work ethic, respect and kindness. The students are encouraged to make good choices in their daily routine and to take responsibility for their behavior. The staff upholds many godly principles and reinforces some of the values my husband and I teach at home. However, I must not assume everything that is taught at this school is good. With any educational institution, the question to consider is this: What is the philosophy *behind* its teachings? Does it line up with God's character and the truth found in the Bible? *"See to it that no one takes you captive by philosophy and empty deceit, according to human tradition, according to the elemental spirits of the world, and not according to Christ"* (Colossians 2:8).

If you look at this world you will find that the things that are important to God, such as generosity, humility, selflessness, and serving others, are of least importance and even despised by this world. Likewise, the things that God calls sin—the love of money, pride, revenge, sexual immorality, and so on—are condoned and even encouraged by this world. Many things that we think and believe about ourselves, our world, and our God are incorrect and have been set in place by the demonic kingdom long before we were born. We need to be alert and constantly on guard to identify the subtle attacks of the enemy. Satan has set up the systems of this world to be in direct opposition to the ways of the kingdom of heaven. He is well acquainted with the operations of God and has the intelligence to twist and corrupt them to spite God. Yet even in the midst of Satan's scams, he can never outwit God. *"The Lord has made everything [to accommodate itself and contribute] to its own end and His own purpose—even the wicked [are fitted for their role] for the day of calamity and evil"* (Proverbs 16:4 AMP).

Dave Ramsey, founder of the money management program *Financial Peace University*, has a session entitled "Buyer Beware." In this lesson he reveals the hidden strategies companies use to get people to buy their products. Corporations spend big money hiring marketing experts who spend hours brainstorming, designing logos and slogans, and strategizing ways to sell their merchandise. They thoroughly study the targeted audience, trying to get *into the mind* of the consumer in order to convince him that he has to have the product. They then advertise in a way that subconsciously links the merchandise with what the purchaser desires: pleasure, glamor, being on the cutting edge, or even normalcy (hinting at the fact that you're *not* normal if you don't have this item). They also study when and where to position their products in the store for the most profit, paying extra for prime shelf space. I'm sure you've heard the candy bar at the checkout counter calling your name. It's right there, easily accessible and slightly overpriced, waiting for you to impulsively grab it. Then there's the stress-free "one click" online purchasing and the "have it now, pay later" financing gimmicks that are all part of the well-thought-out strategies that manipulate and hook the unsuspecting consumer.

If this type of planning and marketing happens in our physical world, then what makes us think it doesn't happen in the spiritual realm? The devil and his kingdom of darkness are also in the business of marketing. The product he is selling is sin. If you really stop to think about it, the enemy markets sin in the same way that companies market their products. If we are unaware, we can easily consume the well-packaged sinful thoughts and ideas of the kingdom of darkness. Undetected, these thoughts take root and start to grow deep in our minds to become a mindset or natural way of thinking. Believing these subtle lies, we will begin to act on them. It would be wise to stop and ask the Commander right now: Lord, where am I "consuming" sin unaware? Where have I been tricked by the evil one in this area? And how has he done this to me?

The satanic world system seeks to steal, kill and destroy all who will fall victim to its beliefs. It would be naïve of us to think that none of these world systems have infiltrated our own belief system. It is crucial that we recognize the message this world is sending so that we are not deceived into believing philosophies that have been set up by Satan and his cohorts. The Bible warns us that many will fall victim to this. *"Now the Spirit expressly says that in later times some will depart from the faith by devoting themselves to deceitful spirits and teachings of demons"* (1 Timothy 4:1). Lord, please keep us from this! We are at war against these world systems. We need to be armed with God's Word so we can quickly respond with God's truth to the ideas and beliefs that seek to enter our minds, taking us captive to do the will of Satan.

All counterfeit religious systems have been set up by Satan and his demons to deceive the human race and lure them away from the one and only true God. Throughout history, numerous false gods and religions have been established to fulfill mankind's need to worship and serve a higher being. The devil loves to take God's truth, manipulate it, twist it and bury a tiny drop of poison in it to deceive mankind—anything he can do to keep us from trusting in Jesus as the *only* way to God. Years ago, a woman recommended that I listen to a pastor's teaching she had really enjoyed. I was not familiar with the man or his teaching, but because of her excitement I told her I would listen to it. Within the first ten minutes of listening, I became very uncomfortable in my spirit. The pastor quoted Scripture and talked about God's love and mercy, but something seemed off. This internal angst became so "loud" that I had to stop what I was doing and ask the Commander what was going on. *Lord, why am I having such a hard time with what this man is teaching? I can't put my finger on anything that he is saying that goes against Your Word, so what's the problem?*

I stopped the recording and looked up all the verses he was quoting. I came to the conclusion that either I was under the conviction of the Holy Spirit and I needed to repent of unbelief in my heart, or this man was saying the right things but preaching with a worldly spirit that riled the Holy Spirit within me. At that point I simply didn't know. Confused, I shut off the teaching and asked the Lord for wisdom. Later that day, I found out that this pastor belonged to a movement that focused on one aspect of God's character, elevating it to the exclusion of others. By teaching a *partial* gospel message, he was actually teaching a *false* gospel message and leading many people down a path of deception. There was no earthly way I could have known that when I began listening to one sermon! This man was saying all the right things, even quoting Scripture to back up his point. It was the Commander Who gave me immediate discernment, and later the confirmation of His prompting. Some of the most dangerous forms of false religion are the ones that appear to be the closest to God's truth. There are countless deceptive religious traps in this world. We need the leading of the Commander and the written Word to help us keep in step with His truth.

Our Culture Is Speaking to Us: What Is It Saying?

The various social systems of this world tend to gauge the value of a person by gender, job status, income, race, physical attractiveness, and a multitude of other surface characteristics. In our western culture, people are infatuated with outward appearance, but our God is not. The world's definition of beauty is different in each culture. What one culture finds extremely beautiful another culture might find ugly and offensive. Our standards can even change from one generation to the next. For instance, in the 1950s in the United States, a size-twelve full-figured woman was considered supermodel material; today, a tall and slender size three is the picture of perfection. Wow! Who can keep up? The biblical view is that lasting beauty is found only in Jesus Christ, and He is the One who bestows *His* beauty upon His children. *"Let the saints be joyful in the glory and beauty [which God confers upon them]; let them sing for joy upon their beds" (Psalm 149:5 AMP).*

As a mother of four children, I spend a considerable amount of time going to various doctor's appointments. I recall one visit when I was browsing through a popular women's magazine in the waiting room. I quickly glanced through it, noticing all the slender models in their beautiful dresses. An article caught my eye about a young music artist's year-long diet that enabled her to have the rock star body she wanted to match her rock star career. It showed the classic before-and-after pictures. I remember thinking that she looked great in her "before" picture and maybe a little too thin in her "after" picture. The article went on to show pictures of the food portions she ate before her diet, in contrast to the tiny portions eaten while on her diet. I was surprised that the portions she ate *before* her diet looked strikingly similar to the portions I eat daily. *Oh dear!* It was meant to be an encouraging article with the message, "If I can eat less, lose weight, and feel great about myself, then you can too!" If I had to sum up my thoughts about this article as I was reading, they would be, *I'm glad you feel good about yourself, sweetie, but honestly, you looked great before you started to starve yourself.* I left a few minutes later and didn't give it another thought . . .

The next day, I unconsciously started thinking about the magazine article and my mind went in the direction of its hidden message. I pondered: *I wonder what it would be like to be so beautiful and wear one of those gorgeous dresses? I would definitely have to look different than I do now. I'd need to be much thinner to look the part. I'd be content to be as skinny as that woman's "before" picture, but if her "before" picture wasn't good enough then I'm certainly not good enough! I bet I eat too much. I should probably start eating less. Better yet, I should skip a few meals to slim down.* These thoughts came with feelings of dissatisfaction with the way I look and disgust with myself for eating too much. This inner dialogue went on for a while until I realized that I was in the midst of a mind battle. You see, when I first read the article I could see the anorexic tendencies in it. But subconsciously, some tiny seeds of doubt were planted in my mind so that the next day those thoughts tried to take root in my belief system to control my behavior. The veiled message in this particular magazine article was that women should be "toothpick thin" in order to be acceptable. Her "after" picture depicted what our culture deems *ideal*, sending women their message of what a "normal, healthy, beautiful" woman *should* look like. But this worldly message simply doesn't match God's perspective. The Word of God says that man looks on the outward appearance but God looks at the heart. This was not the first time Satan had used our culture's standard for beauty to feed me lies and throw me into a mind battle.

I will likely spend many more hours in waiting rooms, and I'll need to be careful in choosing the magazines I read. Every piece of literature is promoting some type of worldview. As Christians we must discern the subtle messages of the enemy coming through the pages of books and magazines, and refuse to allow anything access to our minds that is potentially harmful. Each one of us has different areas of vulnerability—some people could read the very same article and be completely unaffected by it. However, the Commander has personally shown me that looking at this type of magazine opens the door for a spiritual attack on my mind. What might be totally fine for others is not safe for me, and I must be obedient to the Commander to steer clear of my culture's mindset of beauty. What about you? Is the Commander bringing anything to your mind right now that is a danger zone for you? Ask Him to meet you there and give you His instructions.

Guarding Our Minds from Evil

Everything we encounter in this world is sending us a message. We need to ask the Commander to help us discern the spirit behind these things—is it good or evil? Is it truth that comes from the kingdom of heaven or is it deception that comes from the kingdom of darkness? What is the subtle or not-so-subtle message coming through the song, movie, classroom lecture or even the church sermon? One way we can discern the spirit or message behind what we see and hear is by paying attention to the direction of our thoughts during and after the experience. Once again, it comes back to our thinking! Are our thoughts good, positive, pure, excellent and noble, focusing on God and others, bringing us closer to Him? Or are our thoughts dark, impure, judgmental, slanderous and self-consumed, pulling us away from our relationship with God? Our assignment as believers is to take captive the thoughts that come at us. When we do not do this, we unsuspectingly walk right into the enemy's trap. By our disobedience and intentional sin we fall prey to the ambush of the enemy, making us susceptible to one relentless attack after another.

The other night I was about fifteen minutes into a movie when several sexual comments were made by the characters. I felt strongly prompted by the Lord to turn off the movie, but I was nestled in my recliner with a big bowl of popcorn. Too tired to get up, I just sat there hoping the movie would get better. At one point the movie introduced a sexual perversion I had never heard of before. It was presented in a non-threatening way by actually *condemning* the practice at first. The characters responded to it in a shocked and disgusted way that softened the horror of it. However, toward the end of the movie the same sexual idea was revisited, but this time the characters readily accepted it. By the end of the movie, I felt convicted that I should not have watched it. In fact, it was a pretty worthless movie. I didn't fully comprehend the damage to my mind until later that week when I caught myself thinking about the sexual idea presented in the movie. It wasn't that I desired to practice it —my thoughts were more objective, wondering exactly how it was possible to carry out something that grossly perverted. These thoughts entered my mind in such a nonthreatening way that I caught myself visualizing the particular details of how "other people" might carry out this disturbing sexual act before I realized, *Yuck! What am I thinking?*

As soon as I recognized the dark, impure direction of my thoughts, I knew I had opened the door to them by disobeying the Commander and watching that movie. This "lighthearted comedy" had a message of sexual immorality threaded throughout it. Perhaps it was the enemy's agenda to desensitize the viewer to a type of sexual perversion that years from now will be commonly accepted and practiced in our culture. I could have avoided this entire mind battle if I had simply listened and obeyed the prompting of the Commander within the first fifteen minutes of the movie! With every battle we face, even if it is one we initially lose, the Lord is teaching us to be wise and discerning by closely guarding the things we allow in our minds. *"Behold, I am sending you out as sheep in the midst of wolves, so be wise as serpents and innocent as doves"* (Matthew 10:16).

"Be sober-minded; be watchful. Your adversary the devil prowls around like a roaring lion, seeking someone to devour."

1 Peter 5:8

These corrupt world systems have been around for years, and the devil has used them to introduce mankind to countless lies and ungodly mindsets. Even though these world systems might have some positive traits we must never forget who is behind them, and his ultimate goal. Remember, we don't belong here. We must cling to the written Word and the guidance of the Holy Spirit to detect the subtle and deceptive lies of the enemy hidden within the world systems that surround us.

Prayer:

Dear Father,
I thank You that You are always with me. I thank You that it is Your kindness that leads me to repentance. Lord, I invite You into my mind and I give You full and free access to my thoughts. Please help me guard the things I allow myself to see, read, and hear. May Your Spirit of Truth stop me every time I entertain the subtle lies this world desires to feed me. Grant me Your divine discernment to recognize the deceptive message behind the systems of this world. I confess I cannot do this on my own. Father, help me; wake me up spiritually and build in me a dependency upon Your promptings so that discerning between good and evil becomes a way of life for me. God, I trust You and commit this process completely to You.
In Jesus' name, Amen.

Action Steps: Journal your prayers, answers and all the things the Commander reveals to you.

1. Ask the Lord to open your eyes to the messages coming at you this week. Be proactive to read between the lines and discover the voice of the evil one behind the products, organizations and systems of this world.

2. As you watch a movie, glance at billboards, listen to music, play video games, see advertisements, or even think about universities, churches, and businesses you interact with, ask the Lord to talk to you. What are these things communicating? What is the culture saying to

you? What attitudes, behaviors or character traits are being promoted? Are they good or bad? Allow the Commander to show you if you have any of these characteristics in your life.

3. Think of your favorite song. In one sentence, what is its message? Is it a good message? Does it line up with God's character and truth, or does it promote something other than God's truth? If so, what is it promoting? Then make it personal by asking the Commander if any of this way of thinking could be found in your life.

4. Pay attention to your thoughts and emotions during and after your experiences and interactions throughout your day. Allow the Lord to show you anything you expose yourself to on a regular basis that is dangerous for you, and take steps to guard your heart against those messages.

Chapter Five
Identifying Worldly Mindsets

For everyone who has been born of God overcomes the world. And this is the victory that has overcome the world—our faith. Who is it that overcomes the world except the one who believes that Jesus is the Son of God?
1 John 5:4-5

We all enter this world with a childlike innocence that simply takes people as they are. But as we get older the world begins to project its own thoughts and values on us. As I grew up I started to take account of how people looked, and I wholeheartedly adopted our culture's belief that a woman's worth is found in her outward appearance. As a teenager I was constantly hounded with thoughts of being ugly, and dreamed about what it would be like to be extremely beautiful. When I left the awkward middle school years and started high school, I started getting some positive attention for my personal appearance. These compliments fed something in me. I started to place my value as a woman on my physical appearance. As a result, my days were up or down, self-confident or insecure, beautiful or ugly—all based on my perception of how the world defined beauty. I vacillated between *pride* and *insecurity*. Beauty was a fickle, two-sided coin that controlled me constantly but always seemed beyond my reach.

I recall being at the beach "people watching" one day when my Commander asked me to stop and *think about what I was thinking about*. Rewinding my thoughts, I discovered that when I noticed a particular lady I would think, *Oh, if only I looked more like that. Wow, why couldn't I have been made like that? She's so pretty . . . sigh . . . I'll never look like that.* Then as I observed another lady my thoughts flipped to, *Well, at least I don't look like THAT! Yikes! Wow, compared to her I look great!* My "people watching" actually consisted of comparing myself to others and analyzing the competition, my sense of worth bouncing back and forth like a ping pong ball. The Lord has since shown me that I have wasted literally hours of my life by believing this one lie: that my worth is found in my outward appearance.

Mental Strongholds

I embraced this lie and operated in this worldly mindset for so many years that the enemy used it repeatedly to harass and control my thoughts and actions. Any time he wanted to distract me or steal my peace, all he had to do was throw me one tiny thought and I was stuck in a pit of mental quicksand. This one lie had become a mental stronghold for me. *A mental stronghold is a mindset that has become so ingrained that it affects the way we interpret and respond to a situation.* A *worldly* mindset is built on Satan's lies and the temporal values of this world that leave us exposed to his attacks. A *heavenly* mindset is built on the eternal and unchanging authority of God's truth. It is a refuge of safety, protection and rest for us. I now recognize the lie of placing my worth in my outward appearance as what it truly is—a mental stronghold based on a worldly mindset. This kept me from experiencing God's peace in my life when I needed it most. I can fight this worldly mindset only with the power of God's Word daily renewing my mind, tearing down deceptive strongholds and establishing new strongholds based on God's truth. The

"The name of the Lord is a strong tower; the righteous man runs into it and is safe."

Proverbs 18:10

thing about negative mental strongholds is that while we may be able to step back logically and know that what we are struggling with is a lie, the feelings and emotions connected to those lies are so strong they still make us feel powerless to do anything about it. The Word of God is a rock that we can cling to as the Lord helps us navigate through the storm of emotions we experience. We need to be geared up when the lies of this world come against us. Just as every warrior has his weapons of choice when arming for battle, I have a collection of verses attached to my Belt of Truth, that are ready to take down the lies the enemy hurls at me. By reading, meditating on, and memorizing these battle verses, I am equipping myself to tear down the worldly mindset and build up the heavenly mindset.

Let me show you how the Commander led me through the process of renewing my mind, using my example above. As God worked in my heart, I realized that the Lord is my authority on beauty, not my worldly culture. To start building this new mindset, I did a simple word search on "beauty" in the Bible, studying everything I could find pertaining to this topic. Now, when I feel attacked by how the world says I should look, I draw out my battle verses to counteract the lies:

> But the Lord said to Samuel, "Do not look on his appearance or on the height of his stature, because I have rejected him. For the Lord sees not as man sees: man looks on the outward appearance, but the Lord looks on the heart." (1 Samuel 16:7)

> Therefore we do not lose heart. Though outwardly we are wasting away, yet inwardly we are being renewed day by day. (2 Corinthians 4:16 NIV)

> Do not let your adorning be external—the braiding of hair, the wearing of gold, or the putting on of clothing—but let your adorning be the hidden person of the heart with the imperishable beauty of a gentle and quiet spirit, which in God's sight is very precious. (1 Peter 3:3-4)

When I look in the mirror and see grey hair, bags under my eyes, and wrinkles, I can laugh and agree with the verse that says outwardly I am wasting away, but inwardly I am being renewed day by day. This helps me to switch my focus toward thanking God for His inward renewal of me. I have to remind myself that the kingdom of heaven puts little value on my outward appearance, as it has no eternal value. God's focus is always on the heart. I have a choice: Do I focus my mind on the inner beauty that God has freely given me, rejoicing in the heart-work that the Commander is doing in me daily? Or do I focus my thoughts on the uncontrollable, unpredictable world's idea of what I *should* look like with a body that is naturally aging every day? God's truth brings peace and contentment, while the world's lies bring dissatisfaction and an inability to focus on anything other than self-consuming imperfections.

The voice of this world tells me I need to be flawless on the outside in order to be beautiful. This, of course, is never going to happen. If I embrace this mindset, it can easily consume my thoughts and mental energies. No more! I must fight to remind myself what the Bible says about my Savior and what He looked like here on earth. Did you know that Jesus was not considered beautiful in the world's eyes? His physical appearance did not signal He was the long-awaited Messiah.

> *"He had no form or majesty that we should look at him, and no beauty that we should desire him. He was despised and rejected by men; a man of sorrows, and acquainted with grief; and as one from whom men hide their faces he was despised, and we esteemed him not." (Isaiah 53:2b-3)*

Jesus is the Creator of all things, so surely He could have made Himself to be the best looking guy around, but He didn't. Why not? Perhaps He didn't want people to be so focused on His outward appearance that they missed His message. God knows what He is doing, and He gave each of us the physical appearance He wanted us to have for His purpose. To want something different is actually a sinful rejection of God's design and plan. When I find myself at this place mentally, repentance and gratitude are my best weapons.

> *"Submit yourselves therefore to God. Resist the devil, and he will flee from you. Draw near to God, and he will draw near to you. Cleanse your hands, you sinners, and purify your hearts, you double-minded . . . Humble yourselves before the Lord, and he will exalt you" (James 4:7-8, 10).*

Another lie the world whispers to me is, *You don't look as good as you used to.* While I love my kids and wouldn't trade them for anything, I sometimes lament the toll four pregnancies have taken on my body. This thought minimizes the God-given miracle of bearing children. When I do that I must turn to the Word and remember what the Savior endured for me so that He could carry me to new life. Because of Jesus' unconditional love for us, He was beaten to the point of deformity, left with scars that labeled Him as unworthy, and despised by the world. But from God's perspective, these scars were evidence of a sacrificial heart surrendered to His will. They represented the most beautiful, amazing, breath-taking God of all because of His love for us.

Heaven's perspective on beauty is so different when compared to this world. *"As it is written, 'How beautiful are the feet of those who preach the good news!'" (Romans 10:15b).* These are not feet that have just had a pedicure complete with tiny flowers painted on the toenails. These feet are beautiful because they carry the good news of the kingdom of heaven out of a heart filled with love for others. The Apostle Paul also bore on his body the marks of beatings and hardships received while doing the will of God. These scars were a physical reminder of a heart that was devoted to God, and the heart is always what matters to God. Jesus would not have scars if it weren't for His love toward us. It's a good thing He has given me a beautiful new heart in exchange for my old, ugly, hard heart! I don't have to try to make myself beautiful, because Jesus has already done this for me. *"And I will give you a new heart, and a new spirit I will put within you. And I will remove the heart of stone from your flesh and give you a heart of flesh. And I will put my Spirit within you, and cause you to walk in my statutes and be careful to obey my rules" (Ezekiel 36:26-27).* When we embrace the mindset that Jesus Christ has given us true beauty, the worldly standards of beauty will lose their significance. *"Let the saints be joyful in the glory and beauty [which God confers upon them]; let them sing for joy upon their beds" (Psalm 149:5 AMP).*

Lie Alert:

Are you thinking . . .

- I know I have some worldly strongholds but I can live with them; they're not that bad.
- This is too hard.
- I couldn't possibly study and find the Scriptures for myself; that's only for really godly or intelligent people.
- I have no clue where to start, so why bother?
- Experience feelings of dread
——Oh no, what will I find out about myself?
- Feeling overwhelmed——
This is too much to sort through. I just can't do it.
- This isn't worth the trouble.
- I have already tried that.
- That might work for her, but it won't work for me.

There are many types of strongholds that can take root in our souls. Maybe you can relate to my personal battle with outward beauty. Maybe your battle is with jealousy, anger, depression, or another area of struggle. Stop and ask the Commander. What is one of your mental strongholds? Listen for His thoughts. We must first identify our battle before we can fight it. As we begin to tackle our mental strongholds, we cannot be satisfied with a vague understanding of God's truth—we need to own it!

Feelings of worthlessness or pride can hound us in the midst of a confusing battle, causing us to easily forget these biblical truths. By renewing our minds with what God has to say about our worldly strongholds, we can then renounce the lies and proclaim the truth. We can and will train ourselves to think God's way, in the heavenly mindset that will build up a mental stronghold of truth.

Digging up Our Personal Worldly Mindsets

Two major influences that define our worldview are the *society we grew up in* and our *immediate family*. Each of these has shaped who we are and how we relate to others. The foundation of our belief system, which is formed in our early years, is unique to each one of us. Because we live in a sinful world, some of the worldly concepts and mindsets we adopted as children are simply not true when we compare them to our new citizenship in heaven. In order for us to be transformed and firmly rooted in love, we need to let the Father identify and dig up the old mindsets and expose them by the light of His Word.

This transformation doesn't automatically happen as we grow up; we must intentionally ask the Commander to expose any false foundations or mindsets from childhood. *"May Christ through your faith [actually] dwell (settle down, abide, make his permanent home) in your hearts! May you be rooted deep in love and founded securely on love"* (Ephesians 3:17 AMP). As I was reading this verse, I asked the Lord to show me what I was rooted in, growing up in this sinful world. Within a week I experienced three different mind battles that revealed some toxins that were buried in the soil of my belief system: fear, shame, and guilt, which are major motivators in this fallen world. Notice that the Commander didn't just tell me what they were, but allowed me to experience them in specific, well-timed battles. During those attacks, He opened my eyes to see how these three strongholds were embedded in the makeup of my old nature, fueling and motivating many of my decisions and actions. His desire is to have my soul grow in the rich soil of His unconditional love. In order for Him to do this, He had to go back and dig up some old ways of thinking that still affect me today. I once read a bumper sticker that said, "Don't believe everything you think." I was shocked to realize that just because I always think a certain way, it doesn't make it true! We can't do this alone—we must allow the Commander to lead us through this process as He weeds out the lies, uprooting them one by one.

Growing up in a small town, we all knew each other at school. Once you gained a reputation, good or bad, it stuck. By first grade I understood that not everyone was the same, and I'm not referring only to eye color or gender. I began to realize that people fit into different categories. It was not something I was taught, I just came to believe it because everyone else did. As I became aware of these invisible categories, I began to wonder where I fit. You probably remember what it was like. There was the "in" crowd and the "not-so-in" crowd, the class clown, the jocks, the cheerleaders, the brains, the well-to-do, the musicians and the misfits. Once you were labeled, whether by yourself or someone else, that's where you were stuck. Within each group there was constant and unspoken competition, comparison, acceptance and rejection. When you were at the top of the pecking order you felt great about yourself, but when you were at the bottom it was pure misery. You defined others' worth by their abilities and behavior. Likewise, your self-worth was measured in the same way, always dependent on what other people thought of you.

At the end of the school year, the most common thing that people wrote in my yearbook was "You're so sweet, don't ever change!" Anybody else receive this cliché? I think that's what people wrote when they didn't know what to write. This statement reinforced the idea that people liked me *because* I'm a nice person. This belief became a part of my identity, which meant I could never have an "off" day. Once when we were lining up for lunch, a girl asked me if I would be nice enough to get something for her so she wouldn't lose her spot at the front of the line. Doing this favor for her meant I'd lose *my* place in line, but I did it anyway. I knew she was just using me, but I was attached to my identity as a "nice person" and I did not want her to think badly of me. I secretly resented her for this afterward, when I could have simply told her, "No, thank you, you can run your own errand." These false identities can lock us into place, insisting we perform in a certain way. The problem isn't being nice, it's finding my identity in how I act and not in who I am in Christ.

When my older sister attended high school there was a group of boys who would sit on a bench in the hallway rating the girls that walked by. They were scored on a scale of 1 to 10, solely based on their outward appearance. Numbers were shouted out as girls passed by: "6!" "8!" "2!" It was humiliating enough for girls to hear their numbers called out, but even worse was that their peers heard it too. I wonder how many of those girls can still remember today the number hurled at them so many years ago. Often this is exactly what the world does to us. It shouts out its ratings of our success or failure for all to hear. As adults, we may no longer carry the reputation as the straight-A student, the loser who was cut from the team, the star of the drama class or the perpetual last pick in gym. However, we might still possess those same thoughts and feelings that labeled and defined who we were back then. What about you? What was your "title" growing up? Where did you fit in? Ask the Commander to remind you and let you know if it still affects you today. Without these lies being exposed and dug up, these worldly mindsets of worth and false identity will continually fuel and control our attitudes and actions in every aspect of our life. If we accept this worldly mindset as our own, Satan will capitalize on it and bury lies deep in the foundation of our belief systems.

How Family Shapes Our Belief Systems

Another area that greatly shapes the way that we think is our family's values and beliefs. The things that our parents believed in word and deed have so often laid the foundation of our own belief system and worldview, for better or worse. For example, if your family valued musical talent, investing their time and money to place you and your siblings into various musical settings, you might conclude that being musically gifted is of high value in this world. You might even evaluate others based on their musical ability or lack thereof. Each family has a different set of values by which they live. Some families place a high value on athletic ability, work ethic or higher education. For other families social standing in the community is the mark of success, and for still others getting married and having children is viewed as the height of success. These things aren't necessarily bad; in fact, most of them are worthy goals. The problem comes when our worth and identity is wrapped up in our success or failure to achieve these ideals. If we do not measure up to the high standards held in our family, we might be hounded by feelings of rejection and failure to this day.

Our family interactions and our role in the home have also shaped what we believe about ourselves today. You could have been labeled the comedian, the peacemaker, the black sheep, or the strong one that held the family together. Perhaps the perfect-child label was already taken by a sibling, so you opted to be the kid who broke all the rules. These invisible labels might have been self-appointed or thrust upon us, but either way they can become false identities and areas of worth ingrained in our belief system. The key to changing these false labels is to allow the Commander to dig around in the early stages of our belief system and reveal to us areas in which we have falsely based our worth. Is there anything He is bringing to your mind right now? Invite Him into it. Ask the Lord to remind you when those thoughts first started and what lies you have come to believe about yourself as a result.

Often our way of thinking is so deeply rooted in us and so specific to our unique upbringing that it is difficult to identify the lies unless we are face to face with the truth. One faulty belief I accepted in my growing up years was that being in full-time Christian ministry was superior to other forms of occupation. My parents didn't teach me this; I came to this conclusion on my own with the help of the deceiver. Growing up in a family that served in full-time ministry, I embraced the subtle lie that pastors, missionaries and worship leaders were just a notch higher on the value scale than the "average" Christian. I recall an instance years ago when a fellow pastor in my home town "quit the ministry" and returned to his previous job. It was a difficult situation for the church, and my parents rightly grieved over it, but the devil used it to formulate some deceptive thoughts in my mind. I developed the opinion that this man had failed God, and had taken a few steps down on the value scale as a believer because he returned to an "inferior" occupation. I didn't even know I had this false understanding until the Lord revealed it to me years later during a time of conviction. I now mourn over this sinful way of thinking and I'm grateful to God for exposing it, convicting me of my sin, forgiving me and renewing my mind in this area. Holding onto this lie could have been especially damaging in my current role as a pastor's wife. I could easily have allowed the sin of pride and feelings of superiority to destroy the work that He desires to do through me. Believing this sneaky little lie could affect my motive for serving in ministry in the first place, causing me to believe that my value depends on my performance in this area.

The truth is that my value was determined long ago when Jesus gave His life in exchange for mine at the Cross. There Jesus proved and demonstrated that my worth was equal to His worth in the Father's eyes. This is true for all of God's children, regardless of performance or occupation. Our value has been predetermined. It is not what we do with our lives that makes us worth something; it was the exorbitant and excessive price (Jesus' blood) that was paid for us. It has already been settled. Do you believe this? If we don't believe God's truth about our worth, then we will waste our lives trying to prove our value from the world's standards, which is completely unnecessary and sinful.

> **"No, in all these things we are more than conquerors through him who loved us. For I am sure that neither death nor life, nor angels nor rulers, nor things present nor things to come, nor powers, nor height nor depth, nor anything else in all creation, will be able to separate us from the love of God in Christ Jesus our Lord."**
>
> **Romans 8:37-39**

The process of allowing the Commander to expose our worldly mindsets and replace them with heavenly mindsets can be tedious and challenging, and it will certainly be a lifelong process, but it always leads to victory. Being firmly rooted in the deep love of God enables us to be more than conquerors in Christ Jesus. We can move from one victory to another instead of being stuck in the same pit of defeat for the rest of our earthly lives. Seasoned warriors are very familiar with being knocked down or even taking a direct hit, but they also know the pleasure of triumph. It is that joy of throwing off the enemy's chains that keeps them going in the midst of struggle. May we too become well acquainted with the taste of victory and the thrill of a "mission accomplished," so that we never shrink back from the trials we must face.

The Kingdom of Darkness vs. The Kingdom of Heaven

The voice of this world consistently and directly opposes the ways and values of our true home. Nothing in this world will teach us more about God's kingdom than the voice of the Father revealing His Word to us in our everyday circumstances. We need to start thinking very differently now that we belong to God. This new thought process starts by identifying any thought that doesn't match the high standards and operations of the unseen kingdom of heaven. Once we identify these worldly mindsets we must replace them with the truth of the Scriptures. *"But now that you have come to know God, or rather to be known by God, how can you turn back again to the weak and worthless elementary principles of the world, whose slaves you want to be once more?" (Galatians 4:9)*. Let's take a look at a few of the mindsets of this world to see how they contrast with God's kingdom. We must pay close attention to any of these misconceptions that have seeped into our way of thinking.

Being First vs. Being Last

A few years ago there was a popular slogan that showed up on kids' clothing everywhere. It could be found on T-shirts, slippers, key chains and lip gloss. It simply said: IT'S ALL

ABOUT ME! Cute little girls in pigtails sported this popular saying like little divas as they embraced the message wholeheartedly. The voice of this world says, *It's all about you; it's all about what you want and how you feel. You are the center of the universe. Go ahead and do what you want—you're worth it and you deserve it. It's time to take care of you for a change.* We really don't need the voice of this world telling us "me first"—it's as natural as breathing. Calling "shotgun" for the best seat in the car may seem like perfectly normal behavior, but it is entirely contrary to God's way of thinking. *"Do nothing from rivalry or conceit, but in humility count others more significant than yourselves. Let each of you look not only to his own interests, but also to the interests of others" (Philippians 2:3-4).*

It has been said that true JOY comes in this order: Jesus, Others, You. God's very own pleasure gets poured in our laps as we put others before ourselves—this is one of the best-kept secrets, experienced only through obedience. *"And everyone who has left houses or brothers or sisters or father or mother or children or lands, for my name's sake, will receive a hundredfold and will inherit eternal life. But many who are first will be last, and the last first" (Matthew 19:29-30).* I believe we will be very surprised when heavenly rewards are given out as to who is first and who is last. I love how simply John the Baptist sums it up: *"He (Jesus) must increase, but I must decrease" (John 3:30).* In what ways has this worldly mindset snuck in to your way of thinking? Stop and ask the Lord to bring any memories or situations to light in your life.

Work, Work, Work vs. Rest

Sometimes I can hear a voice in my head that says, *Come on, come on, come on! Let's go, let's go! Hurry, hurry, hurry! Move it!* It repeats over and over, urging me to move faster, accomplish more and keep up the pace. It is the voice of performance, and it drags me through the mud like a slave driver with a whip, insisting I achieve more. Even after it expends all my efforts, leaving me exhausted, face down, and spiritually bloody on the battlefield, it still seeks to whip me into submission. It is the voice of the culture I live in and it is never satisfied. *"Do more,"* it says. *"Work harder!"* It never acknowledges what I have accomplished, but only the numerous things that I have yet to do. It beats me up and accuses me of laziness if I take a moment to sit down and rest. This is directly opposite to the voice of our Lord.

> *"Come to me, all you who are weary and burdened, and I will give you rest. Take my yoke upon you and learn from me, for I am gentle and humble in heart, and you will find rest for your souls. For my yoke is easy and my burden is light" (Matthew 11:28-30 NIV).*

And again,

> *Now as they went on their way, Jesus entered a village. And a woman named Martha welcomed him into her house. And she had a sister called Mary,* **who sat at the Lord's feet and listened to his teaching.** *But Martha was distracted with much serving. And she went up to him and said, "Lord, do you not care that my sister has left me to serve alone? Tell her then to help me." But the Lord answered her, "Martha, Martha, you are anxious and troubled about many things, but one thing is necessary.* **Mary has chosen the good portion, which will not be taken away from her."** *(Luke 10:38-42, emphasis mine)*

Wow, what different pictures these two mindsets paint! The world gives us the false promise that if we work hard enough we can earn a rest, but it never delivers on that promise. The kingdom of God invites us to come and rest first. By resting in Jesus we will truly learn how to do the good works He has planned for us. This world operates on an earning-and-deserving mindset, while the kingdom of God operates on a giving-and-receiving mindset: God gives and we receive. It has been said that our entrance into the kingdom of God begins with a great big "It is finished." The work is done because of our Savior, Jesus. As citizens of His kingdom we can stop striving, enter this rest and receive the benefits that He has provided. *"So then, there remains a Sabbath rest for the people of God, for whoever has entered God's rest has also rested from his works as God did from his" (Hebrews 4:9-10).* This amazing rest is a great mystery, and it is only uncovered by our obedience to stop striving and start resting in Him by faith. Do you long for this type of rest? Ask Jesus to come into your striving and show you the way to enter His rest.

Fame/Success vs. Humble/Hidden Things

The world is always ready to elevate us based on its system of success or failure. The kingdom of darkness is infatuated with high positions, titles, wealth, fame and glamorous people. Big, flashy possessions, positions of power, and "name dropping" represent who you are and who you know. The world asks, *What kind of car do you drive? How big is your house? What side of town do you live in? What's your degree? What do you do for a living? What is your title at work? What is your net worth?* We are being profiled even as we mentally profile others, based on the world's standards of success and failure. Are you a blue-collar or white-collar worker? Buy organic or off-brand? Drive an old Ford Pinto or a new Mercedes-Benz? Shop at Bloomingdale's or Goodwill? Whatever you do, or don't do, this world will label you accordingly. You can play this game, but you will never win. Thanks to Jesus, we don't have to! So what will we choose to believe? What do our actions say?

These worldly standards and ideals, whether high or low, do not hold up in our new kingdom. Success in God's kingdom is entirely different from success in this world. Our God sees and highly values the unsung, lowly, and invisible positions and people of this world. Just take a look at where Jesus was born and who His companions were while He was here on earth. He defied the mindset of this fallen world and broke its unwritten rules. Why? Because His kingdom was not of this world, nor did He operate underneath this world's rules and values. Neither should we. Ask the Commander to reveal any areas in your life that He sees as "successful" according to the ways of the kingdom of heaven. Then ask Him if there are any areas you are investing your time, energy, talents in that don't carry eternal value.

The kingdom of heaven exalts the humble, hidden things done in secret with a pure heart.

> *Jesus looked up and saw the rich putting their gifts into the offering box, and he saw a poor widow put in two small copper coins. And he said, "Truly, I tell you, this poor widow has put in more than all of them. For they all contributed out of their abundance, but she out of her poverty put in all she had to live on." (Luke 21:1-4)*

Our world places a high value on being noticed for our "good" works. But the things that are secretly done for God can be the things done exclusively for the praise of the Creator. Every word spoken and every deed done will one day be exposed in the kingdom of heaven. Humble and faithful followers who are found doing the work of God in seemingly insignificant areas may be surprised at how highly they are exalted in their true everlasting home. *"But when you give to the needy, do not let your left hand know what your right hand is doing, so that your giving may be in secret. And your Father who sees in secret will reward you"* (Matthew 6:3-4). And again, *"But when you pray, go into your room and shut the door and pray to your Father who is in secret. And your Father who sees in secret will reward you"* (Matthew 6:6).

Differences Divide Us vs. Differences Unite Us

We tend to be more comfortable with people who are like us. The old saying, "Birds of a feather flock together," really is true. The judgment or fear of others' differences, how they act, dress, or think, can make us want to put a safe distance between us and them. We might view them with skepticism, jealousy and snobbery, thinking that our way must be the best. The kingdom of darkness exploits these differences to continually stir up strife and division among us, leading to prejudices, hatred and hostilities. But the kingdom of God releases us from focusing on our differences, and instead enables us to see other people's unique identities without threat to our own. *"For as many of you as were baptized into Christ have put on Christ. There is neither Jew nor Greek, there is neither slave nor free, there is neither male nor female, for you are all one in Christ Jesus"* (Galatians 3:27-28). Because our value is equally important and securely rooted in Christ Jesus, we are able to see other people as God's creation, and delight in His handiwork and creativity as we enjoy others' personalities, gifts and talents. *"For as in one body we have many members, and the members do not all have the same function, so we, though many, are one body in Christ, and individually members one of another. Having gifts that differ according to the grace given to us"* (Romans 12:4-6a).

When we encounter someone at our job, church or school who thinks, acts, dresses or even smells different from us, we must resist the worldly urge to distance ourselves from them, labeling them by the world's mindset. Instead we ought to move toward them, asking the Commander to give us the ability to see Christ in them. It is a great reminder to know that God loves and delights in them

"But as it is, God arranged the members in the body, each one of them, as he chose. If all were a single member, where would the body be? As it is, there are many parts, yet one body."

1 Corinthians 12:18-20

just as much as He loves delights in us. It is in the DNA of the kingdom of heaven to stop and truly *see* people, discovering what God sees in them. As we develop a godly love and true appreciation for the people who differ from us, we can learn more about our God, the Master Creator who designed each one of us. *"For we are his workmanship, created in Christ Jesus for good works, which God prepared beforehand, that we should walk in them"* (Ephesians 2:10). Is there a person in your life right now who you need to see through His eyes?

Revenge vs. Forgiveness

The world says, *You can't let him get away with that. Don't let her walk all over you! You need to stand up for yourself. No one else is going to make this right but you. Make them pay for what they did.* The kingdom of darkness celebrates revenge. Just look at the many popular movies that are based on a theme of "justified revenge." Picture a movie about a man whose family has been murdered in the opening scene. In the remainder of the movie this vigilante will execute his own justice upon the wicked, as we root for him. It would be unheard of if he simply decided to forgive the man. He probably would be considered pathetic and weak, and there would be an outcry that justice wasn't served. This mindset can sneak into our belief system to keep us from forgiving others and cause us to avenge the wrongs done against us.

> *Beloved, never avenge yourselves, but leave it to the wrath of God, for it is written, "Vengeance is mine, I will repay, says the Lord." To the contrary, "if your enemy is hungry, feed him; if he is thirsty, give him something to drink; for by so doing you will heap burning coals on his head." Do not be overcome by evil, but overcome evil with good.* (Romans 12:19-21)

God designed us to have a strong moral compass regarding justice—our desire to cheer on the wronged man in our fictional movie scenario is based on a God-given desire to see evil punished. Yet, He also commands us to forgive and allow Him to repay evil. Our God treats forgiveness very seriously. Unforgivingness is a grievous, dangerous sin and a significant tool in the enemy's hand against us. *"For if you forgive others their trespasses, your heavenly Father will also forgive you, but if you do not forgive others their trespasses, neither will your Father forgive your trespasses"* (Matthew 6:14-15). Turning the other cheek seems weak from this world's perspective, but it is a sign of godly strength and character not to avenge oneself.

> *To one who strikes you on the cheek, offer the other also, and from one who takes away your cloak do not withhold your tunic either. Give to everyone who begs from you, and from one who takes away your goods do not demand them back. And as you wish that others would do to you, do so to them.* (Luke 6:29-31)

These are just a few examples of how different the kingdom of heaven is from the kingdom of darkness. As believers, we now belong to the perfect, everlasting, ultimate kingdom of the one and only true God. That is why we need to train ourselves to think and act in ways that are true to the nature of our new home. *"Then the sovereignty, power and greatness of the kingdoms under the whole heaven will be handed over to the saints, the people of the Most High. His kingdom will be an everlasting kingdom, and all rulers will worship and obey him"* (Daniel 7:27 NIV). Let us continually study the Scriptures to better understand our true home and operate as citizens in the kingdom of heaven. From this place of belonging we will fight our battles as overcomers just like our Ruler and Savior, Jesus Christ.

Prayer:

Dear Father,
Thank You for dying for me and setting me free from the bondage of sin. I desire that You plant me deeply and firmly establish me in Your unconditional love. I ask that You show me anything that I have been rooted in that is not of You. Please reveal to me any lies that are buried in my belief

system and the worldly mindsets that I've adopted from my childhood and my family. I trust You, God, and rely upon Your divine wisdom to show me what I need to see, and to help me discern my past without becoming bitter.
In Jesus' name, Amen.

Action Steps: Journal your prayers, answers and all the things the Commander reveals to you.

1. Do you recognize any particular category that you seemed to "fit" into in grade school? What were the thoughts and the feelings that accompanied you at this stage of your life? Did you place your worth or value in your ability to perform well in this area?

2. What are some things that your family taught you to value? Where did they invest their time, energy and efforts? What was your "role" in the family? How did others perceive or treat you? How do these values compare with the Word of God? Do these values or labels still affect you today? How?

3. Can you identify any lies you have believed about your worth being dependent on anything other than your relationship to Jesus Christ?

4. If the Lord uncovers a worldly mindset or faulty belief buried in your mind, what are some battle verses you could use to fight those lies?

Chapter Six
Identifying Worldly Cravings

Come, everyone who thirsts, come to the waters; and he who has no money, come, buy and eat! Come, buy wine and milk without money and without price. Why do you spend your money for that which is not bread, and your labor for that which does not satisfy? Listen diligently to me, and eat what is good, and delight yourselves in rich food. Incline your ear, and come to me; hear, that your soul may live.
Isaiah 55:1-3a

I had more than a few sleepless nights when my kids were little, so I started drinking coffee in the mornings to help me stay awake. I didn't like the taste of coffee at first, but I drank it anyway just to help me start the day. As years passed I grew to *love* coffee, especially strong coffee, and you could say I became a bit of a coffee fanatic. I *had* to have my coffee every morning! Soon I was longing for it each afternoon as a treat.

Coffee became more than just a drink for me—it was a comfort and a delight. I looked forward to my cup of coffee and, like a baby with a pacifier, I couldn't go without it. It took years for the Lord to convince me that this had gotten out of hand, that somehow coffee was getting a hold on me and had actually become an idol for me. *What? Coffee, an idol? Oh please!* I would grumble at Him, *What's wrong with coffee, God? It's not a sin. Why do I have to give it up when it's okay for everyone else to drink it?* I'd try to go without coffee for short periods of time, all the while living for the day I could have it again. As pathetic as it may sound, it consumed my thoughts, stole my time, and controlled my actions. When I was bored, sad, lonely, or wanted to celebrate, my first "go to" was a warm, delicious cup of dark roast coffee. (Did I just hear an "Amen"?) It was my "quick fix," and for about fifteen minutes it satisfied me. But the problem was that the high didn't last.

This past year the Lord spoke to my heart and said that He was jealous of the role coffee occupied in my life. He wanted to be my comfort and delight, and my desire for coffee was hijacking my desire for Him. Challenging me to go on a year-long coffee fast, He promised that He could and would give me something better. I made the hard decision right then to believe Him, and I committed that day to have my last cup of coffee for an entire year. I reluctantly sent out a quick email to three close friends, using the spiritual weapon of confession, admitting my sin and seeking their accountability. This cemented my decision and commitment to God.

It wasn't easy, but the Lord was gracious to me. I had to fight the urge to go to the coffee pot and instead go to my Provider. My craving for coffee was an indication that I was needy for *something*. What that was, I didn't initially know. Every time I wanted coffee, I had to stop in that moment and invite the Lord into my cravings. Together we examined my desires and, over time, He taught me how to delight and find comfort in Him. It was hard. God is NOT a "quick fix" but He is both the source and supply for every desire, craving, and need we have. I discovered that in my ignorance, I honestly believed that coffee could meet my God-given deepest needs when instead, He was the only answer for the empty places in my heart. I don't think I would ever have said that coffee was the answer to my emptiness but my behavior revealed my mistaken belief. God created those deep longings inside me and I foolishly tried to fill those longings with something as meager and ridiculous as a warm, comforting cup of coffee. Well, it wasn't working. In God's compassion and mercy He said to me, *No more!* If we are willing to look higher, trust Him with our hearts and obey Him when He says *Stop this*, He will help us and provide the power to accomplish what He asks of us.

> *"Therefore, my beloved, as you have always obeyed, so now, not only as in my presence but much more in my absence, work out your own salvation with fear and trembling, for it is God who works in you, both to will and to work for his good pleasure." (Philippians 2:12-13)*

The cravings we have for the things of this world may seem harmless, but they rob our attention from the heavenly supply of our God. Often it is not our desire that is wrong; it is what we do with it and where we turn to satisfy it. If we are pacified by the resources of this perishing world, we will never tap into the abundance of the kingdom of heaven. Is there anything that is getting in the way of God meeting your longings? Ask the Commander; He will know.

Meeting Our Cravings by the Things of This World

Even though we belong to the kingdom of God, we still live in this world. There are numerous things in this world that have been provided for us as gifts from our Creator. *"So, whether you eat or drink, or whatever you do, do all to the glory of God"* (1 Corinthians 10:31). But what happens when our enjoyment of these gifts gets a little out of hand? Perhaps we begin to develop a passion and longing for them, and before we know it, we cannot do without them. We might not even realize the hold they have on us. Our cravings might start out small or seem entirely innocent, but over time they can grow into monsters, controlling our thoughts and actions.

Glamour, entertainment, popularity, position, money, and possessions are just a few of the things we might pursue in this world to satisfy our longings. Satan has created an illusion, a false promise, that anything we could ever want is found right here in this world. But the reality is that the things of this world cannot satisfy long-term, and all that we acquire here on Earth will ultimately slip through our fingers the day we die. It shouldn't surprise us that the voice of this world lies to us! The dangling delights of this world are fleeting and will eventually perish. The cravings and desires for these worldly things must be submitted to the Lord and placed underneath His authority. If you are getting uncomfortable because the Commander is revealing or hinting at a few things in your life that He wants to talk about—don't run, don't stop reading, and don't pretend you're not hearing Him. Stop and talk to Him about it. Be honest and tell Him why you like them. Allow Him to help you navigate through this.

Ridding Ourselves of Worldly Addictions

Some things in this world we obviously need to steer clear of—things like drug and alcohol abuse, theft and sexual promiscuity. But there are other things that are neither good nor bad in and of themselves—it depends on how we use them. They might be considered blessings from the Lord, but the enemy can use them as snares if they get a hold on us. Food, shopping, sports, chocolate, relationships, Facebook, cell phones, physical fitness, the acquisition of wealth, television, and hobbies are just a few examples of things that can move from a healthy place in our lives into the beginning stages of addiction.

At any given time in our lives, a temptation can creep in and come dangerously close to becoming a false god. We must be in constant communication with our Commander, ready to obey Him when He warns us against seemingly harmless things. There are times in my life when the Commander puts His finger on something and says to me, *This is getting dangerous for you.* As long as we live on this earth our enemy will be seeking opportunities to assault us with worldly cravings. Our God is the ultimate Satisfier, and it is sin for us to reach instead for the things of this world for fulfillment. When we devote more of our time, energy, and thoughts to them than to God, we have essentially become idolaters! *"Little children, keep yourselves from idols (false gods)—[from anything and everything that would occupy the place in your heart due to God, from any sort of substitute for Him that would take first place in your life]"* (1 John 5:21 AMP).

When these worldly cravings grow into addictions, they become spiritual strongholds in our lives. In order to battle these addictions, we need to get quiet before the Lord and ask Him for detailed instructions. The best way to get rid of an addiction is to get addicted to something better. In that way the former obsession becomes bland and tasteless compared to the new, wholesome replacement. When the Commander points to something that needs to go, it means that He wants to set us free and give us something better in its place. If only we would believe Him! As we examine the Bible, we will find that the only "addiction" believers are allowed is an addiction to Jesus.

The question is this: Do we really believe God when He says He can and will satisfy our every need? *"You open your hand; you satisfy the desire of every living thing. The Lord is righteous in all his ways and kind in all his works. The Lord is near to all who call on him, to all who call on him in truth"* (Psalm 145:16-18). God is able to completely satisfy our desires, but the first step is being honest with Him. He is so very near to us as we tell Him with raw honesty about the worldly cravings we battle. Ask Him to reveal to you the core desire or need that is temporarily being met when you go to your quick-fix worldly craving.

Admitting Our Own Neediness

So how do we untangle ourselves from the worldly cravings that get a grip on us? The best approach before an all-knowing God is absolute honesty. *Confession,* agreeing with God that it is sin, and *repentance,* turning away from that sin, are the two primary spiritual weapons we use in this battle. But we must also seek the Lord so that we can decipher what inner need this particular worldly craving is meeting. Who better to tell us than the One Who made us and knows everything about our lives? Ask Him.

I have been surprised to discover that the desires and cravings we have are actually God-given. It is not the longings themselves that are sinful, but rather the things to which we turn to fulfill these desires. For example, God has given us the longing to feel safe and secure. To meet this desire I could take matters into my own hands by continually turning to my sympathetic husband or my warm comfortable bed; I could even turn to a can of Diet Coke or my favorite comfort food. But if every time I experience the neediness of my soul I turn to the physical and tangible things of this world instead of to the Lord, then these things have become idols in my life. The Lord wants to meet our cravings for comfort and safety with the source of all heavenly resources—Himself. It is what you want as well, even if you don't know it yet.

Our God-given yearnings and desires must not be misdirected toward the inferior things of this world. We have already been given unlimited treasures in God's kingdom, and we don't need to pursue the lesser things in this world. When the Lord helps us discover the source of our craving, we will be able to identify the lie that is controlling our behavior and replace it with the truth. If I believe the lie that my husband, or sleep, or food will make me feel safe and secure, then this one lie will control my thoughts and actions, becoming essential to my survival. The truth is that only God can make me safe and secure.

It has been said that the root of all addictions is the need to be loved. The Bible clearly says that God is the source of the love that we crave.

> *"For I am convinced that neither death nor life, neither angels nor demons, neither the present nor the future, nor any powers, neither height nor depth, nor anything else in all*

creation, will be able to separate us from the love of God that is in Christ Jesus our Lord." (Romans 8:38-39 NIV)

Do you believe this? Sitting here, right now, you are loved by God. Nothing in all of creation can keep you from His extreme, intense, and mysterious love. Ask Him how He feels about you this very minute and don't move on until you hear His voice. Trust me, it will be worth it. Wait for His voice, His emotions or the awareness of His presence to fill you. What is He speaking to you? Can you feel His love?

We are never alone in this battle. At any time we can access the love, wisdom and direction of the Commander. Once we have identified the core desire, it is our privilege as citizens of heaven to approach the throne of grace, as the author of Hebrews reminds us, to receive the very thing we are craving in our time of neediness. Then these worldly cravings become godly cravings as we tap into the fulfilling resources of the kingdom of heaven, and are satisfied by the One Who is above everything else.

Throughout our lives here on earth there will constantly be a temptation to meet our needs with things that are easily available around us rather than with God. But if we are willing, the Lord will alert us to the dangers in the battlefield of our minds. The Commander surprised me once by revealing a God-given desire I was trying to fulfill with earthly things. Like many people, I love reading novels, and I enjoyed escaping from my ordinary world into the exciting world of a good book. I was drawn to a certain author who wrote several murder mysteries. I loved the thrill of the unknown and the way this particular author's mind worked. The murders in these books were presented without graphic violence and usually played a minor role in the plot of these books. The bulk of the story was about developing the characters and revealing clues so that the reader could identify the murderer before the unveiling in the last chapter.

Whenever I read one of these books, however, I began to sense the uncomfortable conviction of the Holy Spirit telling me that somehow these books weren't good for me. I really liked these books so I ignored it at first. This prompting became so strong that even though I couldn't really understand the harm at the time, I obeyed the Lord and stopped reading them. Reluctantly, I threw away all the copies I owned. After doing this, I recognized a change in both my demeanor and the atmosphere of my home. I used to struggle with bouts of restlessness and depression, especially after reading one of these books. The Lord revealed to me that even though the murders in these books seemed quite harmless to me, they still affected my mind with a spirit of death and destruction; they invited "darkness" over my spirit and my home. The Lord opened my mind to see His perspective on the enemy of death and the wickedness of murder. These books lured me in with mystery and excitement, but opened the door to dangerous thoughts and ideas.

I asked the Lord, *Why don't I want to give up these books? What's the appeal? What desires are being met when I indulge in one of them?* My marvelous God revealed to me that I was drawn to mystery novels because He created me to crave a good mystery, namely Himself. He placed in me a longing to know hidden truth, and the desire to search for it. This longing is not for a trivial murder mystery novel, but rather for something much higher. Our God is deeply complex and mysterious.

> *Great is the Lord and most worthy of praise; his greatness no one can fathom. One generation will commend your works to another; they will tell of your mighty acts. They will speak of the glorious splendor of your majesty, and I will meditate on your wonderful works. They will tell of the power of your awesome works, and I will proclaim your great deeds. They will celebrate your abundant goodness and joyfully sing of your righteousness. (Psalm 145:3-7 NIV)*

And again, "*He performs wonders that cannot be fathomed, miracles that cannot be counted*" (Job 9:10 NIV).

The Creator gave me this desire so I would seek and pursue Him whole-heartedly. He promises to reveal Himself to anyone who chases after Him relentlessly.

> You will seek me and find me. When you seek me with all your heart, I will be found by you, declares the Lord, and I will restore your fortunes and gather you from all the nations and all the places where I have driven you, declares the Lord, and I will bring you back to the place from which I sent you into exile. (Jeremiah 29:13-14)

It's as if He said to me, *Kori, you want a good mystery? You want excitement? You want discovery? You want to know secrets? Come to Me; I have more than enough for you.* When we find ourselves clinging to the things of this world, refusing to give them up, it may be an indicator that there is a God-given desire in us that remains unmet. Whether we realize it or not, we crave heaven's King and the heavenly assets He provides more than anything else. When we go to the resources of this lowly world instead of the exalted resources of our new home, we are selling ourselves short. We also cheat Jesus out of His rights to love every part of us and meet our deepest needs. We were made for His pleasure and it pleases Him greatly to fit His wealth with our poverty, His plenty with our lack. We must ask the Creator to teach us what we really need from Him instead of the "quick fix" supplied by this perishing world. He will always show us.

Tapping into Heaven's Resources

We can be Christians for many years but still be stuck in spiritual immaturity, not recognizing the ways and the purposes of our true home—the kingdom of heaven. When I think about this I get really angry because this is where I was for many years. I was robbed. What kept me in this immature place, unable to grow the way God intended? I allowed myself to be satisfied with the things of this world. It is a very serious thing to let ourselves be ruled by the cravings and the desires of this world. This is what the Word says:

You adulterous people! Do you not know that friendship with the world is enmity with God? Therefore whoever wishes to be a friend of the world makes himself an enemy of God. Or do you suppose it is to no purpose that the Scripture says, "He yearns jealously over the spirit that he has made to dwell in us"? (James 4:4-5)

Don't miss the character of God here. Can you see the Lord's motive behind this rebuke? His love and craving for us is so strong it's almost inconsolable for Him. Now personalize this: God's desire for YOU makes Him jealous of anything that would keep you from coming exclusively to Him to satisfy you in the depths of your spirit. The fallen world with all its delights is a vicious enemy "promising" you what you want while robbing you blind instead. The love of this world takes you captive, blocking the way to Life, and depriving you of your greatest need and craving—Jesus Christ. Nothing in this world can love you like He can, the way you were created to be loved. Can you blame Him for disturbing and disrupting our shallow contentment with inferior and destructive loves? He is our Savior and Deliverer.

"Do not be surprised, brothers, that the world hates you."

1 John 3:13

I didn't always know this. I didn't realize that this world hates me because of the Spirit of God that resides within me. I didn't have a clue how vehemently this world fought against me in order to keep the light of God's kingdom from penetrating its darkness. The devil wanted me to be so addicted to, and infatuated with, the things of this world that I would never tap into God's resources. He wanted me to be stuck in a state of spiritual slumber, unskilled and unaware, too focused on the things of this world to be a threat to his kingdom.

For though by this time you ought to be teachers, you need someone to teach you again the basic principles of the oracles of

*God. You need milk, not solid food, for everyone who lives on milk is unskilled in the word of righteousness, since he is a child. But solid food is for the mature, for those who have their **powers of discernment trained by constant practice to distinguish good from evil.** (Hebrews 5:12-14, emphasis mine)*

I am so thankful to the Commander for His guidance, His promptings and the power He gave me to let go of some worldly cravings. This discernment between good and evil is a powerful spiritual weapon that is developed by constantly practicing it, and God knows how desperately we need it. We must learn how to identify and say "No!" to the things of this world, and instead say "Yes!" to the things of God's kingdom. We can't have both. This is about our freedom, but more importantly it is about God's glory! Consuming the things of this world dulls our spiritual senses and lulls us into a spiritual state of sleep, making us dormant and useless. Satan knows this all too well, but do we? By God's grace, the more I threw away the trivial things of this world, the more I began to wake up spiritually.

But when anything is exposed by the light, it becomes visible, for anything that becomes visible is light. Therefore it says, "Awake, O sleeper, and arise from the dead, and Christ will shine on you." Look carefully then how you walk, not as unwise but as wise, making the best use of the time, because the days are evil. Therefore do not be foolish, but understand what the will of the Lord is. (Ephesians 5:13-17)

The kingdom is within us—this means that we are to walk as children of light everywhere we go, ushering in this everlasting kingdom. *"From the days of John the Baptist until now, the kingdom of heaven has been forcefully advancing, and forceful men lay hold of it"* (Matthew 11:12 NIV). Forcefully advancing the kingdom of heaven here on earth is our assignment, our purpose and our inheritance in Christ Jesus.

As I began to let go of the things of this world, the Lord began to awaken my spiritual senses. He gave me a yearning to read and study all the verses I could find about the kingdom of heaven—my true home.

> *Fear not, little flock, for it is your Father's good pleasure to give you the kingdom. Sell your possessions, and give to the needy. Provide yourselves with moneybags that do not grow old, with a treasure in the heavens that does not fail, where no thief approaches and no moth destroys. For where your treasure is, there will your heart be also. (Luke 12:32-34)*

It is sinful and spiritually dangerous for us to prize the things of this world and disregard or even reject the heavenly blessings Jesus died to give us. *"Blessed be the God and Father of our Lord Jesus Christ, who has blessed us in Christ with every spiritual blessing in the heavenly places"* (Ephesians 1:3). What are these spiritual blessings in the heavenly places? We'll never know if we don't dig for the treasures found in God's Word. We do not belong to this world, and the way it operates doesn't apply to us anymore. We must fight the sin of unbelief! Do we really *believe* that God can be our safety net, that He can become a dear friend in the midst of our loneliness? Can He be the One to fulfill our need for romance, mystery, excitement or adventure? In so many ways we simply do not believe that God can satisfy us more than the things in this world. The battlefield is in our minds, in the way we think. If there is a "no way, not God" answer to those questions lodged deep down in our belief system, then it will be very hard to allow Him to satisfy our desires. Ask the Lord to dig up those unbelieving thoughts and show you how they got buried there in the first place. Is there a memory He is bringing to your mind right now? Talk to Him about it. What have you come to believe about God that simply isn't true? Our Commander is the only One who can safely navigate us through our unbelief and the sinful passions of this world. He is the only One who can satisfy *all* our needs and desires. The more we allow the Commander to meet us in our neediness, the less appeal the things of this world will have on us. That, my friends, is freedom!

Learning to Live in the Kingdom of Heaven

Our invisible God made this visible world, speaking it into existence. *"By faith we understand that the universe was created by the word of God, so that what is seen was not made out of things that are visible" (Hebrews 11:3).* It's important to understand that Jesus' kingdom seems invisible until we train our spiritual senses to recognize it. We grow up in this physical world, trusting in the things that we can observe with our five senses. Being spiritually dead since birth, our physical senses were all we had access to until we put our faith in Christ Jesus and were made spiritually alive. When we are born into the kingdom of heaven, the Holy Spirit quickens our spirits to new life.

This quickening of the spirit enables us to live as spiritual beings, communicating with a spiritual God and recognizing the unseen kingdom of heaven. *"So we fix our eyes not on what is seen, but on what is unseen. For what is seen is temporary, but what is unseen is eternal" (2 Corinthians 4:18).* At first, as spiritual infants, God's kingdom is not very visible to us. But as we grow to spiritual adulthood we will be able to clearly recognize the unseen realm of God's kingdom all around us. When people asked Jesus about the kingdom of heaven, He explained it this way: *"Nor will people say, Look! Here [it is]! or, See, [it is] there! For behold, the kingdom of God is within you [in your hearts] and among you [surrounding you]" (Luke 17:21 AMP).*

When we use our spiritual senses, we are allowed to *hear* God's voice *(John 10:27)*; we are instructed to *taste* and *see* that the Lord is good *(Psalm 34:8)*; we gain the ability to *touch* or feel Him holding our hand *(Psalm 37:24)*; and we are spiritually able to *smell* the aroma of life in the kingdom of heaven and the stench of death in the kingdom of darkness *(2 Corinthians 2:15-16).* Jesus repeatedly said, *"If anyone has ears to hear, let him hear." And he said to them, "Pay attention to what you hear" (Mark 4:23-24a).* Jesus said this not because He was speaking to people who literally couldn't hear Him, but because He was seeking anyone who had the spiritual ears to listen and understand what He was saying. Jesus was looking for anyone whom His Father was drawing toward Him.

> *No one can come to me unless the Father who sent me draws him. And I will raise him up on the last day. It is written in the Prophets, "And they will all be taught by God." Everyone who has heard and learned from the Father comes to me—not that anyone has seen the Father except he who is from God; he has seen the Father. Truly, truly, I say to you, whoever believes has eternal life. (John 6:44-47)*

Just as an infant born into this physical world must develop his five physical senses to recognize the reality of this world, so we too must use our spiritual senses to recognize the reality of the kingdom of heaven all around us. One of the senses that a baby begins to develop is her sense of hearing; the same is true for the child of God. We must begin to recognize and obey our Father's voice through His Word, the Bible. He is the One who grows us to maturity as we develop our spiritual senses and learn to discern what is good and what is evil.

Dual Vision

The more we wean ourselves from the cravings of this world and recognize the kingdom of heaven as our place of belonging, the more our eyes will be opened to the spiritual realm all around us. *"Therefore, since we are surrounded by such a great cloud of witnesses, let us throw off everything that hinders and the sin that so easily entangles, and let us run with perseverance the race marked out for us"* (Hebrews 12:1 NIV). When I discovered that the kingdom of God is in my heart as well as all around me, I asked the Lord to remove the scales from my eyes, just like He did with the apostle Paul, so that I could more clearly see this kingdom of heaven.

As I was sitting in my living room one afternoon, I looked up to see a family portrait on the wall. The big bay window was directly behind me with a full view of the back yard, and my house was flooded with sunshine. When I looked at the picture in front of me I could see my family with all my kids smiling, while at the same time I could see the back yard in the reflection of the glass. I could either focus my eyes on the family portrait, or I could focus on the reflection of the backyard. The Lord spoke to my spirit: *Kori, I am going to teach you about dual vision. See how you can see the photograph of your family and **at the same time** see the reflection of your backyard in the glass? In the same way, I want to shed My light of truth over you so that you will be able to see what is going on in the physical realm as well as the spiritual realm. I am going to give you dual vision to discern between what is good and what is evil.*

Let me share with you an instance of this "dual vision" from my own experience. Sometimes the Lord warns me about enemy attacks that come against the minds of my children. My children are still young, so they haven't had much practice dissecting the different thoughts entering their minds. On one such occasion, there were three quick interactions with my daughter that happened within a 24-hour period.

First, my nine-year-old daughter walked into the kitchen while I was making supper. She lifted up her shirt and asked me if I thought she had a big belly. I assured her that she had the cutest little belly I had ever seen. She remained unconvinced, saying she thought her belly was fat, and then stuck it out as far as she could to try to prove to me she was indeed fat. The next day in the car I overheard her talking in the backseat. Now, my Darci is *always* talking, so I could have easily missed it when she said, "I think the devil's lying to me. He's telling me that I'm really fat."

Then that night, as we were looking through old family photos, Darci came across a photo of her first birthday. She was clearly enjoying her very own cake—frosting and cake were everywhere. Darci turned to me with a worried expression and asked, "Mommy, how big was that piece of cake that I ate? Was it this big or this big?" She motioned with her hands to show different sizes. I told her that it was a mini cake and that she enjoyed every bite of it. I didn't understand her concern until she said, "Oh, I'm glad it wasn't too big because I ate that whole cake, and just thinking about it makes me want to *throw up!*"

At that moment the Lord began to connect the dots for me, bringing to my mind all three of these short conversations that had taken place within the past day. As I recalled her words, I could see the pattern. I believe the Lord allowed me to recognize that a lying spirit was feeding her thoughts, attempting to gain entrance into my daughter's mind. This vile spirit was attempting to prepare her at an early age for an eating disorder. He was sowing lies, fears and hypothetical solutions into her mind. I believe the evil one's plot was to feed her these lies when she was young so that, years later, she would accept these thoughts as her own and he could establish a demonic stronghold in her life.

The gift of discernment enabled me to see what was going on in the invisible spiritual realm as well as the physical realm. I am so thankful that the Commander allowed me to see this devious attack of the enemy on my daughter *now*, rather than ten years down the road, when she could potentially be dealing with a full blown eating disorder as a young woman because of a demonic mental stronghold that had been built one sneaky little lie at a time. Without the discernment and the dual vision God gave me, I could easily have missed what was really transpiring.

Satan does not fight fair. He loves to attack the young and impressionable by repeating thoughts and ideas until they become a natural part of their belief systems. He might choose to attack us with thoughts, emotions or ideas of death or suicide. Have you ever envisioned creative ways in which you could take your life? These thoughts can come in a non-threatening way at first. Have you ever planned your funeral, imagining

"Be sober-minded; be watchful. Your adversary the devil prowls around like a roaring lion, seeking someone to devour."

1 Peter 5:8

who might be there? Once you get familiar with thinking this way, the ideas can take on a deeper level of darkness. Or have you had disturbing thoughts that targeted your sexuality? *Yuck, I would never do that, why would I even think this? What is wrong with me?* Yet the thoughts keep coming back, each time less repulsive and more acceptable . . . then agreeable . . . then doable. Or what about constant feelings of irritation with everyone and everything for no reason, so that eventually it becomes a normal part of your personality? Where does this come from? Is that your true nature? Whatever the enemy's agenda, he consistently plants these thoughts so subtly and regularly that we assume they are our core thoughts, believing they are a part of who we really are. Once we believe *that* lie, then we being to think of ways to act out "our desires." Do you see how important it is to develop our spiritual senses? Nothing unravels the plots and plans of the enemy like a child of God who spends time with the Commander, learns from Him, and obeys Him without question. We desperately need this dual vision in the daily battles we face.

It will be a lifelong endeavor to stand firm against the enemy of this world and say no to the enticing carrots dangled over our heads. As soon as we fight and defeat one worldly craving, the enemy will likely be prepping us for another one. The good news is that God knows everything about us and can help us to see clearly the worldly mindsets and cravings that we need to address. As we discover and believe in our acceptance, value and significance in Christ Jesus, the lies of this world will lose their potency over our minds. As we learn to depend upon our Father to meet all our needs, the temptations of this world will become less attractive to us. The more we let go of the cravings of this world, the more we will be satisfied with the resources of heaven, enabling us to become more discerning and win one battle after another.

Prayer:

Dear Father,
Thank You that every good gift comes from You to be enjoyed. Help me to glorify You in all that I eat, drink, and do. Thank You for giving me cravings that You alone can meet. Show me the areas that You want to step into and satisfy with Yourself. Show me any idols and give me the power to run to You and not to other things that would take Your place. This process seems hard and overwhelming but I want to be deeply satisfied with You alone. Give me Your instructions and reveal the spiritual battles going on all around me. Train me to be alert to the kingdom of heaven.
In Jesus' name, Amen.

Action Steps: Journal your prayers, answers and all the things the Commander reveals to you.

1. Is there any area in your life that has a strong grip on you? Do you have a craving that is hijacking your desire for God? If so, what is the God-given desire that God wants to meet? Ask Him to help you identify the heavenly resources that you need to let go of this worldly craving. How has this worldly pacifier kept you from maturing spiritually? Ask the Father to grant you the favor to "see" the things He wants you to "see" as you grow up in the kingdom of heaven.

2. Can you think of a time that the Lord granted you discernment to "see" what was going on in the spiritual realm as well as in the physical realm?

3. Ask the Father to *expose* any area of your life in which you love "the world" or "the things in the world" too much. See if there is anything that He is putting His finger on that is potentially harmful to you.

4. After the Commander has pinpointed an area, explain why you are drawn to this "craving" in your life. If you can't explain why, ask the Father to help you dissect this. Think about how often you desire this. What makes you want this? What need does it meet for you? Write it all down!

Chapter Seven
More Spiritual Weapons

We use God's mighty weapons, not worldly weapons,
to knock down the strongholds of human reasoning
and to destroy false arguments.
2 Corinthians 10:4 NLT

Mind battles can be full of confusion and chaos. Most of the time I don't even realize I'm under attack by the lies of the enemy until the battle is well under way, or even *after* it's over. In the heat of the fight I often don't know what's coming at me or where it is coming from. At times, the Commander will instruct me to use one weapon after another before the battle begins to let up. It is important that we know what these tools are and how to use them so we can stand firm and hold our ground even during the chaos. Wouldn't it be great if we were all well-trained warriors, handling our weapons with skill and ease *before* the crazy battle hits? Maybe someday that will be the case but I haven't reached that level of expertise just yet! The truth is, battles will come whether we are prepared or not. Each battle is different and oftentimes it takes a specific combination of these spiritual weapons together to bring about victory. The Commander will let us know when and what weapon to use as we stay in constant communication with Him.

The good news is that the more we identify and fight through the battles in life, the more God-confident and skilled in battle we become. The Commander has given us an abundance of spiritual weapons to fight with and as we get to know Him though the trials we face, He will continually show us how to add His most effective weapons to our arsenals. When we begin to see the degree of weapons provided for us and how dominant and superior they are, we can embrace our struggles instead of hiding, running for our lives, or doing our best to pretend they aren't there. I take comfort in the fact that I'm not the **only** one who has been shaken by the battles I face. Have you ever felt this way? *What in the world is going on? This cannot be happening to me! Not again.* The apostle Peter encouraged the early church with these words: *"Beloved, do not be surprised at the fiery trial when it comes upon you to test you, as though something strange were happening to you. But rejoice insofar as you share Christ's sufferings, that you may also rejoice and be glad when his glory is revealed"* (1 Peter 4:12-13). This verse tells us that trials for the believer are NORMAL and even good for us because they test us! That means we can stop being shocked when they arrive at our doorstep and we can stop wasting time treating them as if they were strange, abnormal or bizarre. May the Commander enable us to move past the urge to avoid or push them away as unwelcome guests. This verse also speaks of joy, but it's not the only passage that connects trial and blessing.

> *Consider it a sheer gift, friends, when tests and challenges come at you from all sides. You know that under pressure, your faith-life is forced into the open and shows its true colors. So don't try to get out of anything prematurely. Let it do its work so you become mature and well-developed, not deficient in any way. (James 1:2-4 MSG)*

This is one way we can turn the shock of the struggle from complaining to thanking God for it. It is a mystery but this opens the door to allow God to use our battles in the most effective way in our lives. James says, "Consider it a sheer gift," because the Commander is up to something we can't see right now through all the pain in the process. These passages hint at the fact that to the degree that we struggle through, that is the degree that we will rejoice when the victory comes. Basically, the harder the battle, the sweeter the victory!

> **WARNING**: Difficulties in life are part of God's gifts to us, even though they never feel like a gift. Satan will tempt us to become angry with God, attacking His goodness and intentions for us, trying to get us to blame Him for all our misfortunes. This attitude causes a breach in our communication with the Commander and leaves us vulnerable to more attacks. We can avoid falling into this trap by immediately THANKING God for our struggles, trials and difficulties, because they are God's way of training us for our own good.

Friends, the battles that you and I face today are a gift of the God of mercy to lead us into greater and greater victories in the years to come. Our faith in Christ will become solidified and we will become veteran warriors, so accustomed to the taste of victory that we are eager for the battle! May our God turn us into expert, battle-ready warriors, three steps ahead of the enemy, anticipating his every move because of the inside information we receive from our Commander. *God, make us Fearless!* May the enemy be defeated even before he has a chance to attack in our lives, and may we learn how to fight for those who can't battle for themselves! So let's look at a few more tools for the battle.

Weapon of Self-Discipline

But I discipline my body and keep it under control, lest after preaching to others I myself should be disqualified. (1 Corinthians 9:27)

But the fruit of the Spirit is love, joy, peace, patience, kindness, goodness, faithfulness, gentleness, self-control; against such things there is no law. And those who belong to Christ Jesus have crucified the flesh with its passions and desires. (Galatians 5:22-24)

For the moment all discipline seems painful rather than pleasant, but later it yields the peaceful fruit of righteousness to those who have been trained by it. (Hebrews 12:11)

A powerful weapon in our arsenal is the weapon of self-discipline, especially when the battle is against our flesh. We must constantly command our sinful nature to sit down and obey God, regardless of what we feel, want or think. When we are tempted to sin we can grab this weapon immediately. We can tell our sinful desires—*No!* For most of us, it is the first word we learned to say, so let's put it to good use and aim it toward our rebellious flesh. There are times I can literally feel my old nature rise up within me like an erupting volcano, demanding my own way! In those times it is a head-to-head battle as I have to tell my "I want my way and I want it now" attitude to bow to the authority of Christ. We can say to our flesh, "Selfishness, I have been given the power to say no to you! Bad attitude, you will not ruin my day! Negativity, shut your mouth today. Offence, I choose to forgive that person. Self-pity, I'm not listening to you." We must also be ready to make a quick decision when tempted to look at something impure or react in slander or spite. You know, it's that moment when you take a deep breath to say something you shouldn't and you get that warning in your spirit that says: *Don't say that. It won't be good if you say that.* But it's the perfect comeback and you *want* to say it soooo badly! It would make you feel so much better if you could just spew out those negative words. In that very moment of decision, we must persistently wield this highly effective weapon until it delivers a death blow to our old nature. The key to successfully using it, though, is practice; without it, we are at a significant disadvantage to the enemy.

We can practice self-discipline every day. To be honest, I indulge my wants and desires way too often. There are things that I want on a regular basis that are not sinful at all so I just do them.

But sometimes, in those moments of decision, I can hear the Commander telling me, *Kori, stop. Wait on this one. Not now.* He has instructed me to use the weapon of self-discipline in simple ways by saying no to something I could buy; something I *want* to buy but choose not to—just to practice dealing with not getting what I want. Or He gives me the opportunity to deny my desire to eat a scrumptious piece of hot lava cake for dessert at a restaurant—just for the sake of strengthening self-discipline. *I know, this sounds like a blast, right?* Or when I have zero desire to get out of my cozy, warm bed in the morning when it's only 5 degrees outside, but I choose to use the weapon of self-discipline to get up an hour early anyway . . . the opportunities to use this weapon are virtually endless!

I'm not making any friends here, am I? Learning to say *no* to our old nature's wants and desires is something we **can** master by the power provided for us in Christ Jesus. When we sharpen this weapon outside of the battle, it will be much easier to wield it in the heat of the battle. Don't be surprised if the Commander calls you to be obedient in a certain discipline where you have to consistently do something that is against all passion, desire, or will. It may seem trivial, unimportant or completely unrelated to anything of true value, but it is His way of training us for the battles that are coming. When we are faithful in the little areas of discipline we will know how to say no to our flesh and continue to say no despite all the whining, rebellious thoughts and attitudes doled out by our old nature.

Weapon of Quietness/Rest

For thus said the Lord God, the Holy One of Israel, "In returning and rest you shall be saved; in quietness and in trust shall be your strength." (Isaiah 30:15)

Come to me, all you who are weary and burdened, and I will give you rest. Take my yoke upon you and learn from me, for I am gentle and humble in heart, and you will find rest for your souls. For my yoke is easy and my burden is light. (Matthew 11:28-30)

So then, there remains a Sabbath rest for the people of God, for whoever has entered God's rest has also rested from his works as God did from his. Let us therefore strive to enter that rest, so that no one may fall by the same sort of disobedience. (Hebrews 4:9-11)

Our lives are full of activity, crazy schedules and constant noise, music, conversation, media, and of course the friendly little "ding" of your phone that goes off 50 times a day alerting you to an incoming message. All of this commotion can deplete our spiritual resources and drown out the voice of our Commander. Sometimes, we need to purposefully take up the weapon of quietness and rest. I highly recommend using this weapon daily to receive your morning assignments from the Commander in His Word. Also, we must be ready to use this weapon to cut through the chaos by carving out an afternoon, an entire day or even a weekend to get away from it all, seeking to rest before the Lord. Training our souls to be quiet, listening for His voice and allowing Him to fill us up with the strength only He can provide is critical as we endeavor to develop an intimate relationship with our Father God.

In January, the Commander instructed me to take out my calendar for the year and *set in stone* one day a month entitled a "Jesus Retreat Day." So every month had one day blocked out specifically to be with Jesus—no agenda, no housework, no kiddos, and no writing or editing. Just a day planned by Him, in His Word, hanging out with Him and writing down everything He wants to tell me. Friends, it is better than a day at the spa! I cannot tell you what my retreat days with Jesus have meant to me; there simply are no words to describe it. I so look forward to this one day a month and I have been told that my face is radiant afterward—that must be Jesus! Obedience to the Commander in this area has been the #1 BEST decision I have made this year. Now, it's not easy; I have to be intentional about it. In fact, I have to **fight** for this day. It's a battle to make it happen but the amazing time spent with Him fuels the rest of my month, not to mention my life!

Rested for the Battle

One week my family and I had just finished a very intense ministry season, where everything was put on hold in order to accomplish this spiritual assignment. Needless to say, the next week I really needed to get caught up on all the normal activities that had been left undone. Grocery shopping, cleaning, answering emails, book editing, meetings, you name it; all of it was hanging over my head and I was scrambling to find the time and energy to do it all. I had a fitful night of sleep where I experienced a panic attack in a bizarre dream, pressuring me about all the things that HAD to be done! It was in the aftermath of that dream that I heard the Commander instruct me to take a week off. *What? I can't take a week off. Who's going to answer all those emails? People are waiting on me to respond, and what about meals for my family? How can I make dinner with no groceries in the house and I'm already two weeks behind on editing and . . .*

Then I heard Him tell me again to REST and this time it came out more as a command than a gentle instruction! I sensed Him prompting me to clear the schedule, cancel the meetings I had that week, leave the emails, postpone the editing *another* week, and stay home to rest. I felt a bit guilty because it seemed irresponsible for me to take a break when so much needed to be done. But I decided to be obedient to His command. After I cleared my calendar for the week and significantly scaled down the meal plan, a huge invisible burden was lifted and I began to focus my attention on doing fun, restful things. As I did, I soon discovered just how depleted I was and realized that I was running on fumes instead of the strength that God provides! Going for a walk in the woods, reading a good novel, watching an action movie with my family were a few things I did to rest up and re-energize. What I didn't know at the time was that I was between two spiritual battles and the Commander wanted me to be recovered, well-rested and ready before the next battle raged. My experience was similar to a coach that takes a key player out in the third quarter to rest, so that he will be ready and on top of his game in the final stages of the game, when it counts most.

We have to trust the Lord and be obedient when He commands us to stop and rest! Entering God's rest is not just a nice option for us; it is a command, and disobedience to this command could cost us greatly. We could lose a victory in a specific battle we are facing if we don't obey His leading to rest. After my week of rest (which, by the way, was amazing, thank you), I was surprised to discover that the world was able to go on without me. Those things that I thought were so important, that had to be done *yesterday*, actually worked themselves out just fine. While I spent the week resting in Christ, He took care of the tiny little details of my life. I was relieved and slightly disturbed to discover that others stepped in and did the things I thought wouldn't get done without me. Sometimes I need to be reminded that God can handle the running of this world just fine without me and that *anyone* but God can be replaced! Honestly, I am glad for this truth—it removes an immeasurable amount of pressure. The weapon of rest that God supplies fuels us for the battles we fight and ushers in freedom from sinful bondage. Maybe that is why it is such a struggle for us to enter that rest—it takes faith in God's promises and obedience to His careful instructions.

Weapon of Forgiveness

And whenever you stand praying, forgive, if you have anything against anyone, so that your Father also who is in heaven may forgive you your trespasses. (Mark 11:25)

Good sense makes one slow to anger, and it is his glory to overlook an offense. (Proverbs 19:11)

Put on then, as God's chosen ones, holy and beloved, compassion, kindness, humility, meekness, and patience, bearing with one another and, if one has a complaint against another, forgiving each other; as the Lord has forgiven you, so you also must forgive. (Colossians 3:12-13)

NOTHING that I know of can shut down or block our communications with the Commander more effectively than withholding forgiveness in our hearts toward another. I have experienced it! That is why throughout this life, the enemy will consistently use people to wrong us at any level, in life-shattering ways as well as trivial and insignificant. Handling the weapon of forgiveness properly can be a potent and a most effective weapon to use against the enemy. We must practice using this tool to quickly let go of any offense committed against us.

One morning after dropping my kids off at school, I was making my way slowly out of the congested parking lot when I came head to head with a hurried driver who obviously thought I was in her way! I could see by her facial expressions and the gesturing of her hands (one finger in particular) that she believed she had the right-of-way and NOT me. I was a little taken aback by her mild display of road rage *and* the fact that I recognized her as a lady from church. I was immediately offended by her behavior that I deemed rude, selfish and anti-Christian. On the drive home, I struggled with conflicting thoughts to let the incident go or to hang on to the offense. *I should extend her some grace,* I thought, *she probably had a stressful morning and was just running late . . . but then again, that is no excuse, she should NOT be acting that way . . . but I've probably been rude to others without realizing it. I should just forget about it.* In the midst of my pondering and mentally replaying of the wrong done against me, it dawned on me that she did have the right-of-way and I had taken a turn directly in front of her. *Whoops, no wonder she was upset at me!* But that thought was quickly replaced by the growing magnitude of her "out of proportion" bad attitude toward me. I was *so* focused on her terrible behavior that I quickly dismissed any wrong of my own. In the midst of my thoughts, I heard My Commander's voice firmly telling me, *Kori, I want you to forgive her and permanently let it go.*

You see, I've learned that a negative experience like this one has the potential for me to start a list of wrongs against this woman. It's like a little sticky note of offence that gets put in a mental file, complete with negative mistrusting emotions. The next time I saw her, those same destructive emotions would flare up even if I had completely forgotten about the incident. Or if I didn't forget what she did to me, I would expect her to do something even more offensive because I have already forever labeled her as a rude, selfish person. The Word of God says that love does not keep a record of wrongs, but our enemy does! He uses things that people say and do to cause us to maintain a mental tally of wrongs. The weapon we use against his devious tactics against us is forgiveness. We must pay close attention to our thoughts, keep a short account and let go of any wrongs that others commit against us, giving these crimes done against us directly to Jesus. When I do, I am surprised to discover that so often other people's wrongdoing against me is more perceived than actual reality.

Within any given week, we will likely encounter someone who is rude to us, hurts our feelings or overlooks us. To be prepared for these offenses, we need to rehearse the following phrase: *I am going to let that go now.* Refusing to forgive is one of Satan's favorite traps for the believer—it causes us to lose sight of God's incredible mercy toward us. When we allow ourselves to get so worked up over the ways others wrong us, our thoughts are quickly consumed. Our minds can be so focused on building a case against another that it can literally block any logical thoughts of our wrong in the situation. In turn, there is no room in our minds to focus on our own sin and, more importantly, what it took to cover that sin: the blood of Jesus. We completely forget God's grace, mercy and forgiveness of our sin, and this is dangerous. Our forgiveness toward others is supernaturally linked to God's forgiveness toward us.

Harboring an Unforgiving Heart

Have you ever gone through a season where it seemed like your prayers were somehow stuck in a "dead zone" with no signal?

My first year of college could be summed up in that way. During my teenage years the Lord seemed so close as He walked me through some very difficult situations, but when I got to college . . . nothing! I had heard from other believers that God is just silent sometimes and there could be many possibilities as to why. So I tried everything I could think of: spending more time with Him, reading the Bible more, confessing any known sin, even fasting. Nothing seemed to restore the closeness of the Lord's abiding presence in my life. To be honest, I got really mad and even offended with God for the first time in my life and resolved to wait out the silence. It was about a year later that the Lord revealed to me that in this case, His silence was due to the sin of my unforgiving heart. Unbeknownst to me, in my last year of high school, bitterness and resentment had crept into my heart in regard to a certain person in my life. This person bugged me and, from my perspective, wronged me greatly! I didn't like her and could barely tolerate her. I held a huge grudge against her.

In my mind this grudge was a completely separate issue from my relationship with God, but I was mistaken. That was a long battle and it took me down for quite a while. It wasn't until I let go of her wrong against me and forgave her that I realized that she really didn't wrong me that badly in the first place. When I could see clearly again, I realized that my behavior toward her was ten times worse than her behavior toward me. I had to repent and seek her forgiveness for my many crimes against her. Bitterness toward her was a slippery slope that led to deception and the inability to hear the voice of God. It opened wide the door to the loud, twisted lies of the enemy, until the Commander instructed me to use the weapon of forgiveness and let go of the offense. I don't ever want to be there again.

Weapon of Giving

Do not withhold good from those to whom it is due, when it is in your power to do it. Do not say to your neighbor, "Go, and come again, tomorrow I will give it"—when you have it with you. (Proverbs 3:27-28)

Bring the full tithes into the storehouse, that there may be food in my house. And thereby put me to the test, says the Lord of hosts, if I will not open the windows of heaven for you and pour down for you a blessing until there is no more need. I will rebuke the devourer for you, so that it will not destroy the fruits of your soil, and your vine in the field shall not fail to bear, says the Lord of hosts. (Malachi 3:10-11)

Whoever is generous to the poor lends to the Lord, and he will repay him for his deed. (Proverbs 19:17)

Now I want you to know, dear brothers and sisters, what God in his kindness has done through the churches in Macedonia. They are being tested by many troubles, and they are very poor. But they are also filled with abundant joy, which has overflowed in rich generosity. For I can testify that they gave not only what they could afford, but far more. And they did it of their own free will. They begged us again and again for the privilege of sharing in the gift for the believers in Jerusalem. (2 Corinthians 8:1-4 NLT)

We are always instructed to be cheerful givers, knowing that all we have has been given to us from the Lord, but there are times in a battle when there is an additional urging from the Commander to give away some of our resources in a very clear and tangible way. Using this weapon of giving can break a hold on us, or even release a much desired blessing from God in the midst of the battle. We are blessed to be a blessing to others, and giving can be such a powerful weapon in our fight against selfishness, coveting, materialism, greed and even depression. We may be surprised to discover that the weapon of giving could be the key to a much-needed breakthrough in our lives.

It was pizza movie night and my turn to go pick up the pizzas. I ordered and arrived at the restaurant within 15 minutes just as they requested, but when I arrived I could hardly find a parking spot. At the entrance I had to push my way through the crowd of people standing around waiting to be seated. This place was busier than I had ever seen it and the atmosphere was hectic and stressful. When I finally reached the counter to pick up my pizzas they informed me that all of their "to go orders" were backed up by at least 15 minutes. Knowing I had to pick up my daughter from work, I told the lady I would come back. Twenty minutes later I returned to the restaurant for my pizzas and once again stepped into an overpopulated, understaffed atmosphere filled with some not-so-happy people who thought THEY had been waiting longer than they should. My daughter and I stood unacknowledged at the counter for about ten minutes. All the while, I could see my pizzas sitting on the "orders up" counter getting colder by the minute.

Take in the scene: A lady hassled a waitress to move her up on the seating list, while other people stood with their arms crossed, tightlipped and fuming. I was getting a bit frustrated myself because at this point all I wanted to do was get my pizzas and get out of there. Then my daughter said to me, "Mom, maybe we're here to bless someone." I laughed because that was NOT what I was thinking at the moment! But her words were convicting and so I asked the Lord in my spirit, *Is she right? Is there someone here You want me to see? Is there someone here You want me to bless?* Then I "opened my eyes" and started looking around, trying to see this situation from His perspective. Almost immediately I saw a frazzled young waitress. I had seen her before but only as a means to help me; this time I tried to look at the situation from her perspective. It had been a long night for her and I could tell by the look on her face that she was in "survival mode." Even as she turned to me and asked what she could do for me, I thought, *God, what can I do for her?* As she rang up my order, I looked into my wallet and saw some cash (not much, but it was something). In that moment, I just knew I was supposed to give it to her. So I looked her in the eye, handed her the money and said, "This is for you. I know it's been a rough night; hang in there." And then we walked out the door with our pizzas.

I believe the Commander knew I needed to give, for her sake and for mine. You see, picking up on the stress of the situation, I could have become self-focused and uptight, opening the door for more negative thoughts and emotions to flood my mind and ruin my evening. But by using the weapon of giving, I was allowed to be a blessing to someone else. Giving to her in her moment of need was a blessing to me, and it changed the direction of my attitude over the rest of my evening. And you'll never believe this, but the pizza we had that night was some of the best pizza we've ever had!

Weapon of Sleep

In peace I will both lie down and sleep; for you alone, O Lord, make me dwell in safety. (Psalm 4:8)

"For I will satisfy the weary soul, and every languishing soul I will replenish." At this I awoke and looked, and my sleep was pleasant to me. (Jeremiah 31:25-26)

But he himself (Elijah) went a day's journey into the wilderness and came and sat down under a broom tree. And he asked that he might die, saying, "It is enough; now, O Lord, take away my life, for I am no better than my fathers." And he lay down and slept under a broom tree. And behold, an angel touched him and said to him, "Arise and eat." And he looked, and behold, there was at his head a cake baked on hot stones and a jar of water. And he ate and drank and lay down again. And the angel of the Lord came again a second time and touched him and said, "Arise and eat, for the journey is too great for you." And he arose and ate and drank, and went in the strength of that food forty days and forty nights to Horeb, the mount of God. (1 Kings 19:4-8)

We need to be on guard against physical exhaustion in the battles we fight. The prophet Elijah became so weary in his battle against the false god of Baal that he lost all perspective—he claimed he was the *only* prophet left, and then begged God to let him die. God's next important instruction for this mighty warrior after the "Call Fire Down from Heaven Showdown" was this: Elijah, lie down and take a nap. When I am battle-weary and physically tired, I am susceptible to all kinds of lies from the enemy. At those times, I can't trust the thoughts running through my mind—I need to sleep! When I wake up well rested, it is amazing to see the difference in my perspective and disposition. Everything that was such a big deal before seemed to shrink in size or work itself out while I was sleeping. At times the best weapon we can wield in the middle of our relentless mind battle is simply to go to bed and sleep! We might think it's the last thing we have time for, but we must regain our strength to stand firm against the enemy.

Nap ≠ Lazy

I have always required more sleep than the average person. I look at high-energy people and marvel at the way God made them. I am also a morning person and I sometimes struggle to stay *alert and enthusiastic* after 8:00 at night. When my kids were little, I would simply put them to bed and go to bed myself. When they got older they started to protest my desire/need to put them to bed at 7:30 each night, often having much more energy at that time than I did. Being exhausted so early every night didn't make me a very nice mother. When the clock struck the magical hour of 8:00, the "Mommy is Closed" sign would go up and my kids could anticipate the difference. Gone was the loving, giving, self-sacrificing mother I once was and in her place was the grumpy, testy nature of my old flesh who just wanted her pillow. It was in this state of mind that I was still trying to complete the duties of a mother and get my kids in bed for the night—not fun for anyone involved.

During that season, a friend of mine told me how the Lord led her to take a short nap in the afternoon while the kids were at school so she could enjoy the evening and late night talks that often take place with her teenage kids. *Wow, take a nap while my husband is working and my kids are in school? Could I? What about all the work that needs to get done? Wouldn't that be lazy? What would people think if they knew I sleep away my afternoons? And what about all the hard-working career moms out there who would love to take naps in the afternoons but can't?* I struggled with these thoughts and many more, but finally had to reject all the guilt-laced feelings of taking a nap when I should be doing *something useful* with my time. As the Lord prompted me toward this, I began to see the wisdom of a well-timed nap that would help me better invest in the lives, activities and conversations of my family. God had to change my way of thinking. Where I once viewed afternoon napping as a lazy, idle thing, I now see it more as a spiritual weapon that enables me to be rested and prepared for the battles ahead. That was years ago, and I don't need afternoon naps anymore; it turned out to be a season of life that the Lord knew I needed. But I've learned when I sense the Commander telling me to stop struggling through the battle and simply sleep, that I need to humbly and willingly carve out time from my busy schedule in order to be obedient to Him.

Weapon of Obedience

Why do you call me 'Lord, Lord,' and not do what I tell you? (Luke 6:46)

Submit yourselves therefore to God. Resist the devil, and he will flee from you. Draw near to God, and he will draw near to you. (James 4:7-8a)

If you love me, you will keep my commandments. (John 14:15)

We are always to be obedient to our God, but there are times in a battle when the Lord will give us detailed instructions to obey

Him quickly and completely. We must be ready at any given moment to swiftly use our weapon of obedience. Whether we obey our Commander will be the deciding factor in the outcome of the battle. There may be times when the Commander prods us to some specific action, and we simply put it off. Even though it might not seem like outright disobedience, our procrastination allows the enemy to gain a foothold in our lives.

I recall a time when the Lord kept reminding me of a sin I had committed years ago. I had already repented of this sin to God and had received His forgiveness, but I had never made it right with the individuals I had wronged. I argued with my Lord that it was too late to do anything about it, but He persistently brought it back to my mind, giving me very clear instructions on how I was to make it right. It finally came to a head when I sensed the Lord telling me that we couldn't go to the next stage in our relationship until I submitted to Him and obeyed Him in this area. This obedience involved the weapon of confession and the payment of funds. Once I had *finally* done what God was prompting me to do, I noticed that I was able to easily resist the devil and make him flee in other areas of my life. It was as if my obedience to God sealed off a "back door" entrance in my life that the devil had been using to tempt and harass me.

Disobedience to those in a God-given role of leadership or authority over us could be another area in which the Commander instructs us to repent and wield the weapon of obedience. Growing up, I had a youth pastor once who was new to our church and started making some changes to our youth group's format that many people were not happy about. Many people felt, and I might add that I did as well, that this youth pastor was clearly making the wrong move and his new ideas were going to affect the youth group badly. I am sorry to admit that I protested by talking behind his back, even stirring up negativity about his motive and character. Of course, I told myself that we were discussing ways in which we could pray for him to make the right decisions! But it was not a mistake that he came to our church and was placed as a youth pastor over the youth group. God is still sovereign over all. What this youth pastor was doing was **not** a sin issue even though I was treating it as such. The real sin issue was my rebellious teenage heart being told what to do by someone who was, in my opinion, a *clearly inexperienced* youth pastor! Change is hard, but not always bad. During that struggle I remember coming across this verse and literally choking on it: *"Obey your leaders and submit to them, for they are keeping watch over your souls, as those who will have to give an account. Let them do this with joy and not with groaning, for that would be of no advantage to you"* (Hebrews 13:17). The Lord instructed me to repent, take this verse to the youth pastor and ask his forgiveness and affirm that I would follow his way of leading the youth group. I still didn't like the changes he made but I learned to trust the sovereignty of God, knowing that He placed that man in authority over me for a reason. If we have a problem with obeying those in authority over us, then our problem is more with the One who set them there in the first place. God might be using them to reveal rebellion in our hearts we didn't even know was there!

Weapon of Serving Others

Do nothing out of selfish ambition or vain conceit, but in humility consider others better than yourselves. Each of you should look not only to your own interests, but also to the interests of others. Your attitude should be the same as that of Christ Jesus. (Philippians 2:3-5)

Humble yourselves, therefore, under the mighty hand of God so that at the proper time he may exalt you, casting all your anxieties on him, because he cares for you. (1 Peter 5:6-7)

But whoever would be great among you must be your servant, and whoever would be first among you must be your slave, even as the Son of Man came not to be served but to serve, and to give his life as a ransom for many. (Matthew 20:26b-28)

In the battle there are times when the Commander will order me to use a weapon that seems strange to me—the weapon of serving others. I can become so consumed with myself and my problems that this weapon can cut through the selfishness and bring about a 180-degree change in my thinking. In the middle of my personal battles I am so near-sighted that it often seems like I am the *only* person in the world who struggles this much, and that my issues are bigger and more important than anyone else's. The lies of self-pity can overwhelm me and make me feel defeated. Thoughts of offense or division are ready to strike, insinuating that others are not sensitive to my plight.

One week I went through a "funk" that just wouldn't go away. I don't know if it was my circumstances, my hormones, or what, but it was bad. Things I could normally handle set me off and I was one tiny trigger away from a blowup or a meltdown. Even as I struggled through this I felt a ton of guilt that my poor family had to be around me when I didn't even what to be around myself. It seemed that grumbling and complaining was all I was capable of accomplishing in a day. I tried to pick up the weapon of worship and use it, but it only helped for a little bit before I was right back in that same funk again. When I get like this sometimes, I tend to want to hide away, lock all the doors and hibernate. I am ashamed of my bad behavior and my lack of strength to overcome it, so I deem myself "unfit" to be around. *Lord, what is **wrong** with me? I hate this place I'm in! I don't want to be here anymore. Help me! Get me out of this, pleeeease!*

Then, right in the middle of my lonely pity party, God instructed me to stop and look to the needs of those around me. *Kori, I want you to spend the day being a blessing to others. Let Me show you how.* He then put some very specific ideas in my mind about whom to serve and how to go about it. *Kori, call your friend and offer to take her out to lunch today. Go to the store this morning and buy groceries for Cheryl; take them to her house because she needs them today. Make a special dinner for your family tonight.* The ideas came quickly and with such great detail and clarity that I knew these were His thoughts and not mine. Did I feel like doing any of this? No! First of all it would require me to get dressed for the day, and that wasn't on my agenda. I was in self-pity hibernation mode and these ideas were the last things I wanted to get out there and do. But I made the choice to lay aside my issues and take up this weapon of serving others. As I began making plans to implement the assignments that God had given me that day, my thoughts began to turn away from: *Woe is me, why do I have to struggle so much? When will I get out of this funk? How long, O Lord, until You deliver me from this dark pit?* With each task the Lord gave me to do, I began to think: *I wonder where my friend would want to go for lunch? What kind of fun groceries should I surprise Cheryl with? What would my family enjoy for dinner? What would make them smile?*

Every time I encouraged and blessed someone that day I was lifted out of my emotional rut. This changed my demeanor and made me want to bless random people I met along the way with a hello, a smile or a word of encouragement. It was just the right weapon at just the right time and the Commander knew it. I am so glad I followed His lead that day! Every battle is different. The reality is that we never know which spiritual weapons are going to be required in the different battles we face. That is why we need to be well skilled in all of them, growing continually in our knowledge and proficiency.

Moving from Defensive to Offensive Battles

I share many of my personal battles, though some of them are quite minor compared to the battles that the persecuted church has faced and will continue to face all around the world. The Lord has taught me not to belittle the trivial struggles we face because with each one He is training us for the bigger trials to come. He is faithful to train us to depend on Him through situations and experiences today so we will be in the habit of depending on Him for the future struggles we will face. Now that we are getting better acquainted with the spiritual weapons God has given us, I want to describe a recent battle where the Commander led me step by step, using multiple weapons in order to stay engaged and ultimately victorious in the battle.

Each year at Easter our church puts on The Promise Production. It uses a cast and crew of about 200 to act out the life, death, and resurrection of Jesus Christ, Broadway style. The last few years my family and I have been in the production but this year I sensed the Commander calling me to invest in the area of child care. Out of all the areas in which I could help, let's just say this was not my first pick, but our God prioritizes children and He made it clear that this was my assignment this year. This meant several late nights overseeing a group of 25 kids, ages 4 to 12, who would be in the production. Four other brave moms joined me in overseeing these kids through several hours of practice and late nights where these kids were up way past their bedtimes.

When the week of the performance finally arrived, there was more than one attempt by the enemy to stir up bad attitudes and rile us to be divided or at odds with one another. I'm going to slow down the battle and give you a play-by-play of what happened one night. The morning of the first performance, I woke up grumpy and couldn't quite shake it all day long. Little stupid things irritated me throughout the day, prepping me for that one "last straw." My family arrived at church a little late that night, of course (trigger for me), and all the other moms were already there. I felt like a major slacker, totally irresponsible, but I greeted them all with a smile, dropped off my stuff and walked into the room full of hyper kids. Still frazzled from the day, I felt unprepared and wasn't even thinking about spiritual warfare.

The moment I walked into the room one little boy hit another boy in the face. *Wow, this is a great start to the next four hours of childcare!* I couldn't let that go unchecked and so I told the boy who did the hitting to sit in a different spot. He replied defiantly, "No thanks, I'm good." Kids blatantly disrespecting my authority is another trigger for me. I replied calmly to him, "Oh yes, you will sit in the other seat." He once again replied with a cool, "Nah, I'm good, I like this chair!" This standoff quickly escalated to a power-play in which I lost my patience, got down on his eye level and told him that he *would* sit in the chair that I told him to SIT in! He must have seen the fire in my eyes because he finally concurred and quickly moved to the appointed seat. As I regained my perspective, I looked around and saw all the other kids staring at me a bit wide-eyed. *Whoops, I probably didn't handle that so well.* Yep, that little 10-year-old boy had hit a trigger where my flesh took over. My inner emotions were so worked up after that encounter that I had to walk out of the room for a moment. I knew that I had lost my patience and blown it, and so I made contact with the Commander. *Lord, what in the world was that? This behavior is not normally like me. I was totally unprepared for that. I had barely walked into the room when that little boy started pushing my buttons. Lord, forgive me, I need your help for the rest of this night.*

After that encounter, the night seemed to go from bad to worse for me. I was hounded with thoughts of condemnation, not to mention some not-so-nice thoughts that kept coming up toward the boy who challenged my authority. Guilt pelted me with these thoughts: *Well, you sure did blow it . . . You're supposed to take care of these kids and show them the love of Jesus, and instead you lost your temper. I bet that boy hates your guts now. He's never going to listen to you again, nor should he after the way you treated him.* I felt like such a failure and so unworthy. These thoughts and accusations almost paralyzed me for the rest of the night and I retreated into shutdown mode, present but not really engaged. I felt like I had nothing to give. These kids, who were normally fairly good, seemed out of control that night. They were violent, disobedient, disrespectful of authority, selfish, and said things like, "I hate you," and "I want to kill you," to each other. At one point, I even got "accidentally" smacked in the face. *What in the world is going on here?* It felt like instead of watching kids, I was merely trying to surviving the night.

The next morning I woke up completely dreading the next four nights with this group of kids. *Why did I sign up for this? What did I get myself into? How can I get out of this?* Even as these thoughts and negative emotions came flooding in, I knew these were not my true feelings but rather what the devil wanted me to think and feel. But even knowing that they weren't true didn't make them any easier to fight through. After I was out of bed and ready for the day, I knew I was in for a morning battle simply trying to bat away one damaging thought after another. I sensed the need to ask my husband to pray for me before he left for work. To do this, I had to work through a few more negative thoughts that said, *Don't bother your husband with that . . . he's got more important things to do . . . don't tell him your struggle, he'll think you're silly . . . he's not gonna want to pray for you anyway.* I did eventually ask him and he prayed over me. As he did, I could feel a lifting of the intensity of the destructive thoughts attacking my mind.

His prayer over me provided a temporary "cease-fire" regarding the negative thoughts assaulting my mind, and with that came some clarity from the Commander. It was then that I realized the previous day had been one play after another by the enemy to set me up for failure. Seeking to lure me into walking in the flesh, he prepared me to fall into his trap when that young boy deliberately disobeyed my simple instruction to sit in a different chair. Because I was distracted and not expecting a battle, I was not geared up for it. Also, any influence that the devil had in the lives of these kids was being stirred up in their thoughts, behavior and attitudes that night. He needed me distracted and desiring to run as far away from them as possible, not standing firm with the full armor of God.

When I realized this, I felt like my Commander said to me, *Kori, Satan threw a punch at you and yes, he won that round. But what are you going to do about it? Are you going to run? Are you going to walk in defeat the rest of this week? Or are you going to stand your ground and fight?* In that moment, I made the choice to get ready for the next round of the fight. *Lord, what do You want me to do?* The plan of action came to my mind swiftly. I needed backup so I took out my weapon of the Body of Christ and quickly explained the situation to a few close friends who I knew would pray. Then I used the weapon of repentance and asked the Lord to forgive me, cleanse me and renew a right spirit in me. After that I began to use the weapon of prayer as I specifically prayed for the boy who had offended me with his disrespect. As I did, the Commander gave me the weapon of discernment, showing me that the "No, I'm good" statement and defiant attitude of this young boy was really just a cover for some pain and fear. I was able to see past his bad attitude to see a scared little boy with some deep hurts. Then the Commander called me to pick up the weapon of obedience as He instructed me to pull this young boy aside and apologize to him for my bad attitude toward him, seeking his forgiveness. Ouch! It was humbling but necessary in this battle.

The next few nights the Commander gave me the ability to see these kids and highly value them in the ways that He does. When they acted up, I had to resist my natural response to handle it in the flesh. Instead He gave me the ability to see past it, look at their hearts, and hear what they couldn't articulate. I was able to speak life into them, recognize qualities and godly characteristics that they had and show them how important and loved they are. As I interacted with them one by one during that time, I realized I wasn't just babysitting these kids while the adults did the spiritually important things. I was in the trenches, training and battling for the future warriors of the kingdom of heaven. Many of them will be great warriors who will do great things for God and even suffer for the sake of Christ. I realized the devil didn't want me, a prayer warrior in the kingdom of heaven, who has the ear and favor of the Most High God, to be anywhere close to these kids.

The last night we were all together, the Lord directed my steps to pray for each one of these kids individually. One by one these kids ages 4 through 12 came over to my corner and let me pray a prayer of blessing over them. I had the privilege of holding their little hands or placing my hand on their heads as I ask God for a lifetime of protection and blessing to be poured out over them. Every prayer was different and unique. I asked each child to tell me what their favorite Bible story was and then turned it into a prayer for them. In those few moments of prayer, I connected with each child as we shared a holy moment of God's presence. I don't know exactly how prayer works but I do believe that those prayers were incredibly potent and that in the time when these kids need it the most, the Lord will honor the prayers that were prayed over them during that night. I didn't know this was going to happen but as I looked back over the situation it is no wonder why the enemy fought so hard to defeat us, seeking to cause disunity. Satan was defeated that week in multiple ways: in my life, in the lives of those kids, and quite possibly in some of the future battles they will face throughout their lifetime.

As you can see, our battles can be quite complex. We must know our Commander's voice and familiarize ourselves with the spiritual weapons the Lord has made available to us through His Word. No struggle we face, big or small, is too hard for Him as we learn to trust His navigational skills.

Prayer:

Dear Father,
Thank You for the struggles in my life. I admit that I don't like them, and long for a carefree life. Someday that will be the case and I look forward to Heaven, but in the meantime help me stay engaged in this spiritual war and fight the battles that come my way. I trust You to train me. Lord, teach me more about the spiritual weapons in this chapter and help me use them with skill and wisdom so that I may experience victory after victory for Your glory.
In Jesus' name, Amen.

Action Steps: Journal your prayers, answers and all the things the Commander reveals to you.

1. Choose a spiritual weapon from this chapter. Research it by looking up all the verses in Scripture you can find about it. Ask the Commander to reveal the spiritual "features" of this weapon and how it

could work in the midst of a mind battle. If the Lord gives you any instructions on how to practice this weapon then be obedient, asking Him to prompt you when and how throughout your day.

2. Choose another spiritual weapon and repeat the above instructions.

3. The next time you recognize that you are in a mind battle, Pray! Ask the Lord to help you use one or more of these weapons: Self-discipline, Quietness and Rest, Forgiveness, Giving, Sleep, Obedience or Serving Others.

4. Allow the Commander to take you through a battle where you begin to use multiple spiritual weapons. Listen for His voice as He brings to mind the different weapons. When you have come through it, document it by writing down the different weapons you used and how they worked together.

Chapter Eight
The Battle Against the Flesh

Now if we have died with Christ, we believe that we will also live with him. We know that Christ being raised from the dead will never die again; death no longer has dominion over him. For the death he died he died to sin, once for all, but the life he lives he lives to God. So you also must consider yourselves dead to sin and alive to God in Christ Jesus.
Romans 6:8-11

Let me introduce you to my flesh. I call her "the old Kori." If you and I only spend a little time together, or if you happen to run into me at Target or at church, you might not see this character hanging around. But if you get close to me, she'll definitely show up and you'll get to see how she operates. I apologize in advance . . . she's not my favorite person to be around!

The old Kori is obsessively consumed with herself. She's sinful, controlling, ugly, highly defensive and selfish, and she constantly demands her own way. She's fearful, judgmental, prideful, and cares way too much about what you might think about her. Even though she thinks herself above it, she is capable of any type of sin given just the right circumstance. If you really got to know her, you wouldn't like her; even I don't like her!

There's a reason why I'm referring to her in the third person; it's because she is separate from who I am now, and she has nothing to do with my new nature in Christ Jesus. And the reason I can tell you about all her ugly, sinful thoughts and actions is this: She is not who I am any more. Spiritually speaking, *she is dead.*

The day I placed my faith in Jesus was the day "old Kori" died. Good riddance to her! As Jesus hung on the Cross, God the Father took my life and seated me inside of Jesus. I was placed so deeply and permanently in Christ that I was hidden in Him and remain in Him to this day. *"For you have died, and your life is hidden with Christ in God. When Christ who is your life appears, then you also will appear with him in glory"* (Colossians 3:3-4). As God the Father poured out His righteous wrath as punishment for my sin, Jesus took the full force of that wrath while covering me and protecting me with His life. When Jesus died, the old Kori, my old sinful nature, was also pronounced dead. All accounts of the debt of my personal sin, the sins already committed and the ones yet to be committed, were settled. My sins were stamped "Paid in Full" and completely canceled out. My death in Jesus brought closure to my old nature and the death certificate for the old Kori was issued. *"For if we have been united with him in a death like his, we shall certainly be united with him in a resurrection like his"* (Romans 6:5).

The death of my old self had to happen before my new birth could take place. *"Jesus answered him, 'Truly, truly, I say to you, unless one is born again he cannot see the kingdom of God'"* (John 3:3). When Jesus rose from the dead, I rose with Him to a brand new life. This was not a remake of the old Kori, who was sinful to the core. This was a new birth with an entirely new nature—the very nature of Jesus Christ. He is my new nature and I am now as good as He is. I, because Christ lives in me, am good to the core. My life and His life are currently wrapped up together, eternally united. His righteousness is now my righteousness. We are one in spirit, righteous in nature. I am not who I used to be. The old Kori came from the bloodline of Adam, sinful and corrupt, but the new Kori comes from the bloodline of Jesus

Christ. He is the firstborn of the new race, and I am one of many in this noble race. I have been made perfect by Christ's sacrifice. Because of this union, I have an entirely new DNA. The royal blood of Jesus Christ runs in my spiritual veins.

For years I completely missed this truth! I thought that the core of me was still bad, evil, and extremely messed up. Mentally, I couldn't separate my sinful behavior from the new person God made me to be. Even as a believer, I thought I was still broken somehow and that it was my responsibility to work hard to fix myself. I mistakenly thought I had to strive, little by little, to make myself more like Christ. This was a deceptive lie from the enemy. The truth is that at the very core of my being, I have *already* been created perfect, righteous and holy. I am good through and through because the very nature of Christ has been given to me. I don't have to "fix" or better myself because Jesus has done it for me by His life and death and resurrection. *"I have been crucified with Christ. It is no longer I who live, but Christ who lives in me. And the life I now live in the flesh I live by faith in the Son of God, who loved me and gave himself for me"* (Galatians 2:20).

My fight is not to strive to become more like Christ; this has already been accomplished. My fight is to resist and say no to my bossy, controlling, sinful old self. Warring in my mind, battling for position, is the old Kori against the new Kori. The old Kori was crucified with Christ and because she is dead, she no longer has the right to rule. She can only take charge if I, the new Kori, allow her to. And she *always* wants to take charge. I have been made perfect and holy. I love God and only desire to do His will because my new nature is the very nature of Jesus Christ. As a new person in Christ I have been given the power to say no to sin. When I mess up and sin, it means that the old Kori rose up and took charge. *"Now if I do what I do not want, it is no longer I who do it, but sin that dwells within me"* (Romans 7:20). By referring to my flesh as "the old Kori," it does not mean that I do not take responsibility for her actions. On the contrary, I can and must take even more responsibility for her behavior because the new Kori has now been given the ability in Christ to silence her.

When I allow a bad attitude, believe the lies of unworthiness, embrace fear, or self-defend by mentally slandering others, I am operating in sin and not being true to my new nature in Christ Jesus. In the midst of the battles, when my flesh shows up "alive and well," I must never forget that is *not* who I am anymore. That is the old Kori, trying desperately to fix, control, protect, and demand her own way.

Even though these two natures war against one another, they can never mix. My new nature can't make my old nature good, and it is impossible for my old nature to taint, pollute or infect with sin the new creation God has made me to be. They cannot co-exist. They cannot share leadership. The one must die and continue dying so that the other may live. Our flesh is a violent enemy to us, seeking to suffocate and conceal the imperishable life of Christ in us. *"We know that our old self was crucified with him in order that the body of sin might be brought to nothing, so that we would no longer be enslaved to sin. For one who has died has been set free from sin" (Romans 6:6-7).*

What my old sinful nature was powerless to do, God did through my union with Christ—He has fully empowered me to live the righteous life I was always meant to live. This is my fight against the flesh: I must daily cling to God's truth, which says I have been set free from my sinful nature. In the heat of the battle, in a moment of decision, I must know and believe that the old Kori has no power over me. She does not have to take charge. She doesn't have to defend me, meet my needs or fight for my rights anymore. As a new creation in Jesus, I have been made whole, protected and completed by my relationship with my Creator. God is the One who has restored my position and my purpose, and He fulfills my every need as I allow Him to sit on the throne of my life.

My daily battle is a choice: Will I let "the old Kori" be in charge, operating independently from God? Or will I, the new Kori, abide in Christ, allowing Him to direct my steps and meet all my needs? God gave us the ultimate gift: His Son, Jesus. All that

Jesus is and all that He has, He desires to pour into us. He calls us to abide, remain, and stay close to Him as He abides in us so that we may be saturated and overflowing with His love. He jealously wants all of us, every single area of our lives, that He may fill us with Himself. This is true for all of God's children, and the enemy does everything in his power to keep us from knowing and believing this powerful truth.

The Origin of Our Sinful Nature

God gave us the ability to think, a will to choose, and emotions to feel. He created us to know Him, and He intentionally gave us needs and longings that He alone could fulfill. Adam and Eve, the first man and woman, were given their identity and purpose from their Creator God. He gave them direction, acceptance, love, and companion-ship with Himself and each other. In union with Him, no doubt they grew in their knowledge of God, their under-standing of His marvelous work in their creation, and their appreciation of how intimately He knew them. They were cherished and wanted. As male and female they were made uniquely separate from one

"Then God said, "Let us make man in our image, after our likeness. And let them have dominion over the fish of the sea and over the birds of the heavens and over the livestock and over all the earth and over every creeping thing that creeps on the earth." So God created man in his own image, in the image of God he created him; male and female he created them."
Genesis 1:26-27

another and given distinct roles for which they were ideally suited. In their perfection they instinctively reflected God's image in their thoughts, actions, attitudes and even their interaction with one another. Under God's perfect leadership and in their union with Him, all was well. They and their future descendants (that's us) were meant to live forever, eating of the tree of life. We were created for the paradise of the Garden of Eden and are made to interact with our Creator, growing in the knowledge and the experience of walking with Him. As offspring of Adam and Eve, living in a perfect world, we were intended to have that same purpose, direction, acceptance, love, uniqueness, and interaction with the One who created us. It is what we were designed and destined for, and it was all good until sin entered into the world through our first parents.

If you look at the human race now, you may wonder what happened to all of that perfection, beauty, and goodness. The forbidden tree is the key to the answer. *"And the Lord God commanded the man, saying, "You may surely eat of every tree of the garden, but of the tree of the knowledge of good and evil you shall not eat, for in the day that you eat of it you shall surely die" (Genesis 2:16-17).* All creation was at their disposal, to use and rule over at their pleasure. The only thing that God instructed them *not* to do was eat of a single tree: the tree of the Knowledge of Good and Evil. This one restriction was for their good because our all-knowing God did not want them, His beloved creation, to experience the wretchedness of evil. Pain, fear, doubt, wickedness, murder, sadness, depression, sin and death all came from the decision to disobey God and eat of this forbidden tree.

> So when the woman saw that the tree was good for food, and that it was a delight to the eyes, and that the tree was to be desired to make one wise, she took of its fruit and ate, and she also gave some to her husband who was with her, and he ate. Then the eyes of both were opened, and they knew that they were naked. (Genesis 3:6-7a)

Everything changed as God's holiness was forced to punish them for their sin. He sent them out of the garden and away from His presence. They not only lost their union with the presence of God, but the only home they had ever known was sealed off as they were banished from the Garden of Eden.

Then the Lord God said, "Behold, the man has become like one of us in knowing good and evil. Now, lest he reach out his hand and take also of the tree of life and eat, and live forever—" therefore the Lord God sent him out from the garden of Eden to work the ground from which he was taken. He drove out the man, and at the east of the Garden of Eden he placed the cherubim and a flaming sword that turned every way to guard the way to the tree of life. (Genesis 3:22-24)

Up to this point they had only experienced the awareness and knowledge of good with their Creator in the garden, but now, cast out into the world, they began to experience the awareness and knowledge of evil. They began to taste fear, experience evil thoughts, and suffer guilt, shame, blame, betrayal, hopelessness and despair. Needs that were once met by their Creator were left unmet, demanding to be fulfilled. In vain Adam and Eve attempted to satisfy their need of love, acceptance, purpose, and companionship outside of God. They literally became slaves to those needs. Wickedness and corruption began to multiply on the earth, because sin was now in the very core of their human nature. Every child that was born to them inherited Adam's sinful nature. The entire bloodline of Adam and Eve was lost, cut off from God and without hope in this fallen world, all because of sin.

We too come from this bloodline. We were born into this world spiritually dead, with sin corrupting our very nature. From birth we too were separated from God, and have sought to serve ourselves, to fight for our own rights, and force others to meet our needs. We were born with Self sitting on the thrones of our little kingdoms. Our whole existence was spent serving, worshiping, promoting, protecting, and seeking praise and acceptance for ourselves. That is, until the Savior, Jesus Christ, came to rescue us from ourselves and set us free from sin and death. *"Remember that at that time you were separate from Christ . . . having no hope and without God in the world. But now in Christ Jesus you who once were far away have been brought near through the blood of Christ" (Ephesians 2:12 -13).*

The Last Adam: Jesus Christ

The Creator's love, which is more incomprehensible than our human minds can fathom, is the power that fueled the work of the Cross. God the Father, in perfect agreement with His Son, had a plan to redeem the human race. Jesus entered the world and became human, fully God and fully man. This is a deep mystery.

The Bible calls Jesus the last Adam.

> *So it is written: "The first man Adam became a living being"; the last Adam, a life-giving spirit. The spiritual did not come first, but the natural, and after that the spiritual. The first man was of the dust of the earth, the second man from heaven. As was the earthly man, so are those who are of the earth; and as is the man from heaven, so also are those who are of heaven. And just as we have borne the likeness of the earthly man, so shall we bear the likeness of the man from heaven. (1 Corinthians 15:45-49 NIV)*

The *first Adam* disobeyed God and brought sin to his entire bloodline, with all of his descendants born in sin and death. We inherited Adam's sinful nature and were born as citizens of the devil's kingdom of darkness, which is condemned to destruction in Hell. The *last Adam*, Jesus Christ, became a man in order to live a perfect life, obey God in everything, and restore righteousness to His entire bloodline. Those who put their trust solely in Jesus are His descendants and have been made new, reborn in holiness and perfection. From His bloodline we have inherited His nature and His citizenship in the everlasting kingdom of heaven.

Jesus died on the Cross and offered mankind the Great Exchange. If we put our faith in Jesus, God will free us from ourselves by putting to death the old sinful nature and exchanging it with the very nature of Christ. Because of this, we can claim His sinless life and all the benefits that go with it. *"Therefore, if anyone is in Christ, he is a new creation. The old has passed away; behold, the new has come"* (2 Corinthians 5:17). We were all spiritually dead once, but Jesus, having been put to death on the Cross and raised again to life, is the source of our new life. He is the first to be brought back from the dead, and by His resurrection we too have been brought back from the dead to new life.

> *". . . and from Jesus Christ the faithful witness, the firstborn of the dead, and the ruler of kings on earth. To him who loves us and has freed us from our sins by his blood and made us a kingdom, priests to his God and Father, to him be glory and dominion forever and ever. Amen." (Revelation 1:5-6)*

We no longer belong to the bloodline of the *first Adam* but we belong to the bloodline of the *last Adam*, with Jesus as our forefather. Because of our new natures, we can once again have relationship with our Creator. And just like Adam and Eve in the garden of paradise before their sin, we can go to God to have our never-ending needs met fully and completely by Him. This is why we are called the Redeemed! This is the good news of the gospel. It's a whole new life we are living now, free from sin and death because Jesus paved the way. But we must first believe this truth! There must be a shift in our thinking that aligns us with this truth in order for us to walk in it.

Defining the Flesh

If it is true that we are good to the core, then why do we still sin? And if we are truly a new creation, then why do we not immediately go to our God for Him to meet our needs? The Bible calls the flesh our "old man" or "old nature." But what is the flesh really, and why is it an enemy to those of us who are sons and daughters of the Most High God? To answer those questions we must go to the Scripture and see the contrast between the old and new nature:

> *Now the works of the flesh are evident: sexual immorality, impurity, sensuality, idolatry, sorcery, enmity, strife, jealousy, fits of anger, rivalries, dissensions, divisions, envy,*

> *drunkenness, orgies, and things like these. I warn you, as I warned you before, that those who do such things will not inherit the kingdom of God. But the fruit of the Spirit is love, joy, peace, patience, kindness, goodness, faithfulness, gentleness, self-control; against such things there is no law. And those who belong to Christ Jesus have crucified the flesh with its passions and desires. If we live by the Spirit, let us also walk by the Spirit. Let us not become conceited, provoking one another, envying one another. (Galatians 5:19-26)*

This is a battle we fight daily against the flesh, and herein lies our struggle. The battle comes when our old nature, the flesh, still seeks to be in charge even though it has been declared dead. From conception, our flesh has fought to meet our needs, fulfill our desires and secure our wants independently from God. The flesh is rebellious, self-governing, and cannot and will not rely upon God in any way. The old nature is incapable of doing anything to please God.

> *For I know that nothing good dwells in me, that is, in my flesh. For I have the desire to do what is right, but not the ability to carry it out. For I do not do the good I want, but the evil I do not want is what I keep on doing. Now if I do what I do not want, it is no longer I who do it, but sin that dwells within me. (Romans 7:18-20)*

The Word of God says that there is nothing good that comes from our flesh. It is only evil, all the time. Even the things that look good still come from a corrupt, self-seeking heart. Since our flesh was our first nature it is our natural default zone to live from the flesh.

The problem is that everything done apart from faith in God is sin. Our fallen nature constantly seeks to promote itself. The flesh will always seek to be in charge and demand to take over. Even though our old nature has been declared dead, we must take the responsibility by the power given us to put it to death daily. Spiritually speaking, there is a past, present and future element to our old nature. Past tense: Our flesh and all its desires have been declared dead when we were crucified with Christ. Present tense: Our flesh is in the process of dying off as we choose to take the power of Christ and daily put it to death. Future tense: When we die, our flesh will give way to LIFE like we

"But I say, walk by the Spirit, and you will not gratify the desires of the flesh. For the desires of the flesh are against the Spirit, and the desires of the Spirit are against the flesh, for these are opposed to each other, to keep you from doing the things you want to do. But if you are led by the Spirit, you are not under the law."

Galatians 5:16-18

have never known before. Our pitiful, sinful flesh will fall away from us like an old shell, never to rise again! In that moment, we might be shocked to discover how much of an enemy it really was to us. But until then, we fight it!

Fighting the Flesh

Whoa, she's a little spitfire! What a temper! I've always had a bit of a temper. I would prefer to call it "spunk" but, in reality, it is sin. As a young girl, when I couldn't get what I wanted, I'd try to control the situation with anger. Although a temper tantrum may not have gotten exactly what I wanted, at least others would take me seriously. Negative emotional outbursts became my normal reaction to most overwhelming or uncontrollable situations. As I got older and learned that this behavior was sinful, my desire to be a good Christian pushed me to put considerable effort into working to eliminate this "flaw." By my early twenties, I thought I had just about mastered my anger issues. I was mistaken; it was simply behavior modification. I needed a heart change.

After my four children were born, the anger resurfaced and my life began to spin out of control. My little ones consumed all my time and energy. I lived in a state of high alert—always looking out for their safety and well-being. Living in "survival mode" left me physically, emotionally, and spiritually drained. Lack of sleep at night and the constant demands throughout the day exhausted me. Fear and anxiety gained a hold, and when I couldn't control a situation, anger was my immediate response. Consequently, stress took its toll on my physical body, and I developed a hormonal imbalance that compounded the problem. Some days I couldn't stop crying, and other days I was terribly angry for no reason. I thought I was going crazy! I felt incredible guilt over my ungodly emotions.

When the pressure became unbearable, I would lock myself in my room and beat the bed in a fit of rage, trying to prevent my kids from witnessing the unbelievable anger that welled up inside of me. I battled fear, anxiety, anger, and self-hatred, all because I was confronted with my inability to handle everything perfectly. I wanted those around me to see me as a good Christian, a respectable pastor's wife, and a loving mother, so I thought I had to hide my secret struggle. I remember being on my face before God, beating the carpet, screaming, "God, I can't do this anymore!" My anger was immediately followed by guilt and shame. I thought, *I'm so glad there aren't hidden cameras in my home! People would get a real show of what a great Christian I am!* This rage intensified as I became angry at myself for being angry. I couldn't understand why I was so sad or upset when I had such a good life. I knew that Jesus was the answer, somehow, but I didn't know how to "fix" me.

Guilty, sleep-deprived and battle weary, I cried out to God for help. He heard my cry and used my desperation to bring me to the end of my own striving. I was stuck in a cycle of trying and failing, shame and defeat. I did not yet understand that I was at war against the old Kori. I didn't know the truth about the controlling and hostile nature of the enemy called my flesh. What I really needed was for the lies to be exposed to the truth, and to discover the right perspective of who I am in God's eyes. I needed a renewal of my mind with the truth of the Scripture.

Our Flesh vs. Our New Creation

There is a complete difference between our old nature and our new nature. We need to restructure the thinking at the core of our belief system in order to fight against the flesh. Whether I believe the truth of God's Word or the lies of the enemy directly affects who takes charge in the situation—the old Kori or the new Kori. The truth of God fuels and empowers my new nature. The deceptive lies of the enemy fuel and empower my old nature.

For example, when we believe that we are unloved, rejected and cursed, our flesh will rise up and take charge to get our needs and wants met. When we think wrong thoughts, wrong behavior follows. Behavior reinforces thinking, and if we believe and think lies about ourselves, we can become caught in a cycle of sinful behavior. If we try to change our behavior without changing our thoughts, we will remain stuck in a cycle of sin. We must go to the source of our thoughts and allow our minds to be changed by the truth of God's Word. Then we will see a difference in our behavior. The result is amazing. If we truly believe God when He says that we are loved, chosen, and blessed, then we will walk in our new nature and not be threatened and interrupted by our old, dead nature. When I get into a situation that makes me feel rejected, there is a moment in the battle when I have a choice to make: Will I believe the lie that I am rejected and allow my flesh to attempt to rectify the wrong, or will I believe and cling to the unconditional acceptance and love of my God? What I choose in that moment will determine who I allow to control my life. Ask the Lord if there are any lies you are believing right now that are creating a crazy sin cycle in your life.

Recently, my husband and I were casually talking about a conference that we thought we might enjoy attending. After researching the when, where and how much it would cost to go, we discovered that we were not the targeted clientele of this establishment. In fact, reading between the lines on their website, we found out that people like us were politely discouraged from coming at all. At first I simply thought: *Oh well, that rules out that opportunity!* But as we moved on to another topic in our conversation, I soon noticed a disturbance in my peace and asked the Commander about it. Sure enough, the subtle lies of rejection had hit their mark. *They don't want you there. You're not good enough, not acceptable. This is an exclusive, elite club and you could never fit in. You're just a nobody.* Once I recognized the battle, it was very important what I chose to believe about myself in that moment. Will I accept the world's measuring stick of position and net worth to determine my value? Or will I believe the truth that I am a favored daughter of the most famous, wealthiest, prestigious God ever and I forever belong to the beautiful, exciting, adventurous kingdom of heaven? So I may be rejected here in this world (Jesus was too) but I am accepted in the place where it really counts.

The Word of God transforms our thinking as we fortify a spiritual stronghold of truth that protects us from the accusations of the enemy. The key is in what we believe to be true. If we believe that we will *never* overcome the sinful nature, we can be trapped in that sin cycle indefinitely. The truth is, our new nature is much stronger and has the power to put the flesh to death because God already did this for us in the death of His Son. This power is not something we have to muster up or pull out of a hat in our own strength. The source of this power is NOT dependent on us, but on God. This limitless power given to us to overcome the sinful nature is none other than the very power that raised Christ from the dead! Resurrection power! If it can raise Christ from the depths of the grave, then what can it do for you and for me? This is something that must be ingrained in our belief system, because so often in our day-to-day life it doesn't *seem* true. And that is where we get stuck. If we do not truly believe that the flesh is dead and that we have been made perfect, holy, and righteous, then we will have a hard time walking in our new natures. The flesh can be assertive, bossy, and extremely controlling, but our new nature must be even more assertive to overpower the flesh by the power of the Spirit. We must not think of our new nature as *only* kind, meek, patient, and submissive. We have these qualities in abundance, but don't forget that we are also to be bold and conquering, haters of sin, and jealous for the glory of God just like Jesus is.

Look at what the Word commands us to do to our old nature:

> Put to death therefore what is earthly in you: sexual immorality, impurity, passion, evil desire, and covetousness, which is idolatry. On account of these the wrath of God is coming. In these you too once walked, when you were living in them. But now you must put them all away: anger, wrath, malice, slander, and obscene talk from your mouth. Do not lie to one another, seeing that you have put off the old self with its practices and have put on the new self, which is being renewed in knowledge after the image of its creator. Here there is not Greek and Jew, circumcised and uncircumcised, barbarian, Scythian, slave, free; but Christ is all, and in all. (Colossians 3:5-11)

"Put to death" is a serious order. It sounds aggressive and intense, more in line with the instructions the Commander gives to His warriors.

But that is not all we are commanded to do:

> Put on then, as God's chosen ones, holy and beloved, compassion, kindness, humility, meekness, and patience, bearing with one another and, if one has a complaint against another, forgiving each other; as the Lord has forgiven you, so you also must forgive. And above all these put on love, which binds everything together in perfect harmony. And let the peace of Christ rule in your hearts, to which indeed you were called in one body. And be thankful. Let the word of Christ dwell in you richly, teaching and admonishing one another in all wisdom, singing psalms and hymns and spiritual songs, with thankfulness in your hearts to God. And whatever you do, in word or deed, do everything in the name of the Lord

Jesus, giving thanks to God the Father through him. (Colossians 3:12-17)

Our God doesn't give us commands to obey without also giving us the power to follow through on those instructions. Because we are chosen, holy and dearly loved, God has given us the capacity to be compassionate, kind, humble, meek and patient. Once again, we don't have to go out and get these qualities—they are already a part of our new nature in Christ, and by the power invested in us we can walk in the ways of righteousness by simply believing what God says is true about us.

God has already enabled and supplied us with the power to complete everything He commands us to do.

His divine power has given us everything we need for life and godliness through our knowledge of him who called us by his own glory and goodness. Through these he has given us his very great and precious promises, so that through them you may participate in the divine nature and escape the corruption in the world caused by evil desires. (2 Peter 1:3-4 NIV)

The question is: Do we really believe this? If we don't then we must repent of unbelief, renouncing our sin, seeking and receiving the Father's forgiveness so that He may cleanse us from any and all unrighteousness.

Freedom in Christ Ministries

We are on a journey with the Commander throughout this life. He is gracious to use others in the body of Christ to encourage and teach us in the ways of truth. The *Freedom in Christ Ministries*, founded by Neil Anderson, has been used by God to teach me His amazing truths about my new identity in Christ. This ministry has a session entitled "Steps to Freedom" where the Lord met me in an indescribable way. The Commander so graciously revealed and uprooted one of the biggest lies of my life—the lie that *I was a worthless nobody*. It was the main root that held together many other lies. Because I wholeheartedly believed this lie, my flesh purposefully set out to "fix" me, or at least make me appear presentable. Secretly I dealt with the fear of exposure, shame and self-hatred. God's amazing grace opened my eyes to the freedom He died to give me.

Freedom in Christ Ministries also has "Truth Statements" from Scripture that clearly spell out Who We Are in Christ. By using the *weapon of declaring* and letting these "Truth Statements" sink deeply into my mind, they continue to completely transform my life. I can feel the Commander's heart in this matter. I can sense His holy righteous anger against the enemy. Even though I was a believer as a young child, I lived in the bondage of sin, missing the truth and freedom that was purchased for me. Proclaiming this freedom that is for all of God's children is part of my assignment in the kingdom of heaven, and I am so jealous for the freedom of my people. I join Moses of old and say to the enemy, the cruel task master: In the name of Jesus, Let My People Go!

My fellow warriors, regardless of how much freedom from sin you have gained, there is more freedom to be had—but we must aggressively fight for it. The Holy Spirit has come and made Himself "one" with our spirit so that our spirit and His Spirit are perfectly interlaced and knit together. *"But he who is joined to the Lord becomes one spirit with him" (1 Corinthians 6:17).* It is that very Spirit that has the power to raise Christ from the dead, and that same Spirit is available to us to say "no" to sin and "yes" to righteousness. *"For the law of the Spirit of life has set you free in Christ Jesus from the law of sin and death" (Romans 8:2).* In the midst of our battles we must choose to no longer walk in the flesh, but rather to walk in the Spirit by faith in the power that fueled Jesus' resurrection from the dead.

Prayer:

Dear Father,
Thank You for setting me free from my sin, my ugliness and myself. You have taken me to the Cross and raised me to new

life. Help me to walk no longer in the ways of my old nature but rather in the new person You have designed me to be. Help me to identify the ways I am allowing my old person to rise up and rule. Show me the lies I'm believing that trigger my flesh, and change the way I think so that it lines up to Your truth.

In Jesus' name, Amen.

Action Steps: Journal your prayers, answers and all the things the Commander reveals to you.

1. Ask the Lord to expose your true thoughts on how you think about yourself. Do you identify more with your old flesh or your new identity in Christ? What is one way of thinking that needs to be renewed by the truth?

2. Is there any area in your life where your flesh has the upper hand, exerting itself over your new nature in Christ? What are you believing about yourself in that situation?

3. Read Colossians 3:5-17 and pray through the passage. Ask the Lord questions and allow Him to examine your life. Do you see more of the old you or the new you showing up in your everyday life?

4. How would you live your life differently if you really believed you are a son/daughter of the Most High God? Would you have the courage to step out in faith and do something God has called you to do? Would you gain confidence in your everyday life? Journal your thoughts.

Chapter Nine
Identifying Fleshly Motives

But I say, walk by the Spirit, and you will not gratify the desires of the flesh. For the desires of the flesh are against the Spirit, and the desires of the Spirit are against the flesh, for these are opposed to each other, to keep you from doing the things you want to do.
Galatians 5:16-17

I love to have people over to my house for dinner, but I don't enjoy all the preparation it takes to get ready for their arrival. I'm not sure why I feel like everything in my house needs to be squeaky clean in order to receive company, but I do! This belief has led to many mind battles in the hours preceding the arrival of my guests. Some women prepare for guests and it seems as easy as breathing for them, while I struggle just to get all the food on the table at the same time. They say that women are natural multitaskers, but I sure didn't get that quality! I find myself frantically picking up toys and shoes, hiding laundry baskets and throwing things in closets that don't belong there. Knowing that company is coming, I see my house with the scrutiny of a tight-lipped, white-gloved inspector with a clipboard. I can suddenly see what was there all along, and I am *horrified*. There's clutter in the corner, fingerprints on the windows, trash cans overflowing, toothpaste in the sink and that week-old mustard stain on the tablecloth.

All of the messes in my house are screaming at me: *You are such a failure! Can't you keep your house clean? What is wrong with you? You should be better than this. They're going to see every flaw and know what a lazy person you are.* This is when the old Kori, fueled by fear and determined to perform well, decides to present our guests with the illusion that she's got it all together. The countdown starts but the list of duties that *still need to be done* keeps growing. The old Kori transforms me into a task-master who no longer sees my children as children, but rather four little workers at my disposal. I point and bark out orders: "You, vacuum the rugs. You, set the table. You, go downstairs and get me a can of olives." They slump their shoulders, roll their eyes, and do a job half-heartedly or wander off and never come back. My voice rises as my desperation grows. Soon everyone in the house is upset and operating in an all-out "Flesh Fest," just minutes before our company arrives. This fight leaves me exhausted, angry and in no mood to entertain guests. Then the shame comes, because at this point I feel like I'm not even worth being around when the guests walk through the front door.

This is a far cry from the relaxing evening I'd envisioned with my friends when I invited them. My house may be perfect and the meal wonderful, but I'm missing out on the real reason for inviting my guests over in the first place. What happened? Why did I allow my flesh so much control? Somewhere along the way I bought the lie: If I can't keep my house clean and my kids in order, then I am a failure as a wife and mother. This lie jolts my flesh to life and drives it into action. Is the old Kori really trying to prove her worth through a clean house and a perfect meal? The truth is that I don't have to prove my worth at all because Jesus has already made me worthy. *"For by that one offering he (Jesus) forever made perfect those who are being made holy"* (Hebrews 10:14 NLT).

So what would it look like for the new Kori to be in charge before the company arrives? Knowing my true value is in Christ Jesus and not dependent on a clean house and a gourmet meal, those things just might take a back burner as my motives and the intent of my heart turn toward God's purpose for the evening. There is a promise in this verse: *"But seek first the kingdom of God and his righteousness, and all these things will be added to you. Therefore do not be anxious about tomorrow, for tomorrow will be anxious for itself. Sufficient for the day is its own trouble"* (Matthew 6:33-34). If my focus is on doing God's will, advancing His kingdom and thinking about how to bless my guests for the evening, then I will walk in my new nature and my focus will be entirely different.

Knowing this in my mind is not good enough—I must practice it. For a short time, the Commander led my husband and me to invite guests over to our house weekly. I had to make a conscious decision every single time to reject my desire to clean like a mad lady and perform well as a hostess, and instead commit myself to seek first His kingdom for the evening. During the preparation I started consciously looking for the Lord's perspective and His purpose for the evening. I prepared for the evening by praying for my family and guests, and asked the Lord to be glorified throughout our time together. When my focus changed, it seemed like all the details that needed to be accomplished either fell into place or became insignificant. There was such a difference as the peace of God covered my home, blessing us all with His presence in our evening together.

The Impure Motives of the Flesh

The flesh is incredibly cunning, struggling to be in charge even in the midst of our godly desires. I was shocked to discover that I could be doing godly things and striving to live for the Lord, yet be operating in my flesh the whole time! When I was growing up, I didn't see myself as significant, and I didn't think others did either; but one thing I *did* receive attention for was my relationship with God. People around me seemed to think my relationship with God was remarkable. My faith in Jesus was a genuine childlike faith, but I didn't yet understand that I was a new creation in Christ Jesus and that everything I needed to live a godly life had already been fully provided for me. My flesh said, *Oh, you want to live for God? You want to be a good follower of*

163

Christ? Let me take over and make that happen for you. I will do it, and I'll do it without God's help!

The flesh is like a spoiled two-year-old defiantly yelling at God, "Leave me alone! I don't need Your help. I can do it all by myself!" The compliments of other people and the desire to be worth something fueled my flesh as the old Kori began to make "being godly" my identity. I worked so hard to earn The Best Christian Ever Award! I was constantly examining myself to find places that needed improvement. I often compared myself to others, and calculated the results. If I believed someone was more spiritual than I was, I'd mentally tear them down in one area or another so that I wouldn't feel inferior. When I did good things or someone complimented me on my spirituality, I felt valuable to God. When I failed and sinned, I felt insecure, unworthy and distant from Him.

There were times, in the pride of my flesh, when I felt that I was doing God a big favor by giving Him my life and that God got a pretty good deal when I "signed up" to follow Him. But all of my striving to please God and be worthy of His love only produced more sin, because it was all done by the power of my flesh. I was trying so hard to do something that in actuality had already been done for me by Jesus.

The old Kori used God and His principles to build a little kingdom of self-righteousness, trying to verify my worth, proving that I was somebody! I am so glad that God showed me my sin by unveiling the selfish ungodly motives of my flesh. I was wrong—in both my beliefs and the motive of my heart. My focus was always on myself and my ability to perform well. I wasted many years trying to fix and perfect myself, going nowhere but deeper into sin. The flesh can only give birth to the flesh.

The truth is that we can all fall into this trap. We need the Commander's instructions to show us when we are trying to live the Christian life fueled by the flesh, rather than the Spirit. It would be such a tragedy for us to work for God our entire lives in the power of our flesh.

> *Now if anyone builds on the foundation with gold, silver, precious stones, wood, hay, straw—each one's work will become manifest, for the Day will disclose it, because it will be revealed by fire, and the fire will test what sort of work each one has done. If the work that anyone has built on the foundation survives, he will receive a reward. If anyone's work is burned up, he will suffer loss, though he himself will be saved, but only as through fire. (1 Corinthians 3:12-15)*

The things that we do in the flesh, independent of God, no matter how spiritual they appear, will all burn up and we will suffer great loss. On the other hand, if we are walking in our new nature, completely dependent upon God, all that we do will be good, enduring the test of fire and last for all eternity. *"Whoever abides in me and I in him, he it is that bears much fruit, for apart from me you can do nothing" (John 15:5b).*

What Begins in the Spirit Can Be Taken over by the Flesh

So how do we know when the flesh is trying to usurp and overpower the godly desires and pure motives of our new nature? All too often, we don't! The old Kori is sneaky and seeks to take control even as I seek to honor God and walk in His ways. What begins in my life with the power of the Spirit can be taken over by my flesh unless I stay closely connected and in constant communication with the Commander. He is the only One who can navigate me through this battle against my flesh.

When my kids started elementary school, I had the great idea that we would all get up early and start the day with Bible time and prayer. As a child I did this with my parents, and even though I was not appreciative at the time, I was very thankful for it later in life. I think I may have glamorized my childhood memory, though, because when it came to having devotions with my own children, the experience was anything but picturesque. It was like pulling teeth to get them out of bed and to the table with their Bibles on time. Many times there was whining, grumbling, bad attitudes, and conveniently timed trips to the bathroom before we were all seated and ready to begin. Next were the fights over how many verses each person would read and who would go first. It didn't seem like anything was sinking into their impressionable little minds at all, except maybe how much they hated this! But I had a rosy picture of them as adults, coming to me in grateful tears and thanking me for leading them in morning devotions all those years ago. This image kept me going.

It all came to a head one morning when I was once again determined to get through devotions, complete with Scripture reading, short quiz and group prayer. Unfortunately for everyone involved, I was the *only* one with this goal! The kids were stomping around with bad attitudes, their bickering was non-stop, and my sinful self saw her chance. The old Kori rose up—and let me tell you, friends, it was not pretty. I completely, totally *lost it*. I pounded the table like an old-fashioned revival preacher, raised my voice to the heavens, and delivered this pearl of wisdom to my children: "KIDS! Shut up and read your Bibles!" They sat around the table, wide-eyed and speechless, wondering where Mom had gone and who'd replaced her with this screeching monster in pajamas. Now that I had their undivided attention, I charged full speed ahead and told my oldest daughter to read the next verse. Ironically, the verse was something about allowing God to be in charge, but by then I was so upset that I refused to listen. I knew that pitching a fit was **not** going to be effective, but I couldn't stop myself. My flesh had gained so much momentum with my outburst that I just kept going, moving us right along from the Bible reading to the quiz and finishing up with a *very* short ceremonial prayer. Okay, done! By the end my son was whimpering, my girls were upset and my ideal Bible time with the kids came to a sorry end.

All I wanted was a meaningful time spent with God and my children—failure! When I cooled off, I repented to God and agreed with Him that my way was not working out too well. On the way to school, I apologized to my children and asked for their forgiveness. Later that morning, I came before the Lord and handed over control of our morning devotions to Him. He surprised me when I sensed Him telling me to end them. *Really, God? You want me to stop having Bible time in the mornings with my kids? But Lord, I want my kids to know You by reading Your Word and spending time with You.* The Lord showed me that my desire wasn't wrong, but that I had taken matters into my own hands. My flesh was trying to force my will upon my children, and I was trying to do something that only God could do. In fact, I probably did more damage by turning morning devotions into a chore for them than I would have by not having morning devotions at all! He reassured me that I could trust Him to speak to my children in His way and in His timing.

At that moment, I had a choice to make: I could operate in the fear of my flesh and continue morning devotions, or I could operate in my new nature with faith and trust God with my hopes and desires for my children. I chose the latter, and my loving Father has proven once again that He is trustworthy! I marveled as I watched God birth in my children the desire to seek Him, creating teachable moments appropriate to each individual child's level of understanding. God met them right where they were and allowed me to walk alongside them, teaching them about Who He is, granting me the very desire of my heart.

Examining the Fruit of Our Works

With the Commander's help we must examine the fruit of our actions to know from which nature we are operating. We cannot examine ourselves without His help. *"I the Lord search the heart and test the mind, to give every man according to his ways, according to the fruit of his deeds"* (Jeremiah 17:10). Sinful reactions, wrong attitudes and ungodly motives are indicators that we are walking in the flesh and not in the Spirit. We need to pay close attention to our thoughts and allow the Commander to alert us when we are doing things fueled by the flesh.

One way He does this is by instructing us to examine the fruit that we produce.

> *Make a tree good and its fruit will be good, or make a tree bad and its fruit will be bad, for a tree is recognized by its fruit. You brood of vipers, how can you who are evil say anything good? For out of the overflow of the heart the mouth speaks. The good man brings good things out of the good stored up in him, and the evil man brings evil things out of the evil stored up in him. (Matthew 12:33-35 NIV)*

Lie Alert:

Are you thinking . . .

- I can accept some flaws about myself; no one's perfect.
- This is just the way God made me.
- I'm a pretty good person, so why try to change?
- I can keep myself under control most of the time.
- I don't want to know my hidden motives; then I'd have to do something about them.

Which nature is operating in us—the old man or the new man? If the Commander shows us that our actions are accompanied by the fruit of anxiety, control, doubt, anger, guilt, shame, judgment, pride, selfishness or self-righteousness, then chances are we are operating in the flesh. Likewise, if He shows us our actions are accompanied by the fruit of love, joy, peace, patience, kindness, goodness, faithfulness, gentleness, self-control, gratitude and humil-ity, we are likely operating in our perfect new nature, fueled by the Spirit.

We must ask the Lord to help us pay attention to our thoughts. We can do many really good things in our lives, but when God uncovers the motive *behind* the motive, we may discover that we were actually promoting ourselves. Now, this doesn't give us permission to stop doing good just because we might have the wrong attitude. Those good works are still good—they benefit the recipients even if our motives are bad. But WE are the ones who lose out in this situation—God knows our hearts, and while

He may allow others to benefit even from our badly motivated good works, He doesn't credit it to us as righteousness. We could work our entire lives, giving all our money to the poor, serving the lowest of the low and suffering for the good of others, all for the glory and fame that it brings to our own names.

> *If I speak in the tongues of men and of angels, but have not love, I am a noisy gong or a clanging cymbal. And if I have prophetic powers, and understand all mysteries and all knowledge, and if I have all faith, so as to remove mountains, but have not love, I am nothing. If I give away all I have, and if I deliver up my body to be burned, but have not love, I gain nothing. (1 Corinthians 13:1-3)*

The pure love that this verse talks about is a love that can only be poured into our hearts by the Holy Spirit, a love that cannot be found in our flesh. Only those who have trusted in Jesus and surrendered their lives to Him have access to this type of love as it flows up from inside of us, springing forth from our oneness with the Spirit of God.

Allowing God to Dig Through Our Motives

It is so easy to assume that we have pure motives when it comes to doing good works. We must once again rely heavily upon the Commander to dig through our motives and bring to light any that might be born of the flesh and not our new natures.

As a pastor's kid and now as a pastor's wife, I have always been in some sort of ministry activity. What I didn't realize was that doing ministry and helping others was meeting a need in my flesh that God had already met for me in Christ Jesus. I didn't comprehend this until He graciously led me into freedom in this area. One year I was heavily involved in several different ministries at our church when I sensed the Commander telling me, abruptly but kindly, to stop everything and simply *come away* with Him. Every time I read Scripture, the passages spoke of people setting themselves apart to be with God. I could tell the Lord wanted this for me. It was as if the Commander called for a "cease-fire" in the midst of a massive battle. The idea seemed overwhelming and borderline impossible. In order to be obedient to Him I would have to eliminate several key areas of ministry—cue dramatic music here—*even the women's board!* This was not easy for me because I felt like I was letting others down. Determined to trust and obey Him, I began to back out of all ministry areas.

I quickly discovered a hole in my life. I felt antsy, and I was afraid I was being lazy. It was incredibly hard for me to *do nothing* for God. I thought I was doing all this ministry exclusively for God, but when He told me to stop and I wasn't okay with it, I had to reconsider that assumption. Then the question became, "Why am I *really* doing all this work?" I felt lost because there was nothing I could point to that displayed or proved my love and devotion to God. There was nothing to gauge my worth as a good worker in His kingdom. I discovered that even though I wasn't trying to earn God's love and favor with all my hard work, I was desperately trying to pay Him back for all He had done for me. Not only is this impossible, it's sinful!

The Father wanted me to stop working, enter His rest and simply let Him love me. Instead of giving God all my time, energy and effort by serving Him, He instructed me to just sit there and do nothing but receive from Him. It wasn't a suggestion; it was a command. I discovered that His supply of love and grace did not run dry or cease because of my lack of work for Him. In fact, the heavenly supply actually seemed to increase; now all my time, energy and effort was focused solely on receiving from Him. The old Kori had to stop striving and get out of the way in order for the new Kori to receive the pure love, grace and anointing of the Father so that the nature of Christ could be revealed in me. This transformed my life and changed my thinking forever. It was such a relief to me to discover that if I never did one more thing for God the rest of my life, it would not and *could not* change His acceptance, approval and unconditional love for me. He loves me for no other reason than the fact that He IS Love! I don't have the words to tell you how personal He became as I just sat there week after week, doing nothing but allowing Him to love me.

The Pruning Process

We will always be in a vicious war against our old nature for as long as we live. The only remedy for our flesh is death. It cannot be rehabilitated. The flesh must die daily in order for our new life in Christ to live and move and breathe. Therefore the antidote to our old nature is embracing the new creation God has made us to be. The flesh cannot put the flesh to death, and we can do nothing apart from Christ. That means we must work with the Lord, obeying Him in all things to daily put the flesh to death. We must be willing to allow the Lord to cut away our old self. This is a painful yet essential operation that He performs in order to bring us into freedom and experience life to the fullest.

> I am the true vine, and my Father is the vinedresser. Every branch of mine that does not bear fruit he takes away, and every branch that does bear fruit he prunes, that it may bear more fruit. Already you are clean because of the word that I have spoken to you. Abide in me, and I in you. As the branch cannot bear fruit by itself, unless it abides in the vine, neither can you, unless you abide in me. I am the vine; you are the branches. Whoever abides in me and I in him, he it is that bears much fruit, for apart from me you can do nothing. (John 15:1-5)

The good news about the pruning process is that when the Commander shows us an area of sin and desires to cut it off, it means that He wants to bring us into freedom, revealing Christ in and through us. He is demanding a response from us: either we repent and experience that freedom, or we remain in sin. The more we embrace His pruning process, the more Jesus Christ is revealed in us.

The Commander's pruning process happens in various ways and on many different levels. One way He exposes and cuts away our old selves is through His Word.

> For the word that God speaks is alive and full of power [making it active, operative, energizing, and effective]; it is sharper than any two-edged sword, penetrating to the dividing line of the breath of life (soul) and [the immortal] spirit, and of joints and marrow [of the deepest parts of our nature], exposing and shifting and analyzing and judging the very thoughts and purposes of the heart. (Hebrews 4:12 AMP)

The Word of God is like a knife that cuts deeply and accurately through our innermost thoughts and motives of the heart. It divides the deepest parts of our nature, revealing to us what comes from the old nature and what is born of our new nature. We are being changed, and the process that Jesus takes us through is sometimes long and hard. There are periods when we need God to cut out the flesh in our lives. God is kind and gentle to do this work in us, and He is willing to allow the pain in our lives, but only for a season. This allows us to have abundant life and grow into a fruitful vine. We have to trust the Father's love for us as He prunes away what is already dead. The flesh will always violently resist the pruning process because it means Self, our old nature that cares nothing for God, must die. God also uses difficult circumstances and close relationships as a scalpel in His hand to apply just the right pressure to cut out the spiritual cancer of the flesh. My husband, children and friends are the people closest to me. God has often used these relationships to expose my sinful nature, giving me the opportunity to choose to submit to God's pruning. The imperfections and challenges of these relationships may be the very things that God uses to cut us the deepest to rid us of our flesh.

This painful pruning process is something that we will resist unless we know God's heart behind it. We can focus so much of our attention on the tool (the person or circumstance) in God's hand, instead of on the love on His face that we become angry at the pain the "tool" is causing. Then our flesh wants to defend itself and jumps off the operating table mid-surgery. Have you done that, friend? When God is performing a life-saving procedure on you, that is the worst thing that you can do! When we don't let Him finish the operation with His healing touch, we remain wounded and bleeding, opening ourselves up to the infections of bitterness and resentment. God cuts so that He may heal. He works with precision and cuts only deep enough to rid us of the sinful flesh in that area. We must embrace this process —as painful as it is, it is essential. Only the Commander sees everything, and we must trust Him when He tells us it is time for His pruning.

The result is Jesus' abundant life in us. The freedom from the bondage of sin is exhilarating as more and more of Christ's nature is revealed in us to glorify God. It enables us to breathe deeply of His grace and frees us to be all He has made us to be— our truest self. It is important to know the Commander's voice so that we recognize His warning when it is time to prune again. Then, instead of fighting Him, we may lie still on the operating table and allow Him to do His work. *"Be still, and know that I am God"* (Psalm 46:10a).

Cutting Away Pride

If we don't actively fight the flesh, it can take charge and even try to take credit for the things the Lord has done in and through us. The new Kori hates pride. When an area of pride starts to creep in and take control in my life, urging me to walk in the flesh and not the Spirit, I want the Commander to take out His pruning shears and cut it off. He is faithful to expose it, and I am committed to repent of it. Pride constantly seeks to destroy and stifle the flow of the Spirit through us.

A good friend and I co-teach a ladies' Bible study at my church. One Monday I was gone and she graciously filled in for me and taught beautifully; she had done this in the past and I was grateful for her gift of teaching. On this particular occasion, however, I heard a lot of feedback from the ladies who attended the class about what an amazing job she had done. That next Wednesday night at church, three ladies in separate conversations told me *again* what a great job she did. By the time the third lady praised my friend's teaching I could feel the pain like a knife in my heart. I thought, *Oh no, they like her better than me. She's a better teacher than I am. People used to say how amazing I was until she came along.* I felt panic, fear of rejection, and loss of worth. The old Kori felt threatened by my friend and her gifts and popularity. My flesh felt the pain of jealousy and the fear of the loss of position and value. But the new Kori was grieved by my thoughts toward my good friend and sister in Christ. In the past when she spoke, I had always been grateful, rejoicing in the gift that God had given her for the rest of us. But this time I felt threatened. I recognized that the pride of my flesh had crept into my role as a teacher at our church, and God was using this situation to expose it. I also knew that God needed to cut this pride out of me before it quenched the flow of the Spirit of God through me.

The next day the Commander urged me to humble myself and use the weapon of confession to sever this pride from my heart. He instructed me to publicly confess my feelings of pride and insecurity to the ladies in the Bible study. Ouch! The new Kori desired to be obedient, knowing that it would be a painful but lethal blow to the flesh. But the old Kori wanted nothing to do with that public humiliation. She assured me that there *must* be a better way. I had a decision to make. It wasn't a fun confession, but the Lord was with me and the ladies in my class were very gracious to me. God's "surgery" was divinely accurate, ridding me of my sinful pride in the gift that He has given me. I didn't even know that it was there until the Commander revealed it to me and gave me specific instructions on how He wanted to get rid of it. It was part of the pruning process the Father lovingly applies to His children, enabling the Spirit of God to flow through us more freely and produce the fruit of the Spirit. This was not the first occasion that God showed me pride in my life, and it probably won't be the last.

What Do We Do With Our Sin?

So what do we do when we discover that we have been operating in the flesh and not being true to our new nature in Christ? When the Commander reveals hidden motives that expose the work of our old sinful nature, we are at a crossroads. When we sin we must take it immediately to Jesus. We cannot take care of our sin any more than we can save ourselves. The Father is the only One who can remove our sin and wash us clean. Let me tell you about a time when the Commander used an incident with my daughter to teach me what to do when I mess up and sin.

"Mommy, I need your help!" As soon as I heard those words I knew something was wrong. My three-year-old daughter was calling for help, her voice full of panic and regret. When I followed the sound of her voice, I came face to face with a locked bathroom door. I begged her to open the door, but I must admit I was not prepared for the sight I was about to witness. The first thing that hit me was the smell. There was "brown stuff" everywhere! It was on the sink, on the wall, the mirror, the toilet, and of course all over her. Piles of brownish wet toilet paper were smeared all over her clothes and the floor. Competing emotions of shock, compassion, disgust, sympathy and horror battled within me, and for a few seconds I was simply speechless. Where to start? What to do? How could I even *begin* to clean this up? It was one of those "mommy moments" that no one prepares you to handle.

We had started potty-training, and she'd been doing a great job. But she had an accident and she didn't want me to know about it. In her shame she tried to hide it from me and did her best to clean it up. But she was only three—of course she was incapable of cleaning it up by herself, and her attempts just made it worse. I surveyed the damage, and then looked at her little face, where I could read fear, shame, and the dread of punishment. Her eyes were searching my face, waiting for my reaction. How would I respond to her big stinky mess? I could see relief wash over her as I reassured her that I loved her. I told her that it was just an accident, she wasn't in trouble, and that I would clean it all up. Forty-five minutes later the bathroom was clean, she was in a fresh pair of footie pajamas and we were snuggled up together on the couch. With a sigh of relief she looked up at me and said, "Thanks for cleanin' up me, Mommy." I cuddled her close as I explained to her that when she has another accident like that again, she shouldn't try to clean it up herself, but instead she should come to me right away so I can take care of it.

My daughter's actions remind me of what I used to do when I messed up. I too would experience shame, try to hide my sin from the Lord and desperately try to clean it up myself. Not knowing the truth of God affected the way I handled sin for several years. Whenever I sinned, I thought that God must be mad at me, so I would stand at a distance for an allotted amount of time, trying to do penance for my sin. After what I deemed a sufficient amount of time, *waiting for God to cool off,* I would come back to Him seeking forgiveness. This was not only unnecessary, it was actually sinful. I didn't realize that this was the old Kori trying to clean up her mess with self-punishment. But we sin when we try to punish ourselves, because Jesus' punishment was more than sufficient. Our actions are telling God that His punishment for our sin wasn't good enough, and we are going to make amends our own way. When we try to punish ourselves for the sin that Jesus already took care of, we belittle Jesus' great sacrifice for us. We then make a bigger mess, sinning even more by not coming to the Father right away and letting Him cleanse us. *"Jesus answered, 'A person who has had a bath needs only to wash his feet; his whole body is clean. And you are clean, though not every one of you'"* (John 13:10 NIV).

As believers we are already made clean by the righteousness of Christ, and when we mess up we are only in need of forgiveness. *"My little children, I am writing these things to you so that you may not sin. But if anyone does sin, we have an advocate with the Father, Jesus Christ the righteous"* (1 John 2:1). Because we are now a new creation in Christ, we don't have to allow our flesh to take charge and sin. But if we do, Jesus, the Righteous One, gives us the grace we need to repent, turn and *immediately* continue to walk in the Spirit. Our flesh tries to hide in shame for fear of exposure and punishment; but from our Father in Heaven, there is none to be had. We may still experience the natural consequences of our sin and poor choices, but since Jesus took our sins and was punished on our behalf, we will never suffer the wrath of God for them. *"There is therefore now no condemnation for those who are in Christ Jesus. For the law of the Spirit of life has set you free in Christ Jesus from the law of sin and death" (Romans 8:1-2).*

"For the grace of God has appeared, bringing salvation for all people, training us to renounce ungodliness and worldly passions, and to live self-controlled, upright, and godly lives in the present age, waiting for our blessed hope, the appearing of the glory of our great God and Savior Jesus Christ, who gave himself for us to redeem us from all lawlessness and to purify for himself a people for his own possession who are zealous for good works."

Titus 2:11-14

I must never forget that when I mess up and sin, that sin is not who I am. Instead, it is the sin living in me, the old Kori. That behavior does not reflect who I truly am in Christ. The reality is that we *will* mess up. Sometimes we'll allow the flesh to take charge and sin, but the Lord has given us the gift of forgiveness—when we confess our sins, it is *His* work, not ours, to cleanse us of all our unrigh-teousness. *"If we say we have no sin, we deceive ourselves, and the truth is not in us. If we confess our sins, he is faithful and just to forgive us our sins and to cleanse us from all unrighteousness. If we say we have not sinned, we make him a liar, and his word is not in us" (1 John 1:8-10).* This is God's grace and it *never* runs dry. There is enough of it for you and me. However deep our sin goes, God's grace goes deeper still, for there is no condemnation in Christ Jesus.

Just like my daughter, we are being "potty trained" to no longer sin as we grow up to spiritual adulthood operating in our new nature. When we mess up we are to immediately go to God so that He can clean us. That way we won't waste time sitting in our sin and trying to take care of it ourselves. This grace of God trains us so that we won't waste a moment in the flesh, but continue walking in the Spirit. Before we know it we are supernaturally walking in areas of freedom that were once areas of deep shame and regret for us. This is a mystery and a miracle that God loves to work in and through us. It is a way of life for every believer as we are being changed from glory to glory. *"But we all, with unveiled face, beholding as in a mirror the glory of the Lord, are being transformed into the same image from glory to glory, just as from the Lord, the Spirit"* (2 Corinthians 3:18 NAS).

Prayer:

Dear Father,
Thank You for setting me free to walk in the Spirit and not my flesh. Show me the areas where I have yet to experience freedom. I trust You to guide me. Show me the areas that I think are completely pure when in reality, my thoughts and actions are independent of You. Help me know the lies behind these situations that allow the "old me" to operate undetected. Dig up the false motives that have been producing bad fruit and redeem them, allowing me to learn how to walk all over again in the new nature of Your Spirit.
In Jesus' name, Amen.

Action Steps: Journal your prayers, answers and all the things the Commander reveals to you.

1. Invite the Lord to examine the motives behind your actions. Pay close attention to any situation or activity

you are involved in that He brings to mind. Ask Him to reveal truth. Is there something you need to step out of doing for a time?

2. Is there any recurring work that you are involved in where your old self keeps showing up? Ask the Lord to meet you there and show you the lies you may be believing about God or yourself that trigger your flesh to take charge. Let Him guide you to truth.

3. Ask the Lord to bring to mind a time you were being "pruned" by Him. Let Him remind you what happened and walk you through the process. How did you do? Was He able to complete the work or is there more pruning He wants to do in that area?

4. Ask the Lord to prompt you the next time you sin, then practice going to Him immediately and confessing it. Repent and receive the Lord's forgiveness, allowing Him to cleanse you from all the effects of that sin.

Chapter Ten
Identifying Fleshly Attitudes

So what do we do? Keep on sinning so God can keep on forgiving? I should hope not! If we've left the country where sin is sovereign, how can we still live in our old houses there? Or didn't you realize we packed up and left there for good? That is what happened in baptism. When we went under the water, we left the old country of sin behind; when we came up out of the water, we entered into a new country of grace—
a new life in a new land!
Romans 6:1-3 MSG

When introducing a new Bible study for the ladies at our church, I designed an invitation on a poster, reproduced it, and then displayed it in prominent places throughout the church building. Three weeks after doing this, I came face-to-face with one of these posters and quickly reread it. Noticing a certain word on the poster, I thought, *Hmm, that word looks a little funny to me. I wonder if I spelled it right.* The next day as I was reading a novel, I came across that very word and my suspicions were confirmed—I had spelled it incorrectly. *Oh no! That poster has been all over the church for weeks! No one is going to want to come to this class because I can't spell and, if I can't spell, they will know I don't know what I am talking about!* I felt dread, embarrassment and humiliation as I envisioned women reading that invitation and labeling me as unintelligent and unprofessional.

From the moment the accusations started, I knew I was experiencing a spiritual attack, but simply knowing this did not stop the overwhelming flood of inferior feelings. I verbally spoke out truth and said, "My qualification to teach this class does not stand on my ability to spell correctly. I am qualified to teach this class because God has called me to it and He has anointed me for it." *"You did not choose me, but I chose you and appointed you that you should go and bear fruit and that your fruit should abide, so that whatever you ask the Father in my name, he may give it to you"* (John 15:16). That helped silence a few of the lies but the battle was not over. That afternoon, as my family and I were walking around downtown, I continued to experience thoughts and feelings of inferiority. It seemed like every person I saw or met was better than me. Everyone looked smarter, more sophisticated, or better dressed than I was. I became so accused and beaten down by these thoughts that I felt like I didn't deserve to walk on the same sidewalk as everyone else. Even in the midst of the attack, I knew these were lies, but I couldn't logically understand why one misspelled word was causing such an intense battle for me.

Later that night, with negative thoughts still swirling around me, I took a moment to ask the Commander for further instructions. He told me to tell my husband about the misspelled word on the poster. I didn't want to do this at first, because my husband is an expert speller, but I told him anyway. When he realized that I had been struggling all afternoon because I had simply misspelled a word, he said, "You're so cute, Kori! It's not a sin to misspell a word. Jesus didn't have to die for that. A lot of people misspell that word and it's not a big deal." My husband gave me the perspective that I needed to end the battle.

The next morning, I could sense that the Lord wanted to talk with me about this battle. I asked Him, *Why was this such a relentless struggle? How could one misspelled word on a poster throw me into such an intense mind battle? Lord, I invite You into this struggle and ask for Your wisdom. Please meet me in this place and give me Your perspective.* As I waited before Him, my thoughts flashed back to a memory from fourth grade. Instead of labeling this as some crazy distraction from prayer, I followed my thoughts back to Mrs. Grover's fourth grade class. At first it was just a vague memory but the more I thought about it, the more the Lord allowed me to remember the details and emotions I experienced back then. The teacher would split the class into two teams for weekly spelling bees. Everyone started by standing at the front of the classroom, but anyone who misspelled a word was finished and had to go back to their seat. The losers had to watch while the winner battled to the end. I **hated** these spelling bees because week after week, I was always the first loser. If by chance I actually knew how to spell the word, panic and embarrassment would fill my mind so quickly that I could only say the first letter before my mind went blank. In this memory, I could see my teammates' facial expressions when it was my turn to spell a word. I could sense their pity and annoyance as, each time, I was the first to be disqualified. I eventually came to the conclusion that I really was a loser. I believed that I was inferior to all the other kids because I couldn't spell.

As an adult woman, I know that a tiny misspelled word on a poster doesn't define me, but the wounded fourth grade girl inside me was experiencing all those negative thoughts and lies all over again. These two situations were mentally connected, but I didn't know this until the Commander revealed these lies and healed me with His truth.

Fleshly Reactions and Attitudes

A fleshly reaction or attitude is simply a sinful response to the circumstances in which we find ourselves. So often it's not something that we think about or plan on doing; it's just the natural response of our flesh. Situations and words trigger trouble spots in our subconscious mind and we react accordingly. We can be walking along in our new nature, full of the Spirit of God, when something happens, setting us off, throwing us immediately into the flesh. Our old nature then takes over and seeks to control our thoughts and behavior. We might think we're acting fine, but the behavior caused by a bad attitude isn't hard to spot. But there are also fleshly sins of the heart that are more subtle, tossing our minds into underlying thought patterns that produce unconscious and unintentional sin. We are often unaware of these heart-level reactions until the Commander points them out and guides us into the truth, but they can do just as much damage as a more visible reaction. Anxiety, worry, fear, ungodly anger, pride, and judgment—these are just a few of the ways we can sin in our hearts by entertaining and believing these thoughts instead of God's truth. It is important that we call sin by its proper name; if we don't diagnose it as sin then we won't battle against it properly.

I used to treat fear too lightly, not recognizing it as sin. I would excuse it by calling it "an area I'm working to overcome." I came to realize that when I entertain, rehearse and give in to fear, I am actually disobeying God's Word! *"Do not be afraid of them, for I am with you to deliver you, declares the Lord" (Jeremiah 1:8).* God repeatedly commands us in Scripture to not be afraid but rather put our trust in Him. When we reject fear and trust God, we are obedient to Him. But when we embrace fear in disregard of His command to trust Him, we disobey Him, and that is sin. For years, I nursed and coddled my thoughts and feelings of fear, not acknowledging them as sin that needed to be repented of and renounced. When I finally realized that *fear is sin,* I began to fight it, forcing my fearful thoughts to submit to the Lordship of Jesus Christ.

Battle Wounds

Imagine you are a soldier on a battlefield, and you've been wounded on your right side. In the midst of the battle people are constantly charging into you. If someone ran into you on your left side, you could very possibly brush it off and continue fighting effectively. But if someone smashes into you on your right side, even the tiniest bump could cause you to suffer extreme pain. Your reaction to someone hitting you on your wounded side would be totally different than on your healthy side. This collision could cause you to recoil in pain or violently lash out at the other person in order to protect the wound from getting hit again. It could even cause you to be paralyzed by the blow, bringing you to your knees in the midst of a dangerous battle.

The same thing can happen to us emotionally in our spiritual war. When an unhealed wound gets hit or even slightly bumped, it triggers a reaction from our flesh. Living in this corrupt world and being born with a sinful nature, none of us has made it through life without being injured in one way or another. Our wounds could be the result of one huge damaging situation, or from small recurring hits to the same spot over the years. Just because you don't have any major injuries or losses in your life doesn't mean you don't have any wounds—even a sliver can be painful and become infected. Big or small, these wounds can become spiritually "infected" and spread to other areas of our minds. Our fleshly nature cannot remove or take care of sin; it can only self-protect with an elaborate, sinful defense system.

Only Jesus can heal our wounds. If our wounds are not treated, they can cripple us and keep us from fighting the fight God has chosen for us. It is through Jesus that God has provided a solution to the wounds we have acquired in this life, even the self-inflicted ones.

> *Surely he has borne our griefs and carried our sorrows; yet we esteemed him stricken, smitten by God, and afflicted. But he was pierced for our transgressions; he was crushed for our iniquities; upon him was the chastisement that brought us peace, and with his wounds we are healed. All we like sheep have gone astray; we have turned—every one—to his own way; and the Lord has laid on him the iniquity of us all. (Isaiah 53:4-6)*

Jesus has taken our sin, sorrows and wounds upon Himself and is well acquainted with our personal injuries, having borne them at the Cross. He is the only One equipped to heal us. This is a powerful verse, filled with truth and healing for us; but how do we apply this often-painful work of Christ to the wounds we have acquired in this life?

When a certain triggering situation occurs in our lives, it can touch a wound, causing a sinful reaction. This tells us that there is an area that needs to be healed by Jesus. Our flesh is a slave to Self, and it defends and protects itself at all costs. We need to know what jolts our flesh into action, forcing it to get ugly and hostile. With the help of our Commander, we can discover our needy and wounded areas so that we can bring them before the Throne, allowing Jesus to cleanse and heal us. There are times when the Lord will allow the same wound to be repeatedly hit, demanding our attention. He does this because He longs to heal us. When we identify a recurring situation that produces fleshly attitudes and reactions in us, we need to use our weapon of divine discernment and have a meeting with the Commander. Sometimes there are too many wounds to count, and we must trust God to direct the healing of our wounds one by one. This is a process. When the Father desires to show us another area He longs to heal, He allows triggers to go off so that we can recognize it. At that time, we have a choice to either allow God to heal us, or to ignore it. If we ignore it, these wounds can continue to be a tool in Satan's hand. Satan will use this hole in our armor to continually attack us, propelling us to walk in the flesh.

Half the battle is recognizing the battle, and the other half is knowing what weapons to use. First, we need to identify the situations in our lives that immediately throw us into a fight against the flesh, tempting us or causing us to sin. They are different for each of us because we all have different mental strongholds. But the Commander is faithful to teach us individually. As we pay attention to our responses to life's circumstances, they will give us indicators about our areas of weakness. If we find ourselves continually over-reacting to certain situations, chances are there is a hidden wound that needs to be cleansed and healed by God's truth and love. These triggers may be connected to old wounds that are crammed full of destructive lies festering below the surface. Without God's help these wounds will never heal. We need to allow Him to dig deep in our memories to reveal these areas and unpack the lies, personal vows and subtle agreements our old nature has made to protect itself. *"The purpose in a man's heart is like deep water, but a man of understanding will draw it out"* (Proverbs 20:5). Remember, you are a deeply complex creation made in the image of God. There is no one better to guide you into truth than the very Spirit of Truth Who knows everything. God created you. He formed you in the womb and knows every little thing that has ever happened to you and how you have responded to it. You can trust Him.

My Personal Triggers

Our mind battles are not neat and orderly but confusing, intense and messy. It is crucial, then, that we know our own personal triggers! The devil will often lay an elaborate ambush where he sets up several different triggers to go off simultaneously in our life, anticipating that we will respond in the flesh and not the Spirit. It is my prayer that while I'm explaining some of the triggers that set off my sinful nature, the Lord would come close and graciously reveal to you some of your own triggers. Over the years, I have discovered that each one of these is connected in some way to an old wound, a lie I have believed or a painful situation in my past.

This is not an exhaustive list by any means, but making this list is the first half of recognizing the battle raging in the arena of my mind. This is part of knowing the terrain and having effective weapons in place when I find myself trapped in a dark, thick forest of fear, resentment or doubt. At one time, the accuser easily targeted these chinks in my armor to distract me and wreak havoc in my life. It was like standing in front of a firing

Situation		Mental State
Being belittled, put down or treated condescendingly by another person with their words, actions or even facial expressions	triggers	anger, panic, feelings of inferiority.
Messes around the house, especially needless ones (for example, one of my kids ripping a piece of paper into a million pieces and then throwing it up in the air like snow—just for fun!)	triggers	exasperation, the need to control, and feelings of failure, defeat and wrath
Being ignored or not being worth someone's time	triggers	pain, anger revenge or withdrawal
My kids bickering ("Did not...Did too...Did not...Did too..."—you know the drill!)	triggers	anger and negativity
Hurting a friend and not being able to fix the relationship	triggers	fear of failure and rejection
Having to talk on the phone or return a phone call	triggers	procrastination, fear of the unknown, panic, dread or guilt
Driving a car in unfamiliar territory (just the thought of it)	triggers	anxiety and paralyzing fear

Being used deceitfully by someone posing as a friend	triggers	feelings of rejection, betrayal, resentment, estrangement from that person, or a desire for revenge
Having to make a decision I don't want to make	triggers	fear of making a mistake and fear of punishment
Having to wear a bathing suit in public—I HATE IT!	triggers	panic, dissatisfaction with my appearance, and a consuming self-consciousness
The thought of being deceived or leading others astray	triggers	debilitating embarrassment, feelings of exposure, horror of inferiority

squad of painful lies, unable to escape and powerless to stop the attack. Because these triggers represented areas where I had been hurt or damaged emotionally in the past, the old Kori immediately rushed in to defend and protect her beloved Self. However, she didn't do a very good job. Now that I am aware of these areas, I have a choice to make when they are triggered. Will I let the old Kori take charge to defend and protect me in that moment? Or will I, the new Kori, allow God to minister to me and trust Him to take care of the situation? With each attack of the enemy I can gain ground or lose it, depending on where I put my hope and trust: the old Kori or God. As long as I am wounded in these areas, the devil has ammunition to use against me as he seeks to control me by building a demonic stronghold in the infection of my past wounds. I must allow Jesus to heal these wounded areas by spending time in His presence, meditating on the truth, and building up an arsenal full of spiritual weapons so I will be ready to bombard the lies with a hailstorm of battle verses.

Our Commander and Medic

So what should our response be when we become aware of a recurring trigger going off in our lives? This isn't an easy process, and like good soldiers we must be proactive to get the treatment necessary for our survival. Our Commander is not only near to guide and instruct us, but He is also ready at any time to be our Medic. Jesus knows our wounds personally, having taken them upon Himself in order that we may be healed.

Allow me to walk you through one of my old mind battles. I want you to see how the Commander enabled me to become aware of an old wound, and how He personally led me into freedom. One year my family and I went away for a much-needed vacation. When we arrived at our destination, my husband got in line at the car rental agency while I watched the kids in the waiting area. I checked my phone and discovered I had a message from a friend in a small group I was leading. She expressed some concerns about a decision that I'd recently made, questioning if it was wise and wondering how it would affect the other ladies in the group. Her manner was very cordial and it was a valid perspective that hadn't occurred to me. She went on to say that she had talked to her husband, that he too shared her concern and would be contacting my husband, the pastor, regarding my decision.

My internal reaction was sheer panic. In an instant, fiery darts of accusations, fears and insecurities were launched in my mind. *You are so stupid! How could you miss this? This is what happens when you try to be a leader. What is wrong with you? This is the worst thing you've ever done. You are in so much trouble. Your husband is going to have to clean up your mess. You are such an embarrassment to him! I bet he wishes he had a better wife.* My mind was hijacked with so many negative thoughts that I couldn't even think clearly. Looking up, I realized that my husband was nowhere in sight, so I gathered my luggage and my two youngest kids and went outside to look for him. Still panicked from the phone message, I stood there feeling stranded, not knowing where to go. More negative thoughts entered my mind: *Can't you pay attention? All you had to do was wait with the kids while he registered for the car and you messed that up too. Now you'll be stuck here with two restless kids for who knows how long until he comes to find you. Serves you right; this is all your fault. What an idiot!*

I sent out a desperate prayer to the Commander for help, as I was *obviously* unable to think clearly on my own. Somehow I managed to follow the signs directing me to the parking lot, which was just around the corner. This should have been my first thought, but the intensity of the mind battle had literally consumed all my brain power. Once I spotted my husband, he became the target for all my frustration and fearful shame. I scolded, "Well, you could have told me you were leaving before you disappeared and left me completely stranded back there!" He looked at me like I had two heads; he had no idea why I was so wound up. Not too surprisingly, my accusation started a minor tiff between us. What a way to start our vacation!

Since I was still believing the lies that my husband would be mad at me (spoiler alert: he wasn't), I didn't want to let him in on my internal struggle. Later that night, when I finally told him, he was surprised by my fear and dread. He assured me that I had in fact made the correct decision, and that he had already addressed my friend's concerns earlier that day. I was surprised to discover that the whole situation was WAY bigger in my mind than it was in reality. I was equally shocked that the whole situation had already been taken care of hours ago. Wow! I felt cheated by the enemy and robbed of several hours of carefree family time. But God had a plan to use this episode to reveal a wound in my life He wanted to heal.

I desperately needed God's perspective to show me what had happened in this mind battle. I set aside some time to get quiet before Him so that I could listen for His instructions. By asking the Father questions and allowing Him to guide my thoughts, He took me back to a memory from when I was eight years old. I had made a decision that got my sisters and me into big trouble. Instead of being punished right away, we had to wait seven hours until my dad got home from work. The Lord enabled me to clearly recall the emotions I felt that day while waiting for my punishment. I remembered the inability to focus on anything else throughout that day except the dread, panic and fear of the reprimand to come. Those same emotions flared up in my mind in the rental car lobby as I listened to the phone message from my friend. In the heat of the battle on vacation day, emotionally I was more like that little girl than an adult woman able to handle a bit of healthy feedback from a friend.

Alone in the Lord's presence, I allowed Him to peel back this emotional scab and permit the festering, infectious lies to pour out: *Oh no, I made a decision and it was the wrong one. If I make a mistake, then I am a failure. I am bad and I will be punished for this. I am not capable of making a good decision. It is better to never take the lead or make a decision because it could be the wrong one and other people will have to pay for my mistake.* The Lord showed me how I had felt incredible shame as a child at leading my sisters in a bad decision that resulted in their punishment as well as mine. When I allowed Jesus to cut open this painful boil, He revealed to me that I had made a vow in my heart that still affected me to this day. He showed me this pact that I'd unknowingly made with myself all those years ago: It is too dangerous for me to make decisions at all, because I'm defective and I make bad decisions that cost others. As a child, after one mistake, I had come to a faulty conclusion that caused me to avoid any and all areas of leadership or decision-making that could affect others. I was paralyzed by the fear of failure.

The Commander allowed this incident at the car rental place to show me an area of healing that needed to take place. Lies needed to be exposed and replaced with the truth. I needed to repent for allowing my flesh to defend and protect me instead of allowing God to fight my battles. An agreement with the enemy had to be brought to the light and renounced in the name of Jesus. When the Healer draws out the poison and drains the wound, He then cleanses it by pouring out His healing balm of love and truth. *"There is no fear in love, but perfect love casts out fear. For fear has to do with punishment, and whoever fears has not been perfected in love"* (1 John 4:18). The Lord also gave me one of my favorite battle verses against the fear of making a mistake. Whenever this trigger goes off and I'm tempted to allow the old Kori to fret over the "what ifs," I defeat the cowardly voice of my flesh by embracing this promise: *"The Lord directs the steps of the godly. He delights in every detail of their lives. Though they stumble, they will never fall, for the Lord holds them by the hand"* (Psalm 37:23-24 NLT). The Lord met me in a very personal way, and it was as if He was saying to me: *Kori, I am completely in charge of your every step and I am the One directing you. There will be times where you will stumble and make a mistake but even in those times I am up to something there. You will make mistakes and you will learn from them. Even though you may stumble at times, I will never let you fall because I am tightly holding on to you. This is not your ability to hold on to me but my ability to hold on to you. We are in this together and I will never leave you for one second.*

These subtle agreements and internal vows are our old nature's way of protecting itself against further pain and hurt. It is part of the flesh's elaborate system of self-protection that operates independently of God. But *it is sin,* and the enemy uses it to create spiritual strongholds in our lives. With these ungodly defense systems in place we will find ourselves in the flesh before we even know it! That is why we must, with the Lord's help, identify those triggers that will immediately awaken our sinful nature. This healing is needed for our survival in the battles that we face. Sometimes we would rather live with the wounds, for fear of what is packed up tight, festering below the surface. Will we give in to the lies of fear because we know there will be pain in the healing process? It is an extremely mature and courageous thing to humble ourselves and submit to God. This process can begin in a time of focused prayer where we allow our Father to take us back to an event, a memory or a recurring pattern in our lives that has shaped us in a negative way. As He walks us through this memory we begin to identify the thoughts, feelings and emotions that are buried in the root system of our beliefs. He reveals any lies that we believed then and are still believing today, and shows us how these lies affect our attitudes and actions. Sometimes God starts at a memory and leads us forward to the present; other times He pinpoints something that's happening now and walks us backwards to show us the source. We must allow the leading of the Commander to guide us through this healing process when we become aware of a trigger that repeatedly sets off a fleshly reaction or attitude.

Prayer:

Dear Father,
Thank You for being the great Healer. Help me become aware of the triggers in my life that make me respond in a way that is contrary to my new nature in Christ. Show me the places that need healing and freedom. I give You permission to take me back to the memories and situations where I believed lies and made agreements with the evil one that do not align with Your truth. Remind me of the emotions and help me identify the specific lies I have believed, and speak Your truth to me.
In Jesus' name, Amen.

Action Steps: Journal your prayers, answers and all the things the Commander reveals to you.

1. Ask the Commander to show you some of your triggers. Begin to make a list.

2. Once you have identified a trigger, get quiet before the Lord and ask Him to show you when this pattern of behavior first started in your life. Invite Jesus to take you there and trust Him to walk you through it.

3. When He brings up a memory, ask Him what you came to believe about yourself in this situation. What did you

come to believe about God? Others? Are these thoughts truth? If not, then you have been given the gift of repentance and you can use the following prayer as a guide.

4. Dear Father, I confess and renounce the lie that _____. I repent for believing this lie and receive Your full and free forgiveness. I take my authority in Christ Jesus and command any demonic influence that has gained access to my life through this sin to leave my presence and never return. Lord, I ask that You come into those empty places in my heart and fill me with Your love and healing through the presence of the Holy Spirit. In Jesus' name, Amen.

5. Ask the Lord if there is anything more He wants you to ask Him or anything He still wants to say to you. Listen and let Him lead you into truth.

Chapter Eleven
Even More Spiritual Weapons

We destroy every proud obstacle that keeps people from knowing God. We capture their rebellious thoughts and teach them to obey Christ. And after you have become fully obedient, we will punish everyone who remains disobedient.
2 Corinthians 10:5-6 NLT

Time is short. Battles rage all around us, and every battle the Commander allows us to experience now is training us for the ones to come. We must be willing to submit ourselves to the Lord for a time of intense spiritual training, arming ourselves to the hilt with spiritual weapons. Here are a few more we can add to our knowledge that will lead us to even greater victory in battle. The victories—or lack of victories—we experience are not just about us. We fight for our freedom, yes, but we are also fighting for the freedom of those in our area of influence because ultimately this is about the glory of our God! The Commander wants to train us not to simply survive these battles, but to be *more than conquerors*, bringing major damage on the enemy as well. If we follow our Commander God, He will teach us to fight through our spiritual battles into whole new incredible areas of freedom and worship in His presence. It is a fight, but it is worth it! We need to train ourselves to think like warriors and stop panicking or grumbling every time we get attacked by our enemy. Victory for every battle has been provided for us as we abide in Christ Jesus. *"No, in all these things we are more than* conquerors through him who loved us" (Romans 8:37). As we train with our spiritual weapons, we will move from barely surviving our trials, to victoriously thriving and forcefully advancing the kingdom of heaven wherever we go. "From the days of John the Baptist until now, the kingdom of heaven has been forcefully advancing, and forceful men lay hold of it" (Matthew 11:12 NIV). Let's take a look at some more spiritual weapons and see if there are any the Commander would have us use this week to fight and overcome the evil one's influence in our lives.

Weapon of Faith

Now faith is the assurance of things hoped for, the conviction of things not seen. (Hebrews 11:1)

The immeasurable greatness of his power toward us who believe, according to the working of his great might that he worked in Christ when he raised him from the dead and seated him at his right hand in the heavenly places. (Ephesians 1:19-20)

Be strong and courageous. Do not be afraid or terrified because of them, for the Lord your God goes with you; he will never leave you nor forsake you. (Deuteronomy 31:6 NIV)

"And I am sure of this, that he who began a good work in you will bring it to completion at the day of Jesus Christ."

Philippians 1:6

Faith is referred to as a shield and it covers us in the amazing, powerful promises of God. But in order to pick up our shield of faith we must know what those promises are, speaking them out at just the right time to block the incoming lies of the enemy. Sometimes in the midst of the crazy battle, I can only recall one verse of Scripture. I hang on to it for dear life, repeating it over and over as my only defense. The good news is that the weapon of faith is more than enough.

In the darkness, we must learn to cling tightly to the promises of Scripture and wait for His rescue, because great power is available to those of us who believe. When all we can see seems to be spiraling into an endless abyss of chaos, this weapon holds us steady and enables us to stand firm on the promise of God's faithfulness. In the heat of the battle, faith in Christ can feel uncomfortable, leaving us squirming vulnerably and without a backup plan. But that is the strongest place I can be, confident in the fact that ONLY God can rescue me and there is no plan B available. How can our faith be tested without situations like these? We must not only believe but experience the fact that God keeps His promises. The weapon of faith can transform the timid or cowardly into the bold and courageous—giving us a God-confidence when facing overwhelming circumstances.

> *And what more shall I say? For time would fail me to tell of Gideon, Barak, Samson, Jephthah, of David and Samuel and the prophets—who through faith conquered kingdoms, enforced justice, obtained promises, stopped the mouths of lions, quenched the power of fire, escaped the edge of the sword, were made strong out of weakness, became mighty in war, put foreign armies to flight. (Hebrews 11:32-34)*

And again, *"Simon, Simon, behold, Satan demanded to have you, that he might sift you like wheat, but I have prayed for you that your faith may not fail. And when you have turned again, strengthen your brothers" (Luke 22:31-32).*

Our faith is built one circumstance at a time. Whenever I am in a battle, struggling to believe in God's word, I have to remind myself of what God has *already* done in His Word and in my life!

Once I faced a potentially confrontational meeting with a person and was, of course, dreading it. Even as I prayed about it, I had nagging feelings that this was going to turn out badly. God promises to never leave me and to turn even the bad things to good for His glory. I knew this truth but struggled to believe it in the midst of the dark cloud of "what if" scenarios whirling around in my mind. But because I have been trained by the greatest of all Commanders, I was reminded to focus on some of my favorite miracles in Scripture. I began to speak them out one by one in my own words. So in the middle of the battle I stopped, pulled out the weapon of faith and declared, "Lord, I trust You! You created the heavens and the earth by the word of Your mouth . . . You gathered all the animals into the ark and brought Noah and his family safely through the Flood . . . You gave Abraham and Sarah a son when physically there was no way . . . You brought the ten awesome plagues on the Egyptians and brought Your people out of slavery . . . You parted the Red Sea . . . You worked through David to take down a lion, a bear and Goliath the giant . . . You restored strength to Samson so that he could defeat his enemies . . . You turned the water into wine . . . You gave sight to the blind . . . You raised the dead . . . You even died and came back to life again!" As my mind briefly visited each miracle, my faith increased. As I focused on how BIG and powerful God is, my struggle from just a moment before seemed so small compared to what the God of the Universe is used to doing. I concluded that my "huge mountain" of a potentially confrontational meeting might be more like a tiny anthill. On God's miracle-scale, my meeting was fairly easy for God to handle.

When I face a crisis of belief—and I do quite often—I have to go back and remember times in the past when God told me to personally believe Him, or step out and do something for Him with no backup plan. Jesus is the author and perfector of my faith. He is the One who started it and He is the One who will build and perfect it. So when I lack faith, I go back and remember the times I could have failed miserably but instead God took over, because my hope was entirely in Him.

Weapon of Salvation

Restore to me the joy of your salvation and grant me a willing spirit, to sustain me. (Psalm 51:12 NIV)

But since we belong to the day, let us be self-controlled, putting on faith and love as a breastplate, and the hope of salvation as a helmet. For God did not appoint us to suffer wrath but to receive salvation through our Lord Jesus Christ. He died for us so that, whether we are awake or asleep, we may live together with him. Therefore encourage one another and build each other up, just as in fact you are doing. (1 Thessalonians 5:8-11 NIV)

For our light and momentary troubles are achieving for us an eternal glory that far outweighs them all. So we fix our eyes not on what is seen, but on what is unseen. For what is seen is temporary, but what is unseen is eternal. (2 Corinthians 4:17-18 NIV)

Therefore, since we are surrounded by such a great cloud of witnesses, let us throw off everything that hinders and the sin that so easily entangles, and let us run with perseverance the race marked out for us. Let us fix our eyes on Jesus, the author and perfector of our faith, who for the joy set before him endured the cross, scorning its shame, and sat down at the right hand of the throne of God. (Hebrews 12:1-2 NIV)

Have you ever been battle-weary? Sometimes I get so fed up at the constant battles I face on a daily basis. I get through one battle and am hit immediately by another one, with no time to recover. At times frustration, spiritual fatigue, and discouragement seek to overpower me and I want to quit— everything! It is in those times that I must take up my weapon of salvation, just like David did, and rejoice that I am destined for heaven! I must remember and stop to celebrate the fact that I will never experience one ounce of the wrath of God or the torment of hell! I can hold out hope that no matter how bad it gets here, this world is the worst of it for me. Salvation is mine, bought by the blood of Christ. I must encourage myself and other believers in this truth. We do not belong to this world; it is a very hostile place for us to live in, but we will not be here forever.

A soldier at war might encourage or console himself with thoughts of home, thinking of loved ones or filling his mind with images of a delicious Thanksgiving feast with friends and family all around. On cold, painful and lonely nights, he does this in order to stay the course, remember why he is fighting the war, and gain renewed strength to get the job done so he can get home. We too are in a foreign country, fighting a long, painful war, with a deep and unexplainable longing for a home we can only dream about. We can take up the weapon of salvation and console ourselves with thoughts of home—our eternal perfect home. We must get into the habit of thinking thoughts about eternity. Read the passages of Scripture about heaven, asking the Lord to fill your imagination with thoughts of eternity. Many believers have gone before us and are awaiting our arrival. Someday soon we will rest from this battle against the world, the flesh and the devil—but not today. Today we fight!

Weapon of Confession

Confess to one another therefore your faults (your slips, your false steps, your offenses, your sins) and pray [also] for one another, that you may be healed and restored [to a spiritual tone of mind and heart]. The earnest (heartfelt, continued) prayer of a righteous man makes tremendous power available [dynamic in its working]. (James 5:16 AMP)

I acknowledged my sin to you, and I did not cover my iniquity; I said, "I will confess my transgressions to the Lord," and you forgave the iniquity of my sin. (Psalm 32:5)

If we confess our sins, he is faithful and just to forgive us our sins and to cleanse us from all unrighteousness. If we say we have not sinned, we make him a liar, and his word is not in us. (1 John 1:9-10)

I was once engaged in a battle with crippling fear in the area of leadership. Self-doubt and insecurities crowded out my ability to hear from the Lord and obey His instructions. The

Commander instructed me to write down all the things I could think of that frightened me—and then *confess them* to a group of ladies I was meeting with at the time. It was an exhaustive list and I was more than a little *afraid* to tell them about my embarrassing lack of confidence, thus solidifying my inadequacies to be a leader. With the Lord's help, I admitted and confessed my sin of fear and asked my friends to pray for me. I was surprised at how quickly this weapon of confession dealt a death blow to the relentless fears that had paralyzed me. When God calls us to confess our sins to one another, He is able to give us clear and detailed instructions as to who, when and how much to share. Wait for His instructions. Take this weapon seriously! It is powerful and often provides immediate relief from the battle. It has been said that sin kept in secret holds its power, but once it is brought out into the light, it can dissolve quickly.

Weapon of Repentance

For Godly grief and the pain that God is permitted to direct, produce a repentance that leads to and contributes to salvation and deliverance from evil, and it never leads to regret; but worldly grief (the hopeless sorrow that is characteristic of the pagan world) is deadly [breeding and ending in death]. (2 Corinthians 7:10 AMP)

And the Lord's servant must not be quarrelsome but kind to everyone, able to teach, patiently enduring evil, correcting his opponents with gentleness. God may perhaps grant them repentance leading to a knowledge of the truth, and they may escape from the snare of the devil, after being captured by him to do his will. (2 Timothy 2:24-26 AMP)

Submit yourselves, then, to God. Resist the devil, and he will flee from you. Come near to God and he will come near to you. Wash your hands, you sinners, and purify your hearts, you double-minded. Grieve, mourn and wail. Change your laughter to mourning and your joy to gloom. Humble yourselves before the Lord, and he will lift you up. (James 4:7-10)

Repentance is key to our salvation and the way in which we are able to enter into eternal life. *"And saying, Repent (think differently; change your mind, regretting your sins and changing your conduct) for the kingdom of heaven is at hand" (Matthew 3:2 AMP).* It is the beginning, yes, but it doesn't stop there; it is also the key to greater degrees of freedom and life. Sin is disobedience to God and His commandments. When we humble ourselves through repentance, turning away from our sin, we return to the safety and blessings found beneath the mighty protective hand of our God. Sometimes we will be stuck in a ruthless battle, fighting with all our energy, using one weapon after another against the enemy, and the battle doesn't seem to be letting up. It may be that only one tool is required—the weapon of repentance. Lodged somewhere in our words, actions or attitudes is a sin that has been allowed to thrive, and it is an open door for our struggle. Whether we have intentional or unintentional sin in our lives, the only way to gain victory is by repentance. Taking up this weapon will be met with great opposition from the world, our flesh and the devil. We must ask the Commander for a godly sorrow that leads to life, not worldly sorrow that leads to death. We need to experience the Commander's grief over our sin in order to fight the independent spirit of our old nature and this world. May we learn to be quick to repent any time the Commander allows us to see sin in our lives.

Weapon of Renouncing and Declaring

For the grace of God has appeared, bringing salvation for all people, training us to renounce ungodliness and worldly passions, and to live self-controlled, upright, and godly lives in the present age. (Titus 2:11-12)

You have multiplied, O Lord my God, your wondrous deeds and your thoughts toward us; none can compare with you! I will proclaim and tell of them, yet they are more than can be told. (Psalm 40:5)

Declare his glory among the nations, his marvelous works among all the peoples! For great is the Lord, and greatly to be praised, and he is to be held in awe above all gods. (1 Chronicles 16:24-25)

In the fight against our enemy, there are times we can begin to drown in the numerous negative thoughts and uncontrolled emotions rushing through our minds. One way we can surface for air is by verbalizing our thoughts and speaking them aloud. When we do this, the Commander will help us separate the truth from the lies. When a lie is exposed and brought to the surface for scrutiny, it loses its power and often seems a bit ridiculous. I might subconsciously be thinking: *If I don't sign up today to bring 35 cupcakes for the 3rd grade Valentine's party, the entire celebration will be ruined, every one of those kids will personally hate me, I'll receive The Worst Mother of the Year Award and probably scar my child for life!* I could be dealing with all the pressure of those thoughts without actually spelling out my fears. Once I verbalize them I can see how irrational they are; they become almost laughable. Then I can use the weapon of verbally renouncing that lie in the powerful name of Jesus.

Other times we will need to speak out a declaration of truth, announcing to God, ourselves, and the enemy that we will believe the truth and put our faith in God alone. When there is a mental stronghold of lies in our minds, the weapon of renouncing and declaring may look something like this: "I *renounce* the lie that I am not valuable or worth anything to anyone and I *declare* the truth that God loves me so much that He gave His Son's life for me." *(John 3:16)* "I *renounce* the lie that I have been abandoned, I'm all alone and no one cares about me and I *declare* the truth that nothing can separate me from the love of God in Christ Jesus." *(Romans 8:37-39)* We can use this weapon by repeating this out loud every morning for a period of time. A recurring lie the enemy has used against me for years is the whispered voice that says, *You can't do that, what will people think of you?* or *They're going to think . . . you're prideful . . . you're ridiculous . . . you're too much . . . you're weird!* Or *Yep, he's probably thinking [fill in the blank] about you!* All the devil had to do was launch just one of these thoughts into my mind and I would stop dead in my tracks, paralyzed by the fear of what others *might* be thinking of me. The Commander led me on a 40-day campaign of renouncing lies and declaring truth that enabled me to tear down the old stronghold of lies and build up a new stronghold of truth. It looked like this:

Overcoming the Fear of Man

(The fear of people's rejection and disapproval, fear of embarrassment and failure in front of others, and the fear of speaking up in the face of people's anger, disappointment, or slander of me.)

> I renounce the lie that my worth/identity comes from what others think and say about me and the fear that it is directly tied to their approval of me.

> I renounce that lie that I must have people think well of me, agree with me and encourage me, in order to be okay. I repent of fearing people and their disapproval more than fearing You, God. I repent and turn away from my pattern of going to man for approval instead of to Jesus to meet my deepest needs.

> I choose to believe the truth that I am already loved, accepted, safe, approved of and set apart for holy purposes. I choose to believe the truth that I am shielded from the disapproval of others because I am hidden in Christ.

I choose to believe the truth that I can go to the Lord at any time and ask Him what He thinks of me. I declare the truth that God is the only One I need to encourage me, affirm me, delight in me and tell me truth.

Renouncing and declaring is also a way of reminding ourselves that truth is to rule our thoughts and emotions, not the other way around. Whatever we think about God, ourselves, or a situation fuels our behavior in that area. If our thoughts are distorted, negative or false, then we will live out what we believe in our hearts, which is bondage. One of my favorite responses to the Commander when He tells me His truth is a verbal, "God, I believe You!" statement. It's simple, but powerful.

Weapon of Ministering Angels

Are they [Angels] not all ministering spirits sent out to serve for the sake of those who are to inherit salvation? (Hebrews 1:14)

Because you have made the Lord your dwelling place—the Most High, who is my refuge—no evil shall be allowed to befall you, no plague come near your tent. For he will command his angels concerning you to guard you in all your ways. On their hands they will bear you up, lest you strike your foot against a stone. (Psalm 91:9-12)

When the servant of the man of God rose early in the morning and went out, behold, an army with horses and chariots was all around the city. And the servant said, "Alas, my master! What shall we do?" He said, "Do not be afraid, for those who are with us are more than those who are with them." Then Elisha prayed and said, "O Lord, please open his eyes that he may see." So the Lord opened the eyes of the young man, and he saw, and behold, the mountain was full of horses and chariots of fire all around Elisha. (2 Kings 6:15-17)

Watch that you don't treat a single one of these childlike believers arrogantly. You realize, don't you, that their personal angels are constantly in touch with my Father in heaven? (Matthew 18:10 MSG)

The Word of God speaks of angelic warriors in the spiritual realm that partner with us to execute God's will. One of their primary roles is to minister to believers. We also know from Scripture that these angelic warriors fight against the demonic spirits of darkness. Our Commander is their Commander. When we are oppressed and hounded by the enemy, we can ask the Lord to dispatch His heavenly warriors to come to our aid. He is able and willing to do this for us! Even in the midst of very dark times we can be confident that our God has not abandoned us. When I am overwhelmed and sense that a relentless vile spirit is attacking me or my family, I often use this weapon, calling out to the Commander to send out the angels to come and fight for us. We can ask God for spiritual insight into the unseen realm just like the well-seasoned prophet Elisha did when he was surrounded by the enemy army. That unique discernment gave God's people the confidence they needed to face their enemy.

Weapon of Peace

Peace I leave with you; my peace I give to you. Not as the world gives do I give to you. Let not your hearts be troubled, neither let them be afraid. (John 14:27)

Behold, the hour is coming, indeed it has come, when you will be scattered, each to his own home, and will leave me alone. Yet I am not alone, for the Father is with me. I have said these things to you, that in me you may have peace. In the world you will have tribulation. But take heart; I have overcome the world. (John 16:32-33)

The Lord is at hand; do not be anxious about anything, but in everything by prayer and supplication with thanksgiving let your requests be made known to God. And the peace of God, which surpasses all understanding, will guard your hearts and your minds in Christ Jesus. (Philippians 4:5-7)

You keep him in perfect peace whose mind is stayed on you, because he trusts in you. Trust in the Lord forever, for the Lord God is an everlasting rock. (Isaiah 26:3-4)

When leaving this hostile world to return to His Father, Jesus—the Prince of Peace—bestowed His own peace upon His followers. This peace is a complete confidence and trust in God that can only be experienced by abiding in Christ—gaining His thoughts, desires, passions and perspective. As we wield this weapon in the midst of a crazy mind battle, we will experience freedom in a way that might seem surreal. Jesus' supernatural peace protects us like a force field, guarding us against fear, panic and despair. This weapon of peace enables us to think clearly and take action swiftly in order to refute the evil lies of the enemy.

Sometimes we need to dig through all our worries to even find the weapon of peace because it has been buried under a ton of cares and concerns. But the Scriptures instruct us to throw each one of those cares on the Commander. That requires sorting through the pile of woes, taking them one by one and forcefully casting them on the Lord. In doing this, we give Him the responsibility to handle those things so that our peace may be restored. This gift of peace is a shield to us and there is nothing in this world that even comes close to comparing to it.

Weapon of Divine Discernment

If any of you lacks wisdom, let him ask God, who gives generously to all without reproach, and it will be given him. (James 1:5)

> But solid food is for the mature, for those who have their
> powers of discernment trained by constant practice to
> distinguish good from evil. (Hebrews 5:14)

> And this is my prayer: that your love may abound more and
> more in knowledge and depth of insight, so that you may be
> able to discern what is best and may be pure and blameless
> until the day of Christ, filled with the fruit of righteousness
> that comes through Jesus Christ—to the glory and praise of
> God. (Philippians 1:9-11)

In some battles, I can't immediately identify the source of the
attack. I can't see what's coming at me in the midst of the
darkness. I only know I keep getting hit, unable even to
distinguish between friend and foe. I am in desperate need of an
aerial view that only the Commander can offer me. He sees and
knows all—past, present and future. He can give me His great
and unlimited wisdom about the very battle I am facing. I need
His godly discernment to peer into the surrounding darkness to
give me His own true perspective on the situation. But in order
for me to receive this instruction, I need to set aside time to sit
and listen to the Commander through His Word. This may
require me to cut some things out of my life in order to meet
with Him. Only then I can hear the life-giving instruction that
the Commander provides. This is where the weapons of quiet
and rest go hand in hand with the weapon of discernment. This
wisdom is not only available over our own lives, but we can ask
for it to be given to others who are in a confusing battle.

When my daughter, Annika, started going to the youth group at
our church it was a hard transition for her. She had thoughts
that nobody liked her, she didn't have any friends, nobody
wanted her there and she just plain didn't fit in! I explained to
her that the thoughts she was experiencing were not limited to
just her, but that the devil uses these exact same lies to keep
people separated and isolated from one another all the time. A
youth weekend retreat was coming up and so she and I spent
some time praying together that the Commander would help

her make friends and reach out to others who seemed alone. In prayer, we believed that the Lord gave us some very specific ways to pray for this youth event. We were both excited to see what was going to take place. Two days after she left I heard a message on my phone late at night. She was crying, "Mom, please pray for me because I'm struggling big-time! God's not answering our prayers. I don't want to be here anymore." She was in a fierce battle, which in turn threw me into the battle as well. I prayed (like only a momma can) for my firstborn to cry out to God and be comforted by Him. The next morning I got a message from our very capable youth pastor's wife telling me that Annika was much better after a heart-to-heart with her.

When Annika came home we spent some time talking about what happen on the trip. She was discouraged and told me several things that happened that she thought were TERRIBLE! Hmm . . . they didn't seem that terrible to me and I thought perhaps there was some confusion over her mind that made her misinterpret these situations. "Annika, let's stop right now and ask God to remove any demonic deception over your thoughts and help you see things that happened this weekend from God's perspective." It was a quick and simple prayer and afterward she casually kept on talking, but her conversation turned from negative to positive. I watched in amazement as the Lord reminded her of one event after another where someone said an encouraging thing to her or chose to hang out with her or asked her to join them. She had an "Aha moment" when she remembered a friend telling her, "Annika, you are such a popular person!" I could see that it was a shock to her to discover that (maybe, just maybe) people do like her after all.

Then the Lord started to connect the prayers that we had prayed *before* the event with situations that happened *during* the trip, showing us how He answered each one. She grew excited and fueled up with joy at the ways she was able to bless others and be an encouragement to them. The cloud of deception had blinded her, leaving her able to see only the few negative things that happened instead of all the good things. She told me,

"Mom, I am so glad we prayed for deception to be removed; otherwise I would have missed out on so much good that God did!"

What about you? Is there an area in your life right now that God is pinpointing? Do you need to ask Him to remove any deception over your mind and help you see this situation from His perspective? I wonder what I'm missing because the enemy has lied to me and I have believed him time and time again. *Help, Lord; show us truth!*

Weapon of Crying Out

This poor man cried, and the Lord heard him and saved him out of all his troubles. (Psalm 34:6)

When the righteous cry for help, the Lord hears and delivers them out of all their troubles. The Lord is near to the brokenhearted and saves the crushed in spirit. (Psalm 34:17-18)

Let my cry come before you, O Lord; give me understanding according to your word! Let my plea come before you; deliver me according to your word. (Psalm 119:169-170)

In my distress I called upon the Lord; to my God I cried for help. From his temple he heard my voice, and my cry to him reached his ears. Then the earth reeled and rocked; the foundations also of the mountains trembled and quaked, because he was angry. Smoke went up from his nostrils, and devouring fire from his mouth; glowing coals flamed forth from him. He bowed the heavens and came down; thick darkness was under his feet. He rode on a cherub and flew; he came swiftly on the wings of the wind. (Psalm 18:6-10)

One of the first social skills kindergarten teachers instill is how to talk at a classroom-appropriate volume, to distinguish between "inside" and "outside" voices. When a student's voice is too loud, the teacher calmly reminds them to use their inside voice. So often when we pray, we have learned to use our "inside" voice only. The weapon of crying out requires us to abandon our inside voice, opting to use our outside voice in prayer. There are desperate times in battle when we need to cry aloud, lifting our voices to the Commander for help. This may seem awkward but it is biblical! The crying out described here is not a silent or halfhearted cry. It is an "outside" voice times ten! As with any weapon, crying out requires practice.

As a mother of young kids, I could tell the different and varying degrees of cries for help that my kids gave. Just by the sound, tone and pitch of my children's voices, I could tell if they were hungry, tired, bored or in a dire need. Loud cries of anguish, panic or desperation always made me stop everything and run to my kids. If the Lord gave me that mother's instinct, and I was made in His image, then how much more does our God feel when He hears one of His children crying aloud? I wonder sometimes if He cannot help Himself but swiftly come to our aid. Whenever we are hungry for more, bored, dissatisfied, upset or especially frightened, we can cry out in the depths of our spirit exactly how we are feeling, to a Father who will meet us there. In fact, God encourages it! *"For you did not receive the spirit of slavery to fall back into fear, but you have received the Spirit of adoption as sons, by whom we cry, 'Abba! Father!' The Spirit himself bears witness with our spirit that we are children of God"* (Romans 8:15-16). The crying out that is talked about in this verse is a literal "cry out," an audible voice full of emotion that is beseeching a Father who is close, loving, intimate and personal. Abba, Father, is a term of endearment from a child who knows and expects immediate help is on the way!

I urge you to adopt this kind of crying out to the Father as a spiritual weapon against the enemy. Don't be shy in raising your voice in prayer to God! You might be surprised at what happens next. If you don't know what I'm talking about, all you have to do is practice this weapon. Jesus went to the Cross so that we can have this personal and intimate relationship with the Father. Let's not be afraid to use this secure weapon of crying out in prayer to our Father who hears and is ready to run to our aid. As we learn to use this weapon with both boldness and respect, we will get an up-close view of our Father's heart toward us. *"He sent from on high, he took me; he drew me out of many waters. He rescued me from my strong enemy and from those who hated me, for they were too mighty for me. They confronted me in the day of my calamity, but the Lord was my support"* (Psalm 18:16-18).

Weapon of Fasting

> *Then I proclaimed a fast there, at the river Ahava, that we might humble ourselves before our God, to seek from him a safe journey for ourselves, our children, and all our goods. For I was ashamed to ask the king for a band of soldiers and horsemen to protect us against the enemy on our way, since we had told the king, "The hand of our God is for good on all who seek him, and the power of his wrath is against all who forsake him." So we fasted and implored our God for this, and he listened to our entreaty. (Ezra 8:21-23)*

> *Then Esther told them to reply to Mordecai, "Go, gather all the Jews to be found in Susa, and hold a fast on my behalf, and do not eat or drink for three days, night or day. I and my young women will also fast as you do. Then I will go to the king, though it is against the law, and if I perish, I perish." Mordecai then went away and did everything as Esther had ordered him. (Esther 4:15-17)*

Fasting is an intense weapon that we can use to humble ourselves and seek the Lord's favor, counsel and protection. It is a period of time where we abstain from earthly food, emptying ourselves in order that God may fill us up even more with His amazing power, strength, wisdom and guidance. There will be times when the Commander will lead us to fight with this powerful, supernatural weapon as the way to push through a specific battle. Queen Esther used the weapon of fasting when faced with the dangerous task of coming before the king of Persia for the lives of her people. She called the Israelites to a fast where they were instructed not to eat or drink for three days while she sought the Lord for direction and favor. We don't know what happened during those three days but we do know that when the time of fasting was over, Queen Esther had a plan. No doubt during her fast, as she sat in silence before the Lord, she *listened* as God gave her ideas and thoughts that shaped her plan of action. How did she know to hold a feast for the king? Where did she get the idea to keep him in suspense all night instead of just presenting her request the moment he asked? The Lord was working through the night to prepare the way for the salvation of her people. What situation are you facing right now where you need this type of detailed instruction? Maybe the weapon you need to pull out is the weapon of fasting.

Weapon of Endurance

Blessed is the man who remains steadfast under trial, for when he has stood the test he will receive the crown of life, which God has promised to those who love him. (James 1:12)

Therefore do not throw away your confidence, which has a great reward. For you have need of endurance, so that when you have done the will of God you may receive what is promised. For, "Yet a little while, and the coming one will come and will not delay; but my righteous one shall live by faith, and if he shrinks back, my soul has no pleasure in him." But we are not of those who shrink back and are destroyed, but of those who have faith and preserve their souls. (Hebrews 10:35-39)

Some battles seem to be all-consuming, painful and never-ending. In those times, we must never forget that God has a purpose and plan in every battle He allows us to experience. With this truth in mind we need to use the weapon of endurance and persevere for a little longer, firmly deciding to stay engaged in the fight. Look at this verse and see how our God builds good things on the foundation of our struggles.

> *More than that, we rejoice in our sufferings, knowing that suffering produces endurance, and endurance produces character, and character produces hope, and hope does not put us to shame, because God's love has been poured into our hearts through the Holy Spirit who has been given to us. (Romans 5:3-5)*

Perhaps our Commander is "irritating" some things in our lives for a reason, even for our good. We have a choice in the matter. When we are the most exasperated, we must endure by rejoicing in our battle and thanking God for it, embracing the character, hope and love God is seeking to produce in us. We must use our spiritual weapon of endurance, patiently standing firm and persisting until the Commander brings us through it. Running this spiritual race and building up stamina is what our Lord is doing in our lives, but the evil one loves to play mind games on us so that we become so confused and exhausted we want to quit. Don't do it; let's keep going.

> **WARNING:** Satan would love for you to quit right now and never get to *The Battle against the Devil* section of this book. Be aware and don't forget that the devil roars the loudest when he's the most afraid. We will have need of endurance in the chapters ahead because the devil and his foul demons HATE to be exposed; rather, he prefers to work undetected in our lives. Once we become aware of him, he often intensifies his attacks. He tries to make us think that fighting him is not worth it and we should give up. He even interjects the thoughts that it is easier to simply let him have his way, or that "just one area" is fine the way it is instead of going through the trouble of kicking out the enemy. This is a serious mistake on

our parts. Stop and pray right now for the weapon of
endurance.

Prayer:

Dear Father,
Thank You for these spiritual weapons. Help me to know how
and when to use them so that I may be even more skilled in
the battles I face. Build my faith, increase my understanding
of heaven, and grant me the humility to confess my sins to
others when needed. Give me the power to repent, renounce
and declare truth, call upon You to dispatch Your angels, live
constantly in Your peace, seek Your divine discernment, learn
when and how to cry out to You, fast, and endure to the every
end.
In Jesus' name, Amen.

Action Steps: Journal your prayers, answers and all the things
the Commander reveals to you.

1. Choose a spiritual weapon from this chapter. Research it
    by looking up all the verses in Scripture you can find
    about it. Ask the Commander to reveal the spiritual
    "features" of this weapon and how it could work in the
    midst of a mind battle. If the Lord gives you any
    instructions on how to practice this weapon then be
    obedient, asking Him to prompt you when and how
    throughout your day.

2. Choose another spiritual weapon and repeat the above
    instructions.

3. The next time you recognize that you are in a mind
    battle, ask the Lord to help you access one or more of
    these weapons: Faith, Salvation, Confession, Repentance,
    Renouncing and Declaring, Ministering Angels, Peace,
    Discernment, Crying Out, Fasting or Endurance.

4. Get alone with the Lord and use the weapon of crying out. If you don't know what to pray about then ask the Lord to give you a subject or desire. Then raise your voice and pour out your heart to the Father. Keep it up until you experience Him moving toward you to meet you in that moment.

Chapter Twelve
The Battle Against the Devil

We know that everyone who has been born of God does not keep on sinning, but he who was born of God protects him, and the evil one does not touch him.
1 John 5:18

"Call to me and I will answer you and tell you great and unsearchable things you do not know" (Jeremiah 33:3 NIV). This verse is so important to me that I've had it inscribed on a wall in my house. Once in a while I spend some time alone practicing the weapon of crying out, with this verse as my prayer: *"Where do you want to take me next?"* Without fail, the Commander will guide me into an unfamiliar area of truth. Sometimes I wonder if He has a whole list of unsearchable things He wants to share with me, and He's just waiting for me to ask!

Shortly after uttering this prayer one day, I felt the familiar prompting of the Holy Spirit to study a new topic: Satan. I have to admit it—I did not want to study Satan! I earnestly questioned the Lord on this. But the Commander insisted, reminding me that I'd just finished telling Him about my hunger for Him to teach and guide me in His truth. Reluctantly, I went to the Scriptures and found every passage I could that referred to the devil, demons, unclean spirits, and the kingdom of darkness. As I allowed the Commander to guide my path through Scripture, I gained a clearer understanding of Satan. I was surprised to learn about the devil's past, his plan for unbelievers, his plan for believers and the punishment awaiting him. The most important thing God taught me through this process was this: *You must not fear Satan, because I have already defeated him!* In fact, I learned that it is actually dangerous for a child of God to fear Satan. *"Do not be afraid of those who kill the body but cannot kill the soul. Rather, be afraid of the One who can destroy both soul and body in hell"* (Matthew 10:28 NIV).

God showed me that when it comes to understanding our enemy, the devil loves for us to fall into one of two extremes—ignorance and indifference toward Satan and the demonic forces, or a dangerous preoccupation with them. Ignorance or casual indifference toward Satan and the demonic forces are a mindset the enemy wants for us. Just because we aren't aware of or don't acknowledge Satan's attacks against us doesn't make them go away! In fact, our ignorance and apathy allow him to work undetected and unchallenged in our lives. The devil would like us to believe that he isn't really active any more, and that he certainly wouldn't attack a "nobody" like me. But he is waiting to ambush us. *"Be sober-minded; be watchful. Your adversary the devil prowls around like a roaring lion, seeking someone to devour"* (1 Peter 5:8). We are children of God, and therefore we are a great threat to the devil and his agenda. We are commanded to "stand firm" and "resist our enemy." Those are fighting words! We cannot afford indifference.

Sometimes this willful ignorance is a result of apathy, but sometimes it is a result of fear. Fear of the devil is the unhealthy dread of anything that has to do with Satan and his kingdom. This fear makes us close our eyes, plug our ears, and hope for the best. This mindset can motivate us to avoid or even forbid the mention of anything associated with the devil, keeping ourselves completely ignorant of and vulnerable to his attacks. But this doesn't take into account the finished work of Christ on the Cross. *"And having disarmed the powers and authorities, he made a public spectacle of them, triumphing over them by the cross" (Colossians 2:15 NIV).* It is wise to know our enemy and his ultimate end so we will not fall victim to him. Satan loves to hold believers hostage through fear of him. But God commands us to fear Him alone! *"The fear of the Lord is the beginning of wisdom, and the knowledge of the Holy One is insightful" (Proverbs 9:10).* Satan arrogantly wants everything that is due to God, including fear. We can unknowingly give the devil honor, worship and control in our lives when we secretly fear him.

On the other hand, believers can become fascinated with Satan, developing an unhealthy interest in his power. This may begin as an apparently virtuous effort to study his ways and tactics, but it results in giving him the time and attention that is rightfully due to our Lord Jesus. We have been naturally drawn toward power and knowledge ever since humanity's first temptation in the Garden of Eden, and in learning about the devil we must not cross that line into sin and obsession. *"Do not turn to mediums or seek out spiritists, for you will be defiled by them. I am the Lord your God" (Leviticus 19:31 NIV).* This extreme is also a form of worship and praise to Satan. We must follow our

Commander so that He can equip us with the spiritual insight we need in our fight against the devil.

The Devil Studies Us

One evening as I was watching football with my husband I noticed something puzzling. Every time the coach relayed instructions to his team through his headset, he covered his mouth with his clipboard. My husband explained that pro sports teams have an entire staff dedicated to scrutinizing game footage, reviewing their opponents' plays and analyzing the statistics. The staff looks for trends in how the team operates in certain situations so that they can prepare their team to anticipate the opponent's plays. Literally thousands of hours of planning and vast resources are poured into pregame preparation. The coaches are aware that they are being watched by the media and the opposing team during the game, and they know that their opponents will do similar study on their team's strategy. To protect the confidentiality of their plays and their communication with the coordinators in the upstairs booth, the coach covers his mouth with the clipboard. I was shocked to find out how much time and energy were dedicated to gaining victory over the other team; all of this over a *football game!*

I sensed the Lord speaking to me: *Kori, see how much time these teams spend studying each other to predict the plays their opponents will most likely run in a given situation? Look at the determination and hours of preparation they invest before they even meet in battle on the field. How much more must I want My children to know their enemy, prepare for battle, and learn the tactics the enemy might use on them? The stakes are far higher than a football game.* I was convicted and sobered by the thought that the devil knows me, analyzes me, and has a favorite set of plays he runs against me in his attempt to defeat me. I was awakened to the fact that I need help understanding the enemy's carefully considered traps, plans and schemes against me, so I asked God: *What kind of "plays" does the devil run on me?* It wasn't too long after that prayer that the Commander began to show me some dysfunctional and recurring patterns in my life that were hindering me from standing firm in the fight and guarding myself against the enemy's tactics. This prayer has led me on a path where the Lord revealed the lies that have infiltrated my mind, and the freedom in Christ that comes when I began to fight against those lies with God's truth.

One way the enemy was stealing from me was in my inability to stay mentally present in the moment. One evening, as I was reminiscing over the day, the Commander gave me an "instant replay" of my thoughts and actions. At breakfast, instead of engaging in conversation with my kids, I was thinking through my 9:00 meeting. During my 9:00 meeting I was partially checked out, already planning my route to stop by three different stores on the way home. That afternoon, when I'd picked up the kids from school, I wasn't fully listening to their "report of the day" because my mind was on my grocery list. When I was actually at the grocery store, I was mentally already at home preparing dinner. While making dinner, I was only partially present because I was thinking about what I was going to do after dinner. It felt like only 20% of my brain was focusing on the task at hand, and 80% was already on to the next thing. Almost all of my mental energy was being spent on the task ahead, instead of being fully engaged in the present. You know, you can miss A LOT when you live life that way! I'm all for planning ahead, but this way of thinking was laced with anxiety and stress.

And this pattern wasn't limited to my day—this way of thinking showed up throughout the seasons of the year. In autumn while the leaves fell, I lamented those lazy days of summer, wondering where they went. I moved through Thanksgiving and Christmas season in a fog, regretting that all the leaves were gone. When January hit, I was mentally ready to start thinking about celebrating Christmas, but by then it was too late. Then I spent the long, cold months of winter wishing for spring. I was either stuck in the past season, regretting that it was over, or jumping ahead and wishing that the current season was now done. Too late or too early, never enjoying the current season. This led to an ungrateful, discontented attitude that could never relish the moment and enjoy what was right before me. I was missing out on so much! I had to repent of this way of thinking, resist the voice of the enemy and ask the Lord to change my mindset in this area so that it matched His truth. As the Lord began to change the way I think, I can now choose to savor the moment and enjoy life in every situation. Joy is available to me no matter where I am or what I'm doing. Today it's cold and windy outside; we are expecting our first snow of the season any day now and I am delighted to be in my warm house, snuggled up with my favorite slippers, eating chocolate and editing this book. I LOVE my life, thank You Jesus!

"Dear children, don't let anyone deceive you about this: When people do what is right, it shows that they are righteous, even as Christ is righteous. But when people keep on sinning, it shows that they belong to the devil, who has been sinning since the beginning. But the Son of God came to destroy the works of the devil. Those who have been born into God's family do not make a practice of sinning, because God's life is in them. So they can't keep on sinning, because they are children of God. So now we can tell who are children of God and who are children of the devil. Anyone who does not live righteously and does not love other believers does not belong to God."

1 John 3:7-10 NLT

God's Power Is Greater

We must understand that Satan's hatred toward us is real and intense. You may ask, "Why is Satan against me? What did I ever do to him?" The answer: You were born . . . and then you were *born again.* Not only is it a burr in Satan's side that the Creator God favored mankind with the gift of His love and the authority to govern this world, but for believers, Jesus stripped Satan and his demons of their authority and returned it once again to the sons and daughters of God. Our God-given authority to rule was reclaimed for us as we were placed inside of Christ Jesus at the right hand of God. What Satan fought so hard to gain was taken from him and returned to us.

The devil hates the children of the Most High God with an ancient and intelligent hatred, but our citizenship in heaven is permanent, and there is nothing he can do to reclaim us. All Satan can do to believers now is to try to deceive us and lure us back into the bondage of sin. We can only sin in our old nature, which is dead and continually dying. The devil seeks to keep us bound. Sin for the unbeliever leads to death, but sin for the believer is unnecessary bondage. Jesus died to set us free from that enslavement! Our freedom and the life of Christ in us is a threat to Satan and his dying kingdom. He uses all his schemes and ancient, corrupt wisdom to keep us from knowing the truth about our righteousness, power, gifts, position and authority as children of God.

The Devil Is Defeated

Jesus came to do the will of His Father. When He obeyed God, even to death on the Cross, Jesus issued a death sentence for Satan's well-laid plans. He is the only One Who could. *"The reason the Son of God appeared was to destroy the works of the devil"* (1 John 3:8). When Jesus entered this fallen world, Satan did everything in his power to tempt Jesus to sin by obeying him instead of His Father God. Satan even tempted Jesus to do good things, like turning stones into bread. But Jesus refused— following Satan's instructions would have meant He was operating outside of His Father's will, which is the definition of sin. Satan offered Jesus everything of this world, including all the world systems, in exchange for one thing: Jesus must bow down and worship him. *"Again, the devil took him to a very high mountain and showed him all the kingdoms of the world and their glory. And he said to him, 'All these I will give you, if you will fall down and worship me'" (Matthew 4:8-9).* Even after being thrown out of heaven, Satan was still obsessed with the throne of God, desirous of the highest power and authority with everyone, even God, subject to himself. Jesus refused him this delusion and used that coveted divine authority to command Satan to flee. Satan's arrogance and fury at once again failing to usurp the throne of God blinded him to what was really going on—the redemption of mankind. Satan focused all his attention on killing Jesus, and he actually thought he succeeded. But Satan was himself deceived, not knowing that it was God's plan all along to put His own Son to death to pay for our sins.

> *For this reason the Father loves me [Jesus], because I lay down my life that I may take it up again. No one takes it from me, but I lay it down of my own accord. I have authority to lay it down, and I have authority to take it up again. This charge I have received from my Father. (John 10:17-18)*

Jesus' work on the Cross proved to be the ultimate defeat of Satan. Jesus stripped Satan of his authority, returning it to the sons and daughters of God. He made it possible for anyone who would trust in Him to be free. We are no longer enslaved to sin and will never pay the penalty for our sin, which is eternal death.

> *When you were slaves of sin, you were free in regard to righteousness. But what fruit were you getting at that time from the things of which you are now ashamed? The end of those things is death. But now that you have been set free from sin and have become slaves of God, the fruit you get leads to sanctification and its end, eternal life. For the wages of sin is death, but the free gift of God is eternal life in Christ Jesus our Lord. (Romans 6:20-23)*

God's kingdom, the very kingdom that Satan desired to rule over, has now become a haven for believers in Christ Jesus. In his plot to kill Jesus, Satan unknowingly played into God's hand, and the kingdom of darkness was utterly destroyed. It was a lethal blow, an ultimate defeat.

So what does the devil do with a fallen kingdom and a death sentence to the Lake of Fire? He is frantic, insane with fury, and seeking to cause as much damage and destruction as possible before he is finally imprisoned. The only tools that Satan has are lies and the illusion of his once "glorious" kingdom of darkness. He is desperate to keep the good news of Jesus' victory from mankind. And for believers, he seeks to twist, distract from

"And having disarmed the powers and authorities, he made a public spectacle of them, triumphing over them by the cross."
Colossians 2:15 NIV

"Since therefore the children share in flesh and blood, he himself likewise partook of the same things, that through death he might destroy the one who has the power of death, that is, the devil, and deliver all those who through fear of death were subject to lifelong slavery."

Hebrews 2:14-15

and steal the truth that Jesus died to give us. Although Satan has been defeated, the fight continues for our allegiance and our obedience. The devil wants our minds, seeking to control our thoughts and then our behaviors. When we disobey God, we are not being true to our new natures. Bill Bright wrote:

God loves you and has a wonderful plan for your life.

Others have added,

Satan hates you and has a terrible plan for your life.

So whose words will we listen to—God's or the devil's? Who will we obey? The devil wants us to think that obedience to God is optional, but it's not. Obedience to God's ways is freedom and life for us, but the devil seeks to keep this truth hidden. He wants us to think that God's laws are merely suggestions, or that they're old-fashioned and restrictive. He constantly seeks to lessen, distort, confuse and trivialize God's commands as he suggests his own deceptive alternatives. Even though we belong to God, we can still choose to walk in the ways of our old sinful flesh.

God says, *"I love you with an everlasting, unconditional love" (Jeremiah 31:3).* The spirit of rejection and unbelief says, *No one will ever love you. Remember what you did? You blew it and God will never accept or love you!*

God says, *"Don't take anything that doesn't belong to you" (Exodus 20:15).* The enemy whispers, *Go ahead and take that item from work; nobody will miss it. This company owes you so much and they've never paid you enough in all your years of service. You deserve it. Besides, where would they be without you?*

God says, *"I have sealed you with my Holy Spirit, established you in the highest position possible and anointed you with power from on high" (2 Corinthians 1:21-22).* Satan says, *You're broken, a nobody, and you can't do anything right. You'll never amount to anything.*

God says, *"Keep the marriage bed holy. Stay true to your husband alone. Don't hurt yourself or him by committing adultery" (Exodus 20:14).* The enemy says, *It's okay, God wants you to be happy. Your husband never loved you anyway. You made a mistake by marrying him and surely this other man is the one you were always meant to be with.*

God says one thing while Satan whispers the opposite. Most believers would never say outright, "I am going to listen to the devil and obey him in this area in my life," but that's exactly what we do in our thoughts and actions. If we aren't paying attention to our thoughts, the lies and deceptions of the enemy are so subtle we can miss them. We may not even realize we're making decisions in the middle of a mind battle! When we listen and obey the voice of the devil instead of God, we are submitting ourselves to the enemy and returning to the captivity of sin. Jesus has already set us free from this bondage through his death and resurrection, but Satan is once again seeking to usurp our God-given authority by luring us into sin. We must be aware of the "plays" the enemy has set up for us. As we wake up from the deception of the enemy, we must take a stand and take back any territory he has gained on us. *"For freedom Christ has set us free; stand firm therefore, and do not submit again to a yoke of slavery" (Galatians 5:1).*

Why We Obey God's Commands

As children of God, we are now a part of His family, and we have the power to say no to sin. Just as in the Garden of Eden, God is very serious about His children obeying His laws because they represent His very best for us. Within His commands are His love, kindness and protection. We must be careful to obey all His commands, not only because He is our Lord and deserves our respect and obedience, but also because obeying His commands keeps us in the safety of His presence, where the evil one cannot mislead and control us.

> *Submit yourselves therefore to God. Resist the devil, and he will flee from you. Draw near to God, and he will draw near to you. Cleanse your hands, you sinners, and purify your hearts, you double-minded. Be wretched and mourn and weep. Let your laughter be turned to mourning and your joy to gloom. Humble yourselves before the Lord, and he will exalt you.* (James 4:7-10)

Obedience to the Father's commands acts like a safety fence all around us. If the devil can get us to believe his lies, stepping out from under the protective covering of God's commands and into sin, then he can gain control and wreak havoc in our lives.

I didn't always understand the significance of God's commands. I felt that some of God's commands were severe, tedious, irrelevant and, quite frankly, optional. This is a common deception of the enemy over the minds of believers. For example, God's warnings not to slander, fear, envy, or withhold forgiveness seemed less important than some of the "big sins"— these seemed excusable, and of course He'd understand if I indulged in them every once in a while. I didn't realize the consequences of my seemingly trivial disobedience, and I needed a renewal of my mind to see the truth. The Commander used my son to teach me why it is so important to obey His commands.

When Kyle was three years old, all he wanted to do was play outside. I was hesitant to let him when his big sisters were at school and not around to watch him. But one day he kept begging, so I finally agreed to let him play outside with strict instructions. I got down to his level, looked him straight in the eyes and very firmly told him he could play anywhere he wanted in our fenced backyard, but under no circumstance was he to go through the gate to the front yard. He readily agreed, and all was well . . . until I heard the doorbell ring! Sure enough, there was my son at the front door, smiling from ear to ear. He was just as proud as he could be that he had found his way *out* of the backyard to the front door and rang the doorbell all by himself, declaring his independence. Well, I wasn't quite so happy. He had disregarded the rules, and I couldn't let it go unpunished. He needed to feel the consequences of his disobedience so that he wouldn't do it again. At his age he couldn't know the dangers that lurked outside the fence—he could get hit by a car, wander off and get lost, or even be abducted. I couldn't expect him to understand, but I could expect him to trust me and obey my instructions.

The same is true of our God. Within the walls of God's commands we find safety, love, blessing and protection. God's best for his people is inside His commandments, not outside.

And now, Israel, what does the Lord your God require of you, but to fear the Lord your God, to walk in all his ways, to love him, to serve the Lord your God with all your heart and with all your soul, and to keep the commandments and statutes of the Lord, which I am commanding you today for your good? (Deuteronomy 10:12-13)

The devil loves to plant negative thoughts in our minds about the pure commands and laws of God. He wants us to doubt God's perfect character and His goodness toward us so that we will reject His ways and chart our own path. Because the devil can't personally curse people whom the Lord has blessed, his only option is to use the same tactics today that he has been using for generations. He casts doubt, suggesting alternatives to God's commands, hoping that we will take the bait. He seeks to lure us outside of the fence of God's safety and protection, taking us captive through worldly temptations and sins that we don't see coming. Once we have sinned against God, either intentionally or unintentionally, we expose ourselves to the open attack of the enemy. Before we can resist the devil, we must first submit to God. We must confess our sins to the Father, repent, and apply the cleansing blood of Jesus to that sin, breaking the mental agreement that we made with the evil one.

To prevent us from shining the light of Christ to the world, Satan seeks to keep us in bondage to the old ways of the flesh. The devil is well acquainted with the Lord's commands, actually using them to set subtle traps to lure the children of God into sin. He knows that God has promised incredible blessings to those who obey His commands, and curses to those who do not.

See, I am setting before you today a blessing and a curse: the blessing, if you obey the commandments of the Lord your God, which I command you today, and the curse, if you do not obey the commandments of the Lord your God, but turn aside from the way that I am commanding you today, to go after other gods that you have not known. (Deuteronomy 11:26-28)

The devil's primary strategy against the believer is to get us to sin and turn away from God's laws, giving him a grip in our lives. He seeks to hijack our authority as believers and control our behavior. The devil is working hard to keep unbelievers blinded to Jesus' salvation and the children of God stuck in sin, ignorant, immature and ineffective in this world. What does it look like when the devil comes to steal, kill and destroy in your life and the lives of those around you? We must study his tactics through the Word of God and study them to see how he is personally attacking us to bring about his desired outcome.

I was peacefully preparing dinner one night when I realized that I'd forgotten to pick up an item at the store. Unfortunately, it was too late to go back and get it. My thoughts began to fill with disappointment at myself for forgetting the one thing that someone had requested. To cope with my feelings of failure, I started blaming others for their fault in the matter. *If only they would have told me sooner,* and *A reminder would have been great too!* My mind was running on what I call "worry auto-pilot." Just then, my daughter came and asked me if she could watch a movie, after I'd already told her no—twice. Her exasperated whine communicated, *My life is so boring . . . I've got nothing to do . . . the only fun thing would be to watch a movie right now.* Her attitude grated on my nerves and I lost my patience, raised my voice and started lecturing her about *her* bad attitude! Then in the same loud, irritated voice, I said, "I am not mad at you!" Abruptly, I stopped and looked at her. I *really* looked at her and she *really* looked at me. We were both being lied to by the enemy. So I said again, much more nicely and with spiritual clarity, "I'm not mad at you, Ella. You are *not* my enemy."

That was a defining moment for me. The Lord removed the veil from my eyes and allowed me to see the well-laid traps of the kingdom of darkness: negativity, anxiety and frustration. Just when I couldn't handle one more thing, someone would step in front of me and receive the full weight of all my frustrations. In this case, it was one of my precious children. My outburst of anger toward her was used by the enemy to feed her lies of disapproval and lack of acceptance from a mother who actually loves and approves of her very much. I could sense that there was a riling spirit repeatedly setting up this "play" against us. I was finally aware of the enemy's tactics. With even greater spiritual clarity I could see that this same "play" had been used on my mother, and could potentially be used against my children when they became parents one day, if I didn't break the cycle.

The Devil Gains a Foothold

Our sin can give the devil an opening into our lives. He tries to get the children of God to take the bait by packaging lies as desirable truth, just like he did with Eve in the Garden of Eden. Sometimes we are deceived and fall into sin unaware. Other times we deliberately choose it. As believers we have the opportunity and privilege to bring our sin to God, confess it and allow the Father to cleanse us from that sin. Then we can immediately return to walking in the power of our new nature. But when we delay and habitually disobey God in a certain area, the devil gains a foothold in our lives.

> *Therefore each of you must put off falsehood and speak truthfully to his neighbor, for we are all members of one body. "In your anger do not sin": Do not let the sun go down while you are still angry, and do not give the devil a foothold.* (Ephesians 4:25-27 NIV)

This passage warns us not to hold on to our anger, but rather repent and confess our sins quickly. As believers it is dangerous to allow a prolonged time of sin in our lives. When we entertain the enticing and often sympathetic lies of these evil spirits, we are actually inviting them into our minds, giving them a foothold. We treat them like welcome guests instead of hostile enemies that are ready to rob us blind. We may not realize it, but we're saying, *Come on in. Make yourself at home. Have a seat; would you care for anything to drink? Let's talk—I'm all ears!* And before we know it, we're engaged in a lengthy conversation with the lies of the enemy—pondering, agreeing, adding our input and chatting like old friends. We embrace these lies as if they are our own original thoughts. Unfortunately, our words and actions soon follow.

In our college years, my husband Craig and I belonged to a church where he worked closely with an older man in ministry. This man treated my husband in a way that wronged and hurt him, and I began entertaining the lies of a spirit of offense and bitterness. It started subtly but quickly grew into the full-fledged sin of unforgivingness. The thoughts I entertained went something like this: *How dare he treat your husband that way! He's supposed to be a godly man and look what he did.* I gave myself the freedom to stew on those angry thoughts, agreeing with the enemy and making these thoughts my own. When I didn't recognize the source of those negative thoughts and take them captive like a true warrior, more lies entered my mind. *I bet other people don't know this side of him.* When people in the congregation spoke highly of him, I'd think, *If others could see his true colors, they wouldn't think he's that great!* Whenever I was around him, the lies and accusations of the enemy poisoned everything this man said, blocking me from hearing anything good. The bitter thoughts flowed quickly: *You've got to be kidding me! How can you talk like a Christian and treat people the way you treated my husband? Practice what you preach, mister!* Fed by the root of bitterness, my thoughts entered even more dangerous territory. I thought up other possible sins this man might be secretly involved in, and I wanted to see him exposed. I wasn't really paying attention to these thoughts, though, and remained unaware of the depth of my resentment until one day when this man's name came up in a private conversation with my husband. Out of my mouth came the most outrageous slam on this man's character. Craig was stunned by my venomous words, and so was I. This was the spiritual wakeup call I needed to alert me to Satan's influence in my mind in this area.

The Foothold Becomes a Stronghold

Without the weapon of repentance and the forgiveness of our sin by the blood of Jesus, the enemy's foothold can become a stronghold. It is a serious thing to slander a brother in Christ, and I was completely and dangerously in the wrong. I had to spend time alone with the Commander and ask Him to search my heart. He showed me the lies I had been embracing and the sin I had fallen into by taking offense and allowing bitterness and resentment to set up camp, opening the door to the sin of slander. If I hadn't repented of my sin and changed my behavior, that sin could have continued to grow, spilling over and poisoning other areas of my life. Left unchecked, this spirit of offense could have gained a massive stronghold, controlling my thoughts and actions and becoming a constant companion throughout the years ahead. The enemy used this stronghold to launch his attacks on my mind, urging me to misunderstand others' intent, taking offense where none was meant and becoming overly sensitive to even the slightest rude comment. I could be mentally tallying up a record of wrongs committed against me, which is sin. *"[Love] does not demand its own way. It is not irritable, and it keeps no record of being wronged"* (1 Corinthians 13:5 NLT).

If I kept believing the devil's lies in this area, I would begin to act on them. Then the enemy would unpack his bags and make himself at home in my life. Once these evil spirits start to gain a stronghold in an area of weakness, they are not polite company. They are rude, bossy, and controlling, and before you know it, they're inviting all of their friends over for a party. Their goal is to introduce more sin, take over other areas of my mind, and gain even more control over me. I need the Commander's help to be aware at the earliest stages when these lies are coming at me, since they may be very subtle at first. So what about when I discover that there is already a spiritual stronghold in some area of my life? What do I do then?

Identifying and Breaking the Stronghold

We need the Lord and the *weapon of discernment* to recognize the enemy's goal in the traps he sets for us. Ask the Commander: What is the nature of the lies coming at me? It could be a spirit that promotes an attitude of complaining, fear, slander, anxiety, rebellion, suicide, gluttony, bitterness, lust, or deception. The enemy studies us. He knows which lies we are most likely to believe, and attacks us accordingly. When we become aware of our sin and God leads us to repent, the enemy doesn't give up easily on the control he had gained in that area. The devil seeks to dominate that area of our minds, ready at any opportune moment to pour out his whispering lies, accusations and deceptions.

In order to destroy a demonic stronghold, we must break the initial agreement that we had with the evil one by repenting and using the weapon of renouncing and declaring. These are internal agreements that we make with the enemy by embracing his lies, allowing him influence in a particular area of our minds. This influence affects our behavior, sometimes without our knowledge. For example, if I subconsciously believe the lie that my worth is directly tied to my success or failure in business instead of in Christ, than anytime something goes wrong in business it feels like a personal attack on my value, opening the door for fear, pride, or anxiety. The enemy has all the ammunition he needs to throw those thoughts of pride in success or insecurity in failure at me to create chaos in my life. Ask the Commander to help you identify the first lie you believed in this area. Claim the work and power of the Cross over that sin, and begin to take back the ground the enemy has taken from you. That can only be done by the weapon of repentance and the forgiveness of our sin by the blood of Jesus Christ. *"In fact, the law requires that nearly everything be cleansed with blood, and without the shedding of blood there is no forgiveness"* (Hebrews 9:22 NIV).

The blood of Jesus Christ breaks the contract with the enemy and frees us from his demonic control. We can also wield the mighty weapon of faith in the promises of God's victory over darkness. We believe that God has already given us the victory in Christ Jesus, and that Satan is defeated in the life of a believer.

Any area of your life that he seeks to control has already been purchased by and claimed for We must fight like might like mighty warriors to take back the footholds and strongholds the devil has occupied in our lives for far too long. This is accomplished by the discernment and power of the Holy Spirit as He enables us to tap into the same power that raised Christ from the dead. This power enables us to breathe deeply of our new nature and reject the ways of our old nature. As we embrace our new self, the old self continually dies off, rendering the influence of demonic activity increasingly less effective. The battle must be won first in our minds by clinging to the turth: *"little children, you are from God and have overcome the, for he who is*

Lie Alert:

Are you thinking . . .

- Is the devil even real?
- I'm sure the devil doesn't even know I exist.
- If he does exist, I'm sure I'm not a big threat.
- Resist the devil? Won't that make him mad at me?
-This is just the way I am, and it certainly has nothing to do with any demonic influence in my life.Christ. *"Or do you not know that your body is a temple of the Holy Spirit within you, whom you have from God? You are not your own, for you were bought with a price. So glorify God in your body"* (1 Cor. 6:19-20)

in you is greater than he who is in the world" (1 John 4:4). The message of this verse alone is powerful enough to take down the greatest of demonic strongholds in our lives.

We need to understand that we are fighting a lying, deceiving, evil presence that works against us with the enthusiastic support of our old nature. He usually targets an area where we have repeatedly operated in the flesh and agreed with the lies of the enemy. *"Submit yourselves therefore to God. Resist the devil, and he will flee from you"* (James 4:7). To rid ourselves of demonic footholds and strongholds in our lives, we must first confess our sin, repent and submit underneath the mighty hand and protection of our great God. Then it is our job to stand firm and resist the evil spirit with our God-given authority in Christ.

Once we have repented of our sin in that area, and reclaimed that ground through the name of Jesus, the attack of the enemy could be even stronger as he seeks to reclaim his lost territory. We need to be ready and geared up for the battle, armed with our spiritual weapons in order to stand firm against the enemy.

The authority of the believer has been purchased at the Cross. It is a God-given weapon to help us resist the devil and be overcomers like Jesus. This authority is ours the moment we are born into the kingdom of heaven, regardless of our physical age or experience. One evening I was enjoying a little uninterrupted quiet time after tucking in the kids, when my 5-year-old got up and sheepishly approached me. "Mommy," he whispered, "there's something scary in my room." Tired from a long day and wanting him back in bed as soon as possible, I began to reassure him that there was nothing to be afraid of. I reminded him that Jesus was with him, and told him to "Just close your eyes and it will be morning before you know it." That's when I heard the Commander's prompting to be spiritually alert. I realized that perhaps there really was something scary in his room, an evil spirit attacking his mind and causing fear. I told my son that because he had given his life to Jesus, he could go back into his room and use Jesus' authority over the devil and tell that scary thing to leave in Jesus' name. His eyes widened and he said, "Okay, but will you come with me?" Hand in hand we went into his room, and he repeated these words after me, "Scary thing, get out of my room, in Jesus' name." I explained to him that it is not because of us but because of Jesus that the evil spirit has to leave. I tucked him back in bed and told him, "If the scary thing comes back, keep telling it to leave in the name of Jesus." But it didn't. Kyle slept peacefully the rest of the night.

A Stronghold of Defeat

Another area the Commander showed me the enemy's influence was in my habitual mindset of defeat. In fact, a stronghold of defeat had gained so much control in my life that it had become my natural way of thinking. The Lord began to highlight a pattern of unfinished responsibilities or projects in my life. I'd start strong on a project with plenty of passion and drive. But about three-quarters of the way through, I'd experience overwhelming or distracting thoughts: *Oh, I don't want to do this anymore! This is too hard. I have better things to do. I'll never get this done! I can finish this later.* Whether it was a simple basket of laundry to fold, a closet to clean or a book to read, I would usually quit just short of completion. Thinking back, I began to notice this pattern woven throughout my life in big and small areas. Sometimes I'd start a project with an apathetic mindset: *I know I'll never finish this! Oh, well!* At other times, I chose not to even begin something for fear of the inevitable feeling of failure when I didn't follow through. The Commander allowed me to see the long pattern of well-placed attacks on my mind, in the middle of a project or just short of the finish line in numerous areas in my life.

The attack was even more intense on the things that God had called me to do—like finishing this book! Even now as I complete these last few chapters, I struggle with thoughts that tell me to quit writing it. *You're a terrible writer. No one will ever understand you. What can you say that hasn't already been said before? You're really just a pathetic NOBODY who can't do anything of real value!* When I indulge these thoughts of defeat, I can envision this book forever tucked away in a file on my computer, unfinished and never making it to print. I have to battle these thoughts with the powerful weapon of the Word of God. *"Being confident of this, that he who began a good work in you will carry it on to completion until the day of Christ Jesus" (Philippians 1:6 NIV).* By the way, if you're reading this, it is proof that our God can overcome the spirit of defeat in my life. He can do it in yours, too!

The Commander helped me realize that this defeatist mindset was more than just a personality trait or a character flaw—it was a demonic influence in my life. I had repeatedly stumbled in this area in the past by listening to the whispering lies of defeat, and it had become a stronghold for the enemy. This understanding has helped me to be able to fight and reclaim the area of defeat and turn it into victory. I still experience occasional attacks as the spirit of defeat seeks to regain its stolen ground. When this happens, it can be intense, but by using the weapon of faith I choose to believe that defeatism is NOT a part of my new nature! *"I can do all things through him who strengthens me" (Philippians 4:13).*

We may find that the devil focuses his attacks on us during certain times of the year or seasons in our lives. The Commander revealed to me that the dread and depression I experience almost every time I return from a trip or vacation is the result of demonic activity. I'm thankful to arrive home, but I just want to hide from all the normal responsibilities of my everyday life. I become overwhelmed with feelings of abnormal sadness and fatigue. I'm unmotivated, and the thought of facing people makes me want to hide. This may seem like a common response to the end of a vacation, but the Commander has shown me that there's something more at play here. What is the fruit of it—good or bad? Is it really normal or is it a well-timed attack from the enemy? Looking back through my life, I can remember many instances when this "cloud of darkness" settled over me the first few days after returning from a trip, leaving me vulnerable to further attacks of the enemy. Now that I know about it, I can anticipate it and fight it with the weapons the Commander provides. The weapons of thankfulness, endurance and the name of Jesus have been helpful to me in this battle.

Author's Note: As I edit this chapter a year after I wrote the first draft, I can tell you that the Lord has completely set me free from the cloud of darkness that use to loom over me after a trip. I hardly remember what that was like anymore! It gives me hope, and it encourages me to ask the Commander: *What are some other areas in my life where an evil presence has repeatedly attacked me? Show me and help me fight for freedom.*

What Are Satan's Favorite "Plays" Against You?

I pray that you will learn to identify the areas of demonic influence in your life as well. Ask the Commander to help you discern the "plays" the enemy has targeted you with, both now and in the past. At first you may think that these areas are simply a normal part of your life or just a part of your personality, but the Commander can help you discover which areas are actually the result of demonic influence. It is my prayer that as I've shared a few of the areas where the evil one has sought to influence or control me, the Lord will reveal to you some areas in your own life that need to be fought for and reclaimed for the glory of God. Satan is defeated and we must not fear him, but we must be aware of his tactics against us. Where has the enemy been operating undetected in your life? The Commander will help you identify them and lead you into victory! He has already defeated Satan and the kingdom of darkness is already crumbling. Remember, His divine power has given you everything you need for life and godliness.

Prayer:

Dear Father,
Thank You for defeating the devil and setting me free to live for You. Show me the areas where I am still in bondage by believing the lying voice of the evil one. I long to be free and grow increasingly into more areas of freedom. Set me on a path where You reveal one by one the areas the enemy still has influence in my life. Show me the key lies that keep me in submission to him instead of You. As I repent of those lies I ask You, Jesus, to sever all those ties and fill me with Your Spirit instead.
In Jesus' name, Amen.

Action Steps: Journal your prayers, answers and all the things the Commander reveals to you.

1. How do you feel about studying the devil? Does it make you nervous? Do you think it's sinful to talk about or study the devil in Scripture? Bring any concerns you have to the Lord and ask Him to help you.

2. Now that you know that the devil is defeated and subject to your authority in Christ, how does this change the way you think about him? Do you experience less fear?

3. Ask the Lord to show you the areas in your life where there has been demonic influence. Are there any "plays" the evil one runs on you? What are the whispered lies of the enemy in those situations?

4. Take a moment and ask Jesus to speak truth into those areas of your life. Listen for His voice. Ask Him how He feels about the enemy's attacks toward you. Are there any instructions He is giving you?

Chapter Thirteen
Identifying Generational Strongholds

I am the Lord your God, who brought you out of the
land of Egypt, out of the house of slavery. You shall
have no other gods before me. You shall not make for
yourself a carved image, or any likeness of anything
that is in heaven above, or that is on the earth beneath,
or that is in the water under the earth. You shall not
bow down to them or serve them; for I the Lord your
God am a jealous God, visiting the iniquity of the
fathers on the children to the third and fourth
generation of those who hate me, but showing steadfast
love to thousands of those who love me
and keep my commandments.
Deuteronomy 5:6-10

When my oldest daughter was in grade school she began to
develop frequent stomachaches. I noticed they became
heightened when she was anxious about something. At the age
of seven she was having panic attacks just from thinking about a
class project or a short presentation at school. I tried to help her
by talking her through it, but it soon became evident that this
paralyzing fear wasn't coming from a rational cause. We prayed
and memorized battle verses, but the panic attacks continued.

Before long her daily stomachaches started keeping her from eating properly. She could only eat small amounts of food at a time, and within minutes of swallowing her first bite, she was doubled over in pain. This went on for months. We took her to the pediatrician, and then to a specialist who ordered tests to find the cause of the pain, but the diagnosis was always inconclusive. The specialist finally told us that many kids have mysterious stomachaches, and the best way to deal with it was to teach her how to cope with the pain. As a mother, this advice was simply not good enough! I hated to see my little girl in so much pain. I used my weapon of crying out to the Lord for help. *God, You know everything. What is going on with my little girl? Why is she in so much torment and pain? Please help us! Please come to our aid!*

One day I came across a verse that talked about the sins of the fathers being visited upon the children. The Commander stopped me right there and immediately brought Annika's stomachaches to my attention. I was seeking an answer regarding my daughter's upset stomach, but this wasn't the answer I was expecting. *God, are you saying that my daughter is suffering because of some sort of sin in my life? How could this verse apply to me? I don't hate You, God—I love You!* I was surprised at this idea, but I needed an answer so I asked the Lord, *If this is true, please reveal this sin to me.* During the next few months, the Lord started connecting some thoughts for me. He reminded me that when Annika was a baby she was extremely colicky and was often inconsolable in her discomfort. The Lord also brought to my memory that when I was a young girl, I used to get stomachaches at extremely stressful times in my life. I had completely forgotten about that! I also had a vague memory of my grandmother taking a drop of antacid on her first bite of every meal. She would laugh along with her grandkids at her strange habit, saying, "I like food, but it doesn't like me." It slowly began to dawn on me that my daughter wasn't the first one in the family to suffer from physical symptoms of stress and anxiety. All of the evidence led to the realization that the sin of fear and anxiety was rampant in my life and in the lives of my family on my mother's side.

It wasn't just my daughter—this sin of worry, fear and anxiety affected multiple members of my family. This particular spirit of fear had attacked my daughter before she was even aware of spiritual attacks. Likewise, I was living with constant thoughts of worry, fear and stress that were so normal to me that I didn't even know it was sin. This demonic stronghold over my mind was so ingrained in me that I didn't realize there was another way of living. My unrealized and unintentional sin had left the door wide open for the spirit of fear to launch an early attack upon my young daughter. It is important that we recognize the work of the enemy over our family line and seek to stop these generational strongholds through repentance before they are passed on to our children and grandchildren. I would never say that I hated God, but my actions spoke louder than my words as I repeatedly bowed down and served the spirit of fear. Much of the truth the Lord has revealed to me in this chapter has been born out of the desperate cry for my children to be released from the bondage of fear, rejection, worthlessness, negativity and control. With Annika, the Lord was faithful to lead us every step, using our spiritual weapons and battling through with discernment and truth. It wasn't easy, but today she is totally free from the anxiety that led to those debilitating stomachaches. And God used this struggle in her life at an early age to train her to run to Him, rely on His instructions and fight for victory.

Generational Strongholds

A generational stronghold can be defined as the demonic activity over a family unit or bloodline that seeks to have dominion from generation to generation. In many cases, these forces of darkness have gained access to a particular family line through unrecognized sin of a member of that family. It is true that a believer cannot be completely taken over by a demonic presence, but that doesn't mean that believers can't be harassed or even controlled by an evil presence in a certain area of their lives. We have the Holy Spirit within us, and we are instructed to abide in Christ just as He abides in us, walking in our new nature. We are to stop sinning and remain in the unconditional love of God. However, if we sin repeatedly in a certain area, we give the devil a foothold, creating an opening for demonic control in our lives. Even if the sin is unknown or unintentional, its ongoing presence in our lives can build up an evil stronghold which gives the enemy the liberty to attack our descendants to the third and fourth generation.

The kingdom of darkness takes this word of the Lord very seriously. Scripture says that when a man sins and goes against God's law, that sin is "visited" on his children to the extent of the third and fourth generation of those who hate Him. This "visiting" is not the same as suffering the consequences of our ancestors' sin. *"The soul who sins shall die. The son shall not suffer for the iniquity of the father, nor the father suffer for the iniquity of the son. The righteousness of the righteous shall be upon himself, and the wickedness of the wicked shall be upon himself"* (Ezekiel 18:20). It is clear that each person is accountable for what he does, and the responsibility for the sin that he commits will be upon himself alone. However, that doesn't restrict the long-term effects of the father's sin upon his children. When we think of the word "visit," we can think of someone coming to our house for a social call, hoping to come into our home. They want to come in and be with us, but we have a choice in the matter. We can either open the door and let them in, or keep it shut and tell them to find another place to stay.

Let's say a grandparent of ours repeatedly sinned in the area of jealousy. This sin became a mental stronghold for them, and they never acknowledged or repented of it. Now, during our lives, a spirit of jealousy may be ready and waiting, seeking an opportunity to present us with the same lies and temptations that our grandparent fell victim to years ago. This may start when we are young, occurring over and over (as in the case of my daughter and the attack of fear in her life), or it may wait several years for a surprise attack. Sometimes these harassing spirits go dormant for a while, waiting for an opportune moment to attack with their lies just like Satan did to Jesus. *"And when the devil had ended every temptation, he departed from him [Jesus] until an opportune time" (Luke 4:13).*

When I was confronted with an intense mind battle several years ago, I experienced this firsthand. I started being plagued with adulterous thoughts. I was horrified and recognized immediately that these were not my own thoughts or desires. It is important that we know that not every thought that enters our minds is ours! Being happily married and totally in love with my husband, I couldn't understand why I was being bombarded by these appalling notions. After a few days of battling these lies, I pleaded with the Commander to show me where this was coming from and why this was happening to me. He brought to my mind one of my ancestors who had cheated on her husband, having an affair that resulted in emotional pain and regret for the entire family. As I pondered this, it dawned on me that I was probably being hounded with the *exact same lies* she entertained and acted upon all those years ago. Even though I didn't commit her sin, this adulterous spirit was "visiting" me, seeking to gain an opening in my life. To close that door, the Commander instructed me to repent of her sin just as He instructed the Israelites to repent of their fathers' sin.

> *"But if they will confess their sins and the sins of their fathers — their treachery against me and their hostility toward me, which made me hostile toward them so that I sent them into the land of their enemies — then when their uncircumcised hearts are humbled and they pay for their sin, I will remember my covenant with Jacob and my covenant with Isaac and my covenant with Abraham, and I will remember the land." (Leviticus 26:40-42 NIV)*

I had to repent of her sin and renounce the work of the enemy over my life as a result of that sin, and break the hold in the power and authority of the name of Jesus.

As I've said before, half the battle is recognizing the battle; the other half is knowing what to do about it. We must be aware of the enemy's schemes over our family line so that we recognize when the attack is being launched over our minds. Let's say the doorbell rings, and we look through the crack in the door and find the whispering lies of *slander, gossip* and *complaint* standing on our doorstep. They've got their bags packed, just waiting for us to open the door so they can move in and take over our lives. Because a certain sin has established a generational stronghold in our family line, it can seek to "visit" over and over again, attempting to gain a new stronghold in our generation by wearing us down. We can resist the temptation and refuse sin an entrance, or we can give in to that sin and open the door, allowing Satan to gain a foothold. That foothold can quickly develop into a stronghold—Satan has enjoyed the hospitality of our ancestors, and he boldly expects it to continue.

Each one of us is responsible for our own decisions. The concept of generational sin is not a guarantee that we will automatically succumb to the sins of our forefathers, but it does mean we may be more prone to those patterns of sin. We have a choice when temptation comes. In the case of Cain, sin was hiding outside his door seeking to grab him, but he still had the choice to rule over it. *"The Lord said to Cain, "Why are you angry, and why has your face fallen? If you do well, will you not be accepted? And if you do not do well, sin is crouching at the door. Its desire is for you, but you must rule over it"* (Genesis 4:6-7). We must be aware of this principle in the unseen realm so we are not taken off guard by the recurring generational sins of our forefathers. We can be more predisposed to fall victim to a particular sin in our lives because it has been allowed to "visit" us repeatedly due to the unrepented sin of our ancestors. The enemy, desiring to keep his evil presence in the family line, will continue to look for an entrance into our lives until the generational stronghold is recognized, broken by repentance, and renounced by the authority of the name of Jesus Christ.

King David's Bloodline

The Bible tells the tragic history of King David and his family line. We see how the sins that David committed were repeated in the lives of various members of his family. In 2 Samuel 11, King David committed a sin that greatly affected not only himself and his family but ultimately the entire nation of Israel. King David coveted another man's wife, Bathsheba, and committed adultery with her. When Bathsheba became pregnant, King David plotted to cover up his sin. Under false pretense and posing as a friend, David devised a plan to murder Bathsheba's husband and take her as his own wife. As a consequence of David's sin, God pronounced a curse on his family that his descendants would be plagued by violence and war. His sins of covetousness, sexual impurity, conspiracy, betrayal and murder were "visited" upon his children as the same sins showed up repeatedly in their lives. His sons always had the choice to do what was right, but they opened the door to the sin crouching outside, committing many of the same mistakes and sins as their father David.

With each of his sons the circumstances were slightly different, but the same type of sin was involved. Notice how many times this grouping of sins committed by David with Bathsheba shows up again in the lives of his children. David's oldest son Amnon coveted his half-sister Tamar, and secretly plotted to lure her into his bedroom, posing as a doting brother; he then betrayed her by raping her and leaving her destitute. Covetousness, manipulation, betrayal and sexual immorality were all evident in this situation. Another of David's sons, Absalom, hated his brother Amnon for what he had done to Tamar, and two years later he took his revenge. Absalom deceived his father into thinking that all was forgiven and threw a party inviting Amnon, but at the height of the celebration Absalom had Amnon murdered. Absalom was estranged from King David for years and bitterness built up in his heart. Furthermore, Absalom coveted David's throne and conspired with leading men to betray his father and take it by force. King David was driven from his palace while Absalom committed adultery with

David's remaining concubines. Absalom was ultimately murdered and David was restored to his throne, but not without great loss to king and nation. King Solomon, David's son and successor, also fell victim to sexual indulgence that led to him taking 700 wives and 300 concubines. These forbidden foreign wives turned his heart away from the one true God, taking the entire nation down a path of idol worship for generations to come.

A Stronghold Gains Power from Generation to Generation

A snowball effect results when sin breeds sin. Once a particular demonic stronghold is in place, it seeks an opportunity to strengthen its hold, inviting more sin and increasing control. The following verse discusses unclean spirits with different levels of strength, and their tendency to band together in order to double their efforts.

> *When the unclean spirit has gone out of a person, it passes through waterless places seeking rest, but finds none. Then it says, "I will return to my house from which I came." And when it comes, it finds the house empty, swept, and put in order. **Then it goes and brings with it seven other spirits more evil than itself, and they enter and dwell there,** and the last state of that person is worse than the first. So also will it be with this evil generation. (Matthew 12:43-45, **emphasis mine**)*

We see this in cases where demonic strongholds have flourished in a family line for countless generations. Once an evil presence is well established in a family line, it seeks to expand to other areas of sin and demonic oppression in the family so that the next generation becomes even more wicked than the last, bringing even more of the righteous wrath of God on the bloodline.

*And when you tell this people all these words, and they say to you, "Why has the Lord pronounced all this great evil against us? What is our iniquity? What is the sin that we have committed against the Lord our God?" then you shall say to them: "Because your fathers have forsaken me, declares the Lord, and have gone after other gods and have served and worshiped them, and have forsaken me and have not kept my law, **and because you have done worse than your fathers**, for behold, every one of you follows his stubborn, evil will, refusing to listen to me. Therefore I will hurl you out of this land into a land that neither you nor your fathers have known, and there you shall serve other gods day and night, for I will show you no favor." (Jeremiah 16:10-13, **emphasis** mine)*

God's Provision is Our New Bloodline— the Blood of Jesus

Our Savior provided a way of escape for us by changing our family tree, or "bloodline," spiritually speaking. Even though many of us had excellent earthly fathers, they were powerless to keep us from inheriting their own sinful natures. That is something only a perfect, sinless Father God could do. Because of Jesus, we now belong to the family of God, where every member of the family has been declared justified, righteous, and holy in His sight. *"For those whom he foreknew he also predestined to be conformed to the image of his Son, in order that he might be the firstborn among many brothers" (Romans 8:29).* We are born of God, and Jesus is the firstborn among us. We belong to His family, and God is our Father.

As obedient children, do not be conformed to the passions of your former ignorance, but as he who called you is holy, you also be holy in all your conduct, since it is written, "You shall be holy, for I am holy." And if you call on him as Father who judges impartially according to each one's deeds, conduct yourselves with fear throughout the time of your exile, knowing that you were ransomed from the futile ways inherited from your forefathers, not with perishable things

such as silver or gold, but with the precious blood of Christ,
like that of a lamb without blemish or spot. (1 Peter 1:14-19)

We no longer have to follow the sinful ways passed down to us by our forefathers, because we have a new Father and the blood of Jesus Christ runs in our royal veins. We have inherited His holiness and have been empowered to walk in that holiness even as we live as exiles in this fallen world. This is what the Savior accomplished for us in our fight against the world, the flesh and the devil. Our flesh was corrupt and spiritually dead, but we have been given a new nature and new life. The enemy visits our corrupt bloodline with the sins of our fathers, but we now belong to a new family with the one perfect, holy God as our Father. There is hope for us because through the precious blood of Jesus we have overcome this world and its ruler, the devil. The death and resurrection of Jesus totally destroys the sin contract and subtle agreements we have made with the enemy regarding our sin. And with the authority we have been given in Christ Jesus, we have the power to throw off these oppressive spirits and their whispering lies to reclaim the ground the enemy has taken from us.

There is no forgiveness of sin without the blood of Christ. *"Indeed, under the law almost everything is purified with blood, and without the shedding of blood there is no forgiveness of sins" (Hebrews 9:22).* God has provided a solution to the enemy's grip over us: The blood of Jesus cleanses us from all our sin.

> *But if we walk in the light, as he is in the light, we have fellowship with one another, and the blood of Jesus his Son cleanses us from all sin. If we say we have no sin, we deceive ourselves, and the truth is not in us. If we confess our sins, he is faithful and just to forgive us our sins and to cleanse us from all unrighteousness. If we say we have not sinned, we make him a liar, and his word is not in us. (1 John 1:7-10)*

In listening to and agreeing with the lies of the enemy, we make a mental contract with him, shaking hands with him and letting him influence our thoughts and actions, but it is an influence he has no right to have. When we recognize and agree with God that those thoughts and actions are sin, confessing and repenting of those sins, the shed blood of Jesus cleanses us from all unrighteousness and dissolves our "agreement" with the presence of evil in our lives.

The weapons of confession and repentance are absolutely necessary to break the generational strongholds of sin. When we confess and repent of our sin and the sins of our forefathers, Christ Jesus forgives the sin and casts it far from us. Then the enemy no longer has the liberty to "visit" us or our children. The contract is broken and the curse of sin is lifted because of Christ's death and resurrection. Once again, obedience to God's commands and staying inside the safety fence of His love and protection are God's best for us. *"Repent therefore, and turn again, that your sins may be blotted out, that times of refreshing may come from the presence of the Lord" (Acts 3:19).* We are commanded to be obedient in everything so that Satan won't be able to outwit us.

> *The reason I wrote you was to see if you would stand the test and be obedient in everything. If you forgive anyone, I also forgive him. And what I have forgiven — if there was anything to forgive — I have forgiven in the sight of Christ for your sake, in order that Satan might not outwit us. For we are not unaware of his schemes. (2 Corinthians 2:9-11)*

The Commander will give us insight into the devil's ways and schemes as we walk in close fellowship with Him. All who belong to the family of God love to abide in Christ and do the will of their true Father.

Identifying the Generational Strongholds over Our Bloodline

Disobedience to God's commands brings devastation upon us and our children. These generational strongholds must be identified and reclaimed by the blood of Jesus Christ. Some of these strongholds (violence, depression, suicide, lying, physical or verbal abuse, stealing, addictions, pornography) are obvious, showing up again and again in different members of the family. There are also the less-obvious generational sins—strongholds of pride, anger, selfishness, suicidal thoughts, unbelief, self-sufficiency and hatred. We need to identify the sins and destructive mindsets that have been passed down to us by our forefathers and repent of those sins, finding renewed life in forgiveness. Just because we can't see the spiritual realm doesn't make it any less real. Satan's kingdom is well-organized and intricately ordered, with the demons assigned specific duties and levels of rank.

> *Put on the full armor of God so that you can take your stand against the devil's schemes. For our struggle is not against flesh and blood, but against the rulers, against the authorities, against the powers of this dark world and against the spiritual forces of evil in the heavenly realms. (Ephesians 6:11-12 NIV)*

They are well acquainted with the family tree and are familiar with the sins of our ancestors. These evil spirits seek to build a continued presence over the bloodline. While we may not know their exact battle plan, we can see the evidence of their attacks as they attempt to gain access to the descendants in the family line. They are constantly seeking influence and control, targeting both children and adults with attacks based on birth order, gender, personality or any other characteristic which provides an opportune moment. Without the intervention of Jesus Christ and the power of the Cross, each generation becomes more and more controlled by evil, acting increasingly wickedly toward God.

My Personal Generational Strongholds

With the guidance of the Commander, I have become aware of areas of sin in my family line that are more than just coincidence. The weapon of discernment has allowed me to notice behaviors and attitudes in myself and my children that at first glance may seem like just a part of our personalities, but are actually demonic activity in disguise. I'd like to share a few of these with you, starting with the stronghold of gluttony. This might not necessarily be constant overeating, but rather an obsession and a habit of indulgence regarding food. Not everyone in my family is affected by this but it definitely has a strong vein running through my family line, and I was "visited" by this mindset early on. Some people eat to live, and some *live* to eat. I grew up with the second definition! Even now when we gather for holidays, we plan in advance the delicious meals that we're going to be eating. It's not so much about the quantity of the food as it is about the quality. We love to eat *good* food, and we all have our favorites. There's nothing wrong with enjoying a good meal, but we get preoccupied with food planning, food preparation, food presentation—food, food, food!

Although this way of thinking about food has been passed down to me, I have personally embraced it wholeheartedly, and for a long time I thought this was a normal way of thinking. It was surprising to me to discover how a friend of mine regards food. She could eat a bowl of rice every night for dinner and be just fine. I jokingly tease that she's no fun to go out to lunch with because her attitude toward food is more about function than pleasure. It seems pretty boring to me, but there's a flip side— her appetite and cravings for food do not control her. She is free from that type of bondage and idolatry—the god of food. Even though I adopted this mindset from my family, I can't simply blame them and say this is just the way I am. I must take responsibility for how I have sinned in my gluttonous mindset toward food.

Food brings me great joy, but it is a false joy. The subtle and evil trade-off is that it also controls me. So often a sin that has been passed down from generation to generation is a sin we're simultaneously fighting on three fronts—the world, the flesh and the devil. The world repeatedly lures us toward a particular sin; our flesh continually craves and takes control in this area; and the devil persistently "visits" us, ambushing us with his venomous lies. Let's study this three-pronged attack, using the example of my battle against the stronghold of gluttony.

World: The country that I live in is a man vs. food, super-sized culture, promoting as much of any type of food one could want. All I have to do is drive across town and I have countless choices of food to eat, including my favorites: the burger-and-fries diner downtown, the authentic Mexican dive with the monster burritos, the best pizzeria in town, and oh—don't even get me started on the bakeries! Yes, I know I have a problem. When the Commander calls me to fasting and prayer for a period of time it can cause borderline depression for me because food brings me so much (false) joy.

Flesh: I also fight my own sinful nature in the area of gluttony. Growing up, I looked forward to a Little Debbie snack every day after school. My mom, sisters and I all enjoyed this special treat as we sat around the table and talked about our day. My flesh readily embraced food as the answer to all my problems. The Commander showed me that while I was processing the moments of my day, whether they were good, bad, boring, embarrassing, or exciting, I was always savoring a Little Debbie snack. The enemy obtained an increasingly strong hold on me in this area as I learned to associate the processing of my emotions with comfort eating. I learned this habit as a little girl, but I still have a tendency to do the same thing today. I know now that anytime I am bored, sad, anxious, or even wanting to celebrate, the old Kori wants to turn to food instead of God.

Devil: From the very beginning of my life, a vile spirit of gluttony has been crouching at my door, seeking an entrance and tempting me with thoughts like, *Oh you poor thing, it's too bad that happened to you. You deserve a treat!* Or, *Why don't you make yourself a nice cup of hot chocolate? That will make you feel better.* Or perhaps, *You need to celebrate this—let's order pizza!* Entertaining and repeatedly acting on these "helpful suggestions" allowed the sin of gluttony to gain a grip on me, and if I had remained unaware, it could have continued to control me.

The deceiving spirits lured me with the false god of food, manipulating me to turn to this idol—instead of Jesus—as the answer. It began as a foothold and through the years became a significant stronghold. Each time I chose to listen to Satan and his lies, I rejected God and His truth. For far too long I sinned against God and allowed the spirit of gluttony more and more control in this area. There's no way I can gain freedom from this except through the gift of repentance and the forgiveness of my sins. I must believe that the blood of Jesus breaks the demonic influence gained over me when I agreed with Satan for years that food is the answer to everything. With the sinful agreement broken, I can then take back the ground that the enemy has occupied for far too long in my mentality about food. But it is and will continue to be a battle. I must use my weapons of renouncing and declaring: I must continually renounce the lie that food will make me happy and is the answer to all my problems, and faithfully declare the truth that Jesus is my joy and the fulfillment to all my desires.

A second generational stronghold is the mindset of negativity, evidenced by the "glass half-empty" perspective that I can see running through my family. Some of my family members are more vulnerable to the lies of the enemy in this area than others. This stronghold comes with thoughts of, *Poor me. Not again! What a terrible day! This is too hard. Why does everything bad always happen to me? Everyone's against me!* Disappointment, annoyance, exasperation, dissatisfaction and even sadness accompany these thoughts. One of the benefits of godly discernment is the awareness of not only the demonic attacks over our own minds, but also the attacks against our children. I discovered this firsthand when this generational stronghold targeted one of my daughters. I can recognize its attack just by observing her behavior. It comes and goes, seeking to gradually gain a hold on her. When these thoughts come over her mind, it's like a whirlwind of lies that blinds her from seeing anything good in her life. It's so strong that she can't even listen to reason, sinking in a pit of negativity. I wish I could break this hold over her, but it's already gained some ground in her young life. This is her battle. But as her mother I can see that this is not who she is; this is not a part of her new nature in Christ Jesus. This is an attack on the joy and peace that Jesus died to give her. Even though she may not be fully aware of what is going on, the Commander is allowing these attacks so that He can train her even at this very young age to recognize these negative thoughts and take them captive. In the flesh I would love to stop these attacks; however, the Commander is teaching me how to fight beside her, interceding for her in prayer and training her how to walk through these mind battles with her God-given spiritual weapons. As much as I hate to see these attacks of the enemy on my children, I know that they will need every ounce of training the Commander sees fit to give them to grow strong and firm as warriors in the armies of God. The truth will set her free.

My family has also been targeted by a generational stronghold in the area of rejection. I can definitely see it in my own life and in the reactions and responses of other family members. It is not like we all took a class on how to misinterpret situations and people—whether in words, behavior, or in actions—which we tend to personalize as direct attacks on our character. Looking back across my family, I can quickly identify this pattern of thinking that surfaces repeatedly. One of my daughters has been attacked by this mindset since she was very small. She consistently misunderstands or misreads a situation with thoughts of rejection: *They don't like me. She won't play with me. They are excluding me. I never get to go to Grandma's house. Everybody hates the picture I colored.* She accuses others of rejecting her before they even get the chance! When she thinks that someone may not like her, she often responds in a nasty, self-protecting way. Her attitude alone can make people reject her, thus making the perceived rejection a reality. I've seen this mental stronghold attack her again and again, skewing her perspective and causing the enemy's thoughts to come out of her mouth as if they were her own. These lies of rejection are coupled with hurt, anger and defiance. But, like all of us who fight against our personal spiritual strongholds, this is not who she is! This is the old nature believing the lies of the enemy. The truth is that she is accepted, loved and wanted by her family and by her Creator. As with her sister, the Lord enables me to identify the moments when these attacks are happening and spoon feed her the truth of her identity in Christ. This is her battle, but she is not alone in it. The truth will set her free!

Blessings of God to a Thousand Generations

The curse has been lifted. The Cross changed everything for us. God has mercy on the disobedient and pours out His unconditional love on the obedient.

> *You shall not bow down to them or serve them; for I the Lord your God am a jealous God, visiting the iniquity of the fathers on the children to the third and fourth generation of those who hate me,* **but showing steadfast love to thousands of those who love me and keep my commandments.** *(Deuteronomy 5:9-10,* **emphasis** *mine)*

In His mercy, He limits the visiting of iniquity of the sinner to extend only to the third and fourth generation of their descendants. But notice the outpouring of blessing He bestows upon the future generations of those who love Him and keep His commands. For the obedient children of God, what comes knocking at the door of our descendants is God's love, gifts and blessings. This is not limited to the third and fourth generations but extends to a thousand generations for those who love Him. That includes our spiritual heritage as well, our new family tree, the bloodline of Jesus Christ. Our love and obedience to the Father will affect and influence our brothers and sisters in Christ for years or even centuries to come.

We must never forget that our battle is not only about us. Our obedience or disobedience to God is crucial to future generations in the body of Christ. We have the power through the choices we make to bring God's blessings to thousands of generations. Likewise, we could personally be receiving God's favor, love and blessings because of other believers' acts of obedience and faithfulness to God that go back ten, a hundred or even a thousand generations. In my case, the love of God and the obedience to His commands of one of my unknown ancestors may very well have played into the blessing of being born into a home where Jesus was exalted, worshiped and taught. Some things we just won't know this side of heaven.

You may be influencing thousands simply by the decisions you make in the secret battlefield of your mind. The stakes are high when it comes to recognizing and reclaiming these areas of generational strongholds. You must believe the truth that you fight as a holy, righteous victor, because *that is who you are*. No matter how difficult or overwhelming the generational strongholds of the enemy may seem, the truth is that our Father has set you free!

Prayer:

Dear Father,
Thank You for the gift of family. Thank You for all the love, care and blessings that have been given to me through my family. Help me honor them and at the same time take an honest look at how the enemy has influenced the members of my family in ways that have negatively affected me. Lord, show me these things so that I may be set free to walk in truth. I wait for You to expose the enemy in the situations of my life, connecting the dots and revealing the ways You want to bring about the healing I need so that I may live for You.
In Jesus' name, Amen.

Action Steps: Journal your prayers, answers and all the things the Commander reveals to you.

1. Ask the Lord to bring to your mind any areas of sin that are evident in the lives of your family members that still affect you today.

2. Pay attention to any battles that keep resurfacing in your life this week. Ask the Lord to show you any patterns among your parents or grandparents that are similar to your thoughts and behaviors. Ask Him to guide you into truth and show you the best weapons to fight with.

3. Are there any battles you are experiencing right now where you have to fight the world, your flesh and the evil one all at the same time?

4. When the Lord reveals some generational sin, repent of that sin. You may use this prayer:

Dear Lord,
Thank You for revealing to me this area of sinful dysfunction. This is not who I am and not consistent with my new nature. I repent of _____ and the sin of my ancestors and receive Your full and free forgiveness. I command any and all demonic influences who have gained access to my family line through that sin to leave me (and my children) alone and never return. Lord, come into those broken and vacant places and fill me with Your Holy Spirit. Instead of struggling with that sin, I desire the fruit of the spirit to flow out of my life in Christ.
In Jesus' name, Amen.

Chapter Fourteen
Identifying Territorial Strongholds

Go therefore and make disciples of all nations, baptizing them in the name of the Father and of the Son and of the Holy Spirit, teaching them to observe all that I have commanded you. And behold, I am with you always, to the end of the age.
Matthew 28:19-20

I was a woman on a mission: I had a short span of three hours to visit seven stores. Having left my kids with the babysitter, I was ready to plow through the list of stores, finish my shopping and get home just in time to make supper. Two of those stores landed me at the local mall. Unfortunately they were at opposite ends of the mall, so after finishing in the first store, I walked the length of the mall to get to the other. As I passed each storefront, I could see my reflection in the glass. My thoughts took a turn as I evaluated my appearance. *Wow. You look like a worn-out mommy. Why didn't you fix up a little before you went out in public?* I looked around and noticed the newest fashions displayed. *When did you get so far out of style? Look at your outfit. You've had that shirt for what—three years? Why don't you buy something new for a change?* I passed a hair salon and glanced in to see a row of ladies getting their hair done. *When was the last time you took the time to get your hair cut and styled? Did you even **do** your hair today? You should take better care of yourself.*

That mind battle stuck with me the rest of the evening and into the next day as I subconsciously pondered these negative thoughts. I was content at home taking care of my family and enjoying life, never feeling that my appearance had become worn out or lacking in any way because I didn't have the latest fashions. I was satisfied with my appearance until I stepped foot in the mall. From one end of the mall to the other I was assaulted by lying spirits of discontent and self-awareness, all pointing to my "need" to buy something to make me feel better about myself. At the time, I was not aware that specific types of evil spirits could be assigned to certain places with a particular agenda and goal. The devil and his demons calculatingly weave together the various mindsets of the world and our sinful nature so that they work in tandem against us. The Commander used this very battle to open my spiritual eyes to the territorial strongholds constructed by the kingdom of darkness.

Biblical Glimpses into the Spiritual Realm

There are spiritual forces of good and evil in the invisible domain all around us. The Word of God gives us glimpses of angelic warriors in the kingdom of heaven and the spiritual forces of evil in the unseen realm. Whether we recognize it or not, there is a fierce fight taking place all around us. Daniel, a prophet of God, inquired of the Lord for wisdom with prayer and fasting. After three weeks, an angel came to him to deliver a message: *"The prince of the kingdom of Persia withstood me twenty-one days, but Michael, one of the chief princes, came to help me, for I was left there with the kings of Persia, and came to make you understand what is to happen to your people in the latter days"* (Daniel 10:13-14). Before the angel left he said, *"But now I will return to fight against the prince of Persia; and when I go out, behold, the prince of Greece will come. But I will tell you what is inscribed in the book of truth: there is none who contends by my side against these except Michael, your prince"* (Daniel 10:20-21). This angelic messenger from God had been in an intense battle against the principalities of darkness presiding over the region of Persia. For twenty-one days he was unable to get away until Michael, one of the chief angelic princes, came to his aid so that he could deliver the message of God to Daniel. He goes on to explain to Daniel that his battle is far from over and he will return to fight against the prince of Persia, and that even the prince of Greece will come. These are the rulers, authorities, cosmic powers and spiritual forces of evil in the heavenly places.

In 2 Kings we get another look at the invisible angelic armies of God. The prophet Elisha and his servant awakened early one morning to discover that their city was surrounded by an enemy with horses and chariots. Seeing that there was no chance of escape, the servant became fearful.

> *"Alas, my master! What shall we do?" He (Elisha) said, "Do not be afraid, for those who are with us are more than those who are with them." Then Elisha prayed and said, "O Lord, please open his eyes that he may see." So the Lord opened the eyes of the young man, and he saw, and behold, the mountain was full of horses and chariots of fire all around Elisha. (2 Kings 6:15b-17)*

The horses and chariots of fire were the unseen angelic armies of the kingdom of heaven sent to protect Elisha. His servant was unable to see them until the Lord opened his spiritual eyes.

The Word of God reveals to us that there are well-organized forces in the invisible realm, with different levels of rank, degrees of power, positions and assignments in the kingdom of heaven and kingdom of darkness. When Jesus walked this earth and entered various towns, He was met by these unseen forces. Some territories welcomed and received Him wholeheartedly while others rejected Him and His ability to save them, even pleading with Him to leave. Mankind's openness to the gospel of Jesus Christ is influenced by the dominating forces of good or evil residing over the area.

> *In their case the god of this world has blinded the minds of the unbelievers, to keep them from seeing the light of the gospel of the glory of Christ, who is the image of God. For what we*

proclaim is not ourselves, but Jesus Christ as Lord, with ourselves as your servants for Jesus' sake. For God, who said, "Let light shine out of darkness," has shone in our hearts to give the light of the knowledge of the glory of God in the face of Jesus Christ. (2 Corinthians 4:4-6)

Territorial Stronghold of Darkness

In the book of Mark, the author describes an incident that happened when Jesus and his disciples entered the region of the Gerasenes. As soon as Jesus stepped off the boat he was met by a man who was bound by a powerful evil spirit. This demonized man fell down before Jesus, and crying with a loud voice said,

"What have you to do with me, Jesus, Son of the Most High God? I adjure you by God, do not torment me." For he was saying to him, "Come out of the man, you unclean spirit!" And Jesus asked him, "What is your name?" He replied, "My name is Legion, for we are many." And he begged him earnestly not to send them out of the country. (Mark 5: 7-10)

The spirit that tormented this man immediately recognized that Jesus was the Son of God. This spirit of darkness was consumed by fear knowing that Jesus, the Creator of all, completely trumped his authority in this region. In this encounter this vile spirit revealed to Jesus that he was called Legion, meaning "many." This wasn't a small or insignificant presence, but rather a demonic stronghold of darkness that kept the people in this area in bondage. Legion also greatly feared that Jesus would force him to depart from this particular country, his home. He begged Jesus not to send him out of this area because it was his abode of rank and strength, his personal fortified area of darkness here on Earth. Jesus allowed him to stay in the area but cast him out of this man, setting him free from the grip of the evil spirit. When Legion came out of the man, he went into a herd of pigs, causing the entire herd to run off a cliff to their death.

*The herdsmen fled and told it in the city and in the country.
And people came to see what it was that had happened. And
they came to Jesus and saw the demon-possessed man, the one
who had had the legion, sitting there, clothed and in his right
mind, and they were afraid. And those who had seen it
described to them what had happened to the demon-possessed
man and to the pigs. And they began to beg Jesus to depart
from their region. (Mark 5:14-17)*

Instead of being overjoyed that the local crazy man was now in
his right mind and had been set free from the demonic spirit, the
people rejected Jesus and begged Him to leave their town. From
this passage we can see that this country was an area dominated
by spiritual darkness that kept the people in fear and sin. This
oppression prevented them from recognizing and receiving
Jesus.

Territorial Stronghold of Sexual Immorality

There are times when a certain physical area is occupied by a
particular demonic stronghold. The devil seeks to gain an
entrance through the sins of people, past and present, and build
up his influence there. If it is a place where much sin abounds,
then it is very possibly an area dominated by demonic forces. It
could be a concentration of evil with a strong presence of
division, sexual immorality, materialism, addictions, or even
sickness and disease. There are times we will be able to discern
if we are in a territorial stronghold of evil simply by paying
attention to our mind battles. Some time ago my family and I
took a road trip across the United States. Having started early in
the morning, we stopped for lunch and then began the
afternoon stretch. The kids had settled in their car seats with
their blankies, so I closed my eyes for a quick rest while my
husband took his turn at the wheel. Instead of dozing off, I
found myself thinking some bizarre sexual thoughts. These
thoughts weren't normal thoughts for me or even a familiar
mind battle. Then I started to remember movies I had watched
years ago with "that one bad scene in it." Instead of pushing
those thoughts away, I had an unusually strong desire to replay

those sexual scenes in my mind. I tried fighting these thoughts but the urge to give in and let my thoughts take me down this path was remarkably strong. In that moment, I had to make a decision: Do I indulge in a sexual fantasy and experience the shame of my sin? Or do I ask the Commander for help? Taking a deep breath and throwing off the mental fog, I asked Jesus for help.

It was then that He brought to light the different billboards along the highway advertising adult video/book stores. Thinking back to the past hour, I realized we had passed four or five of these advertisements as well as the stores that were easily accessed from the interstate. For there to be so many adult stores within such a short distance of each other meant there must be a large clientele. I began to understand that in the spiritual realm this was a breeding ground for lust, impurity and sexual perversion that targeted the people passing. That is why my mind battle was so strong—I was being targeted as I traveled through this area. Though I would never dream of stopping at one of these stores, I was still being attacked by the territorial presence of this stronghold of sexual immorality. The initial impure thoughts triggered old memories in my mind of the sexual scenes in movies I had allowed myself to see. The enemy took advantage of any agreement I had previously given to this sin in order to trip me up as I passed through this territory.

Territorial Place of Light

God's Word tells us in John chapter 4 that Jesus entered a town of Samaria called Sychar, where He met a woman at the well. In the midst of their conversation, Jesus revealed to her that he was the long awaited Messiah. In that short interaction her eyes were opened and she wholeheartedly received Jesus as Savior, running off to tell the whole town about Him. Scripture says that as a result, *"Many Samaritans from that town believed in him because of the woman's testimony, 'He told me all that I ever did.' So when the Samaritans came to him, they asked him to stay with them, and he stayed there two days" (John 4:39-40)*. The doors were wide open as the people came to Jesus and asked Him to stay with them. Why is it that the region of Gerasenes was so closed to Jesus while the town of Sychar was so open to Him? I believe the answer lies in this next verse. While the woman at the well went to tell the town about Jesus, He took a moment to teach something to His disciples:

> "Look, I tell you, lift up your eyes, and see that the fields are white for harvest. Already the one who reaps is receiving wages and gathering fruit for eternal life, so that sower and reaper may rejoice together. For here the saying holds true, 'One sows and another reaps.' I sent you to reap that for which you did not labor. Others have labored, and you have entered into their labor." (John 4:35b-38)

Jesus tells His disciples that others have labored in the town of Sychar by sowing seeds beforehand. As a result, Jesus and His disciples were reaping a harvest of souls into His kingdom for eternal life. This territory and the people who lived there were open to the gospel and ready to embrace Jesus because it was an area prepped for the gospel. Unseen forces of angelic warriors were pushing back the kingdom of darkness so that these people would be able to see the Savior of their souls—they were hungry and ready for Jesus, the Messiah. The whole territory came to see Jesus, put their faith in Him and begged Him to stay with them.

Spiritual Battleground

The Apostle Paul experienced this same spiritual warfare as he went from town to town preaching about Christ. Some areas were hostile to the message of Christ and violently persecuted Paul. Other areas welcomed his message with open arms and many were saved. After Paul faced much discouragement with areas closed to the gospel, the Lord came to him and encouraged him with these words,

> And the Lord said to Paul one night in a vision, "Do not be afraid, but go on speaking and do not be silent, for I am with you, and no one will attack you to harm you, for I have many

in this city who are my people." And he stayed a year and six months, teaching the word of God among them. (Acts 18:9-11)

God is telling Paul that in this city He has many of His own followers who obey His commands and host the Holy Spirit within their hearts. Spiritually speaking, there was a breakthrough of invisible angelic forces that ensured Paul's safety in the midst of the darkness. Wherever we live, we can walk in and out of places—schools, stores, offices, restaurants—that experience this unseen battle of spiritual forces. This is our mission . . . *"And this gospel of the kingdom will be proclaimed throughout the whole world as a testimony to all nations, and then the end will come" (Matthew 24:14).* We are not here simply to enjoy life and survive the onslaught of attacks against us but rather to join others in pushing back the kingdom of darkness wherever we go, obtaining our orders from the Commander, remaining alert and fighting offensively through prayer.

Territorial Strongholds

There are times the Commander will alert us to the ruling territorial spirits over a place so that we do not fall victim to their attacks. There is a favorite spot my family likes to frequent on vacation. It's a beautiful, sunny, resort area that caters to retirees, vacationers, and seasonal residents who winter there. Anything that money can buy is available in this area because the majority of people who visit here have time and money to spare, or at least live like they do. Our first time there, the Lord revealed to me a ruling spirit of selfishness over the area. There is a strong mindset of entitlement and indulgence that says, *I've worked hard; now it's time for ME.* Of course, not everyone in this area is affected by this mindset but the temptation is definitely there. You wake up in the morning and decide what you want to do based on how you feel. There are so many options to choose from—you can walk the beach, sit by the pool, go to a nice restaurant, shop, get pampered at the salon, read a book or take in a local attraction. The worldly voice of the area says, *I deserve to do what I want to do, eat where I want to eat, and have the best of the things I enjoy.* Without my being aware of it, this worldly mindset was starting to affect my way of thinking. If I didn't get to go to a certain restaurant I would pout, or if the server was taking just a little too long, I'd get impatient. One day when my family arrived at the pool, it was quite busy and there were a limited number of vacant lounge chairs. I found myself disgruntled at people's selfishness as they took up more chairs than they needed, often leaving their belongings for hours while they were nowhere to be found. This left other people sitting on the ground or having to go elsewhere to find a place to sunbathe. Instead of being grateful and overjoyed at simply being on vacation with my family, I mentally focused on those selfish people, judging them for taking up all the chairs to hold their bags, towels, and sunglasses.

I found myself getting to the pool earlier the next day to seize a good spot, reserving more lounge chairs than I needed just in case I wanted to move when the direction of the sun changed. What was happening to me? I was blind to my own selfishness because I was so focused on judging others, and it was robbing me of my peace and joy. Now, when my family goes back to this vacation destination, I am aware of the ruling spirits of selfishness and indulgence in the area and ask the Lord to put a guard over my mind. I also fight, using the spiritual weapons of gratitude and thankfulness, praying for others to be blessed as they enjoy their vacations.

Forces of Good and Evil at War

At times the Commander will give us discernment to alert us to what is happening in the spiritual realm. We must pay attention to our thoughts and the different lies that come at us as we move in and out of different areas, not only for our spiritual protection but also to know our assignments. Some places are hostile to us as carriers of the life of Christ and other places are open and welcoming. There are areas of demonic activity in places that can affect us, attack us or rile the Holy Spirit within us. There are areas where the sin of division, disunity, rivalry, hatred, or discord is dominant and controls people on various levels in their relationships, marriages, employment, churches, and schools. We need discernment to be aware, alert and watchful so that we do not fall into the trap of the enemy.

Several years ago while visiting a church in another town, I immediately connected with the people as we worshipped God together. However, when the pastor began to give his message, I experienced a mind battle I didn't initially recognize. At first a wave of fatigue came over me and I felt like I could barely keep my eyes open. I had to stifle a few yawns and physically shake my head a few times just to stay awake. It was a fight to pay attention to what the pastor was saying. When I focused I could tell that it was a good message, delivered with clarity, conviction and love. But each time I engaged in the message I again drifted off mentally, tuning out his words and becoming distracted by trivial things. I contemplated what I wanted for lunch after the service. I lost a full five minutes envisioning myself in the Chinese food buffet line, selecting my favorite things to eat. *I wonder how much longer the pastor is going to preach, because I'm hungry!* Once I realized what I was thinking, I chided myself and forced all my attention back to the pastor. I could tell he was a gifted speaker and was preaching a vital, life-giving message of freedom . . . The next thing I knew I was gawking at the architecture of the building and admiring the beams on the ceiling. *I wonder what year this building was built?* Snapping back to the sermon, I thought, *What is my problem?*

I wanted to pay attention to what the pastor was saying but for the life of me I couldn't concentrate. Once I realized I was being attacked by one distraction after another I used my weapon of prayer and made contact with the Commander, asking Him to protect my mind from any outside forces of evil that were feeding me these thoughts to distract me from the message of the gospel. I experienced immediate relief as the Lord blocked the attacks and alerted me to what was going on in the spiritual realm. Once I was able to pay attention I started to look around with spiritual eyes at the people in the congregation. I noticed that some looked distracted, bored or even zoned out. Some were sneaking glances at their watches or trying not to nod off.

It was almost like I could sense the congregation was just being tolerant of the message, politely enduring it until the pastor was finished. This made me wonder if they were getting hit with the same spiritual attacks that I had experienced. As soon as the sermon was done I could "see" and "feel" a waking up of the people as the oppression of the demonic distractions lifted.

With the weapon of divine discernment I could see that God had gifted this congregation with a leader who was anointed to preach the truth. The pastor was preaching the pure and powerful Word of God but the devil's counterattack was to make sure that the truth didn't penetrate the hearts and minds of the congregation. I could sense this was not the first time this had happened to this congregation. Later, alone with my Commander, He gave me a specific prayer for this pastor and his church. It was then that God revealed to me that this wasn't just a chance visit to this church, but an opportunity to join in spiritual warfare on behalf of my brothers and sisters in Christ.

Jesus Will Build His Church Through Us

Jesus promised that He would build His church. I cling to and rest on this promise. But I also join Him in this work as I daily receive His instructions. *"And I tell you, you are Peter, and on this rock I will build my church, and the gates of hell shall not prevail against it" (Matthew 16:18).* This verse depicts the gates of hell as being unable to succeed against the aggressive attack of the body of Christ. Those bound in darkness and destined for hell do not have to stay locked up as the church—that's you and me—violently push against its doors. You may ask why the church is storming the gates of hell. We are going after our inheritance! The souls of the saints are the inheritance of the Lord. As co-heirs with Christ, His inheritance is our inheritance. He invites us to join Him in going after the lost, sowing seeds of prayer, proclaiming truth and pushing back the enemy, so that He can transfer people out of the kingdom of darkness and into His kingdom of light. We need to know our battle positions and our assignments so that we may bring Christ into the places in which we live, shop, and frequent. We must have the mindsets of warriors, not just able to defend ourselves when we get attacked, but on the lookout any time the Commander wants us to push back the gates of hell. Often we don't have to go out of our way to plant seeds of prayer or reap a harvest. Everywhere we go we need to be asking the Commander, "Why am I here? What do You want me to see?"

> *You are the light of the world. A city set on a hill cannot be hidden. Nor do people light a lamp and put it under a basket, but on a stand, and it gives light to all in the house. In the same way, let your light shine before others, so that they may see your good works and give glory to your Father who is in heaven. (Matthew 5:14-16)*

Recently my church organized a "Love Your City" community outreach that involved sending teams of families and individuals to schools, parks and retirement homes to complete various service projects. My family was part of a team sent to a thirty-five-year-old ball park on the outskirts of town. Our assignment was to paint doors, stain wood and replace the boards on the bleachers. I found myself working next to a woman who had invested years of her life at this ball park and who was a key voice in lobbying for its renovation. She welcomed our team wholeheartedly and enthusiastically told me about the fundraising that enabled the community to put in the playground equipment and the new splash pad. Walking the grounds, I was impressed with the design and layout of the park and was surprised at how many people were there enjoying the facility. The park had a sense of community pride, unity and safety that reminded me of my childhood. As I walked around I was positively drawn to the park and had the desire to come back for a family picnic on a sunny summer day. This woman I had just met began to share with me her future dreams for the park. During the conversation she briefly mentioned that she had a degree in a certain field but wasn't using it because apparently God had other plans for her, one of them being the renovation of this community park.

It was then I realized this wasn't just a side project for this woman. It was a God-birthed, prayer-soaked dream and assignment for her. I knew that my teammates and I weren't there simply to paint and stain wood but also to encourage this woman and sow seeds of prayer over this park. Clearly God had a purpose and a plan for this territory and I could sense in my spirit His favor already evident over this park. The invisible forces of good were prevailing here and I prayed that God would continue to set up a guard of angelic warriors all around the perimeter of the park to ban the evil one from this place. I asked the Lord that this place would be a haven of safety, relaxation, laughter, relationship-building, and family time for the people in this community for many years to come.

Everywhere Your Foot Steps

Listen to the words that the Commander gave to the mighty warrior Joshua.

> I will give you every place where you set your foot, as I promised Moses. Your territory will extend from the desert to Lebanon, and from the great river, the Euphrates—all the Hittite country—to the Great Sea on the west. No one will be able to stand up against you all the days of your life. As I was with Moses, so I will be with you; I will never leave you nor forsake you. Be strong and courageous, because you will lead these people to inherit the land I swore to their forefathers to give them. Be strong and very courageous. Be careful to obey all the law my servant Moses gave you; do not turn from it to the right or to the left, that you may be successful wherever you go. Do not let this Book of the Law depart from your mouth; meditate on it day and night, so that you may be careful to do everything written in it. Then you will be prosperous and successful. Have I not commanded you? Be strong and courageous. Do not be terrified; do not be discouraged, for the Lord your God will be with you wherever you go. (Joshua 1:3-9 NIV)

When the people of God went out to claim the territory that God had given them, they had to fight for it. It was theirs because God had declared it to be so, but the enemy was still occupying their God-given inheritance. The same is true for us. In their case, their inheritance was land for which they were instructed to fight. In our case, we fight for the souls of people.

We too have been given this commission. Everywhere we set our feet God will give us the land as our inheritance. It is the people, our future brothers and sisters in Christ for whom fight, that are our spiritual inheritance. Our territory is the neighborhood we live in, the church we attend, and the places where we shop. There is a divine reason that we live in the house that we do, work at the job we have and frequent our favorite coffee shop or restaurant. Yes, we need a house and a job and a place to shop, but it is so much more than that. There is a spiritual purpose as well and it is the priority here. It's not all about us.

Perhaps you moved into a subdivision that is dominated by an unseen presence of addictions, or you have a job at a company that has bought into the worldly mindset of fame and success. What if you work next to a person who struggles with a stronghold of rebellion and they are constantly talking down the authority figures in their lives, including your boss? You need to be aware of their battle so that your co-worker's unrecognized battle doesn't get a foothold in your thinking. You need to be ready for the lying spirits and the mind battles that you might find yourself fighting against in these places—not just to protect yourself but also to pray protection over others and usher in the Spirit of God that is inside of you.

An example of this in the Bible is the apostle Paul. He was a tent-maker by trade, but his *real* job was proclaiming and spreading the Word of God everywhere he was sent. Say you're a soccer mom, spending hours at games and carpooling players all over town. That's just your cover job; your *real* assignment is to pray over and invest Christ into the players and families with whom you interact, having godly discernment to see the spiritual warfare all around you. It is the people of God who host the divine presence of Jesus that brings forth the kingdom of heaven in this world. We are on assignment!

The Commander has sent me to join prayer teams at my kids' school and with ministries in my community and church. He has instructed me to prayer-walk in my neighborhood and frequent different businesses in order to encourage and pray a covering of protection or blessing over those places. After having been involved with a school for eight years, investing hours of time and prayers there, God is reassigning our family to a new school and neighborhood. On the surface, it may simply look like a change of a school and a new address but spiritually speaking it is a reassignment for us in the armies of God. Even now I'm asking the Commander, *What do you want me to see? What do you want me to know? How do I pray? Why here? Why now?* I will wait on the Commander and I am confident that He will let me know when I need to know.

Faithfully Fighting Our Daily Battles

As I stated at the beginning of this book, my intent is to help us become aware of the attacks of the enemy and learn how to **defend** ourselves against his attacks, standing firm as we engage in this spiritual war. However, this is only half of the training. Yes, we must learn how to defend ourselves but we must not stop there. The Commander must train us how to fight **offensively** and reclaim the territory for His glory and His kingdom. As warriors in the armies of God we are to live with the mindset of advancing the kingdom of heaven wherever we go. This is our fight and we must own it! *"From the days of John the Baptist until now the kingdom of heaven has suffered violence, and the violent take it by force"* (Matthew 11:12). It says the violent take it by force—those who are focused, intense, bold, strong, fearless, skilled, confident and fixed upon the victory. If we have never thought of a Christian as being a violent person, then maybe we need to rethink this and allow the Commander to renew our minds.

When I breathe deeply of my new nature I can feel this holy, righteous, aggressive fight in me. I *want* to fight and I *want* to win! I don't want to stand on the sidelines and watch others accomplish valiant deeds in this spiritual battle—I want to be in the thick of it. The old Kori can be a bit competitive and she selfishly doesn't like to lose at cards, but that is nothing compared to this violent anger I feel against the enemies of my God and Commander! I am jealous for His glory to be known and seen by all. I so badly want people to know Him, but even more than that I want Him to be known. He is worthy of it.

In all our training to learn how to defend ourselves against the attacks of the enemy we must never lose sight of the fact that the war is way bigger than our own personal battles. If our main goal as soldiers is simply to be safe and remain alive, chances are we could be excessively cautious, fearful and self-consumed in this fight. This is not how we are to be.

> *Therefore do not throw away your confidence, which has a great reward. For you have need of endurance, so that when you have done the will of God you may receive what is promised. For, "Yet a little while, and the coming one will come and will not delay; but my righteous one shall live by faith, and if he shrinks back, my soul has no pleasure in him." But we are not of those who shrink back and are destroyed, but of those who have faith and preserve their souls. (Hebrews 10:35-39)*

This is why we cannot do this fight alone. If we try, we simply won't make it. Many have gone before us and many will come after us to struggle, fight and forcefully advance the kingdom— but for now it's our turn. Someday we will rest from this fight, but until then, we keep on fighting. We fight with all the strength that our Commander provides for us. My prayer for us is that we will finish strong to the very end, unto our last dying breath, bringing our God the highest glory possible with our lives and joining the Apostle Paul in saying,

"I have fought the good fight, I have finished the race, I have kept the faith. Henceforth there is laid up for me the crown of righteousness, which the Lord, the righteous judge, will award to me on that Day, and not only to me but also to all who have loved his appearing" (2 Timothy 4:7-8).

Prayer:

Dear Father,
You created the Earth; all that is in it is Yours, reflecting Your magnificent glory. The seas are Yours because you made them and formed the dry land with Your own hands. What a beautiful and well-suited planet You have given us. Even with the beauty surrounding us, still creation is imperfect and our enemy desires to spoil and steal glory, all of which is due to You! He seeks to deceive me in an attempt to lure me away from You. Now that I know enemy forces occupy certain places, please show me where those places are in my life. Tune my spiritual ears and eyes to reveal the hidden schemes of the enemy. Lord, help me to soundly defeat my enemies, that I may gain more freedom in my life.
In Jesus' name, Amen.

Action Steps: Journal your prayers, answers and all the things the Commander reveals to you.

1. In prayer and by searching through Scripture, ask the Lord to reveal to you any spirits that have claimed your home as their territory. After they have been revealed, use your authority in Christ to remove them from your home. You may need to repeat this process over the course of the next month or so.

2. Spend time in prayer, asking the Lord if any of these territorial spirits gained entry through sin, watching certain movies, reading certain books, playing certain games, etc. When the Lord shows you these

things, confess them to the Lord and repent. Then remove them from your home.

3. As you go about your life over the next few weeks, pay attention to your thoughts. What do you think about at the grocery store? What about the mall? Do you fall into certain thought patterns after visiting certain restaurants or friends? It may well be that certain spirits hang around these places of business or people. Once you are aware of them, you will know how to prepare ahead of time, making you less susceptible to the enemy's tactics.

4. When you become aware of territorial strongholds in areas where you live and interact, be proactive in praying for wisdom and protection. You might pray this prayer:

Dear Father,
Thank You that You have made a way for me to be in the world but not of it. I want to be a light in the darkness that advances Your kingdom and brings You great glory. Protect me from the evil that is all around me by the power of Your blood. Help me be aware of, but not taken out by, the whispering lies of the evil one that reside in the places I live, work, walk and where You send me. I trust You when You say that "greater is He that is in me than he that is in the world." Grant me Your angelic warriors to be on all sides of me so that I may accomplish the assignment You have for me in the midst of this present darkness.
In Jesus' name, Amen.

Chapter Fifteen
The Battle Plan

You then, my son, be strong in the grace that is in Christ Jesus. And the things you have heard me say in the presence of many witnesses entrust to reliable men who will also be qualified to teach others. Join with me in suffering, like a good soldier of Christ Jesus. No one serving as a soldier gets entangled in civilian affairs, but rather tries to please his commanding officer.
2 Timothy 2:1-4 NIV

Every good soldier must have an action plan in place before the battle comes, and the same is true for us as warriors in the armies of God. I cannot emphasize this enough. To recognize the battle is one thing, but to train and prepare so that you may be ready for it is a sign of a mighty warrior. So the question is: What is your biggest battle right now? Is it a relationship, job, finances, resentment, or fears about the future? We must know ourselves and the various areas in our minds that take us down a mudslide.

We are constantly changing and so are our circumstances. Our battle last week may not be our battle today or three years from now. We need the Commander to help us daily, moment by moment, year by year. We will gain victory over some conflicts and rarely have to face them again, but others will come back to test us again and again. So what's your battle plan? You must have one. This chapter is designed as an interactive, face-to-face time spent alone with your Commander. Together, you will identify your specific struggles and put in place a Battle Plan *before* the fight hits. This will take some time and effort on your part but it will be well worth it. Like getting up early to go to the gym, it will require you to prioritize and endure, but the benefit comes later when the battle hits. I am not asking you to do anything that I wouldn't, so after I wrote this chapter I personally walked through each section, inviting the Commander to examine my life right where I am now. The examples I give throughout the book came from the things He revealed to me as I waited on Him to expose the hidden lies I have believed and reveal the truth.

Writing out a Battle Plan is necessary because it helps you define your fight and train in advance with the most effective weapons to help you be victorious. Also, when we are surrounded by dark lies, we can tend to forget everything we have previously learned. I'm not sure how this happens but it has happened to me so often I have learned to anticipate it. When the Battle Plan is written out, complete with the lies I've believed and the Scripture to counter those lies, it's like a lifeline and usually cuts the duration of the battle by half. You could think of it as building a spiritual "playbook" to counter the plays the enemy runs on you. It is not a once-and-done project, but rather a continual process of learning how to meet with your Commander and get your instructions from Him.

In asking the following questions, don't try to think through them by yourself. Invite the Commander into your mind to answer them with you. It can be hard and exhausting to answer questions that pertain to the heart. They require deep thinking, listening, and sometimes remembering painful memories, but the One who lives in us knows all and is completely trustworthy. Ask Him. It may surprise you that He has a lot to say directly to you, in a very personal way.

Start with the Spiritual Weapon of Prayer:

Dear Father,

Thank You for being my Commander and leading me into truth and victory. I ask You to examine my life and answer these questions for me. Join me in this process. I wait for Your voice to help me see the battle and put together a Battle Plan that will be the most effective way to fight the battles You allow to come my way. Help me to be faithful and complete this Battle Plan so that when the battle comes, I will know what to do.

In Jesus' name, Amen.

Worldly Mindsets

See to it that no one takes you captive by philosophy and empty deceit, according to human tradition, according to the elemental spirits of the world, and not according to Christ. For in him the whole fullness of deity dwells bodily, and you have been filled in him, who is the head of all rule and authority. (Colossians 2:8-10)

Identify the Battle: Jesus, what worldly standard or human tradition have I believed in the past that You want to bring to the surface right now?

_____

_____

_____

Jesus, what are the specific lies/bondage that Satan wants me to believe and remain stuck in, instead of being filled with Christ in those areas?

_____

_____

_____

Lord, lead me to truth. What is one passage of Scripture that counters this lie?

_____

_____

_____

Jesus, speak to my heart: What is true about me as a citizen of the kingdom of heaven?

_____

_____

_____

What spiritual weapons do I have that will most effectively help me win this battle *when* it comes at me?

_____

_____

_____

Worldly Cravings

Do not love the world or the things in the world. If anyone loves the world, the love of the Father is not in him. For all that is in the world —the desires of the flesh and the desires of the eyes and pride in possessions—is not from the Father but is from the world. And the world is passing away along with its desires, but whoever does the will of God abides forever. (1 John 2:15-17)

For the grace of God has appeared, bringing salvation for all people, training us to renounce ungodliness and worldly passions, and to live self-controlled, upright, and godly lives in the present age, waiting for our blessed hope, the appearing of the glory of our great God and Savior Jesus Christ, who gave himself for us to redeem us from all lawlessness and to purify for himself a people for his own possession who are zealous for good works. (Titus 2:11-14)

But far be it from me to boast except in the cross of our Lord Jesus Christ, by which the world has been crucified to me, and I to the world. (Galatians 6:14)

Identify the Battle: Jesus, what things in this world am I drawn to, do I crave and desire to consume, instead of You?

_____

_____

_____

Lord, please show me what triggers that desire. Am I bored, tired, overwhelmed, or feeling needy for comfort, excitement, or safety?

_____

_____

_____

Lord, has this thing become an addiction or stronghold for me? *(If you don't know, try giving it up for two weeks; then you'll know!)*

_____

_____

_____

Jesus, reveal to me the core desire I have tried to meet by repeatedly going to this thing in the world.

_____

_____

_____

Jesus, what is the truth? How have You provided for this desire/need in my life?

_____

_____

_____

What are some Scriptures and Spiritual Weapons You want me to use to counter this lie and win this battle when it comes my way?

_____

_____

_____

Fleshly Attitudes

So be done with every trace of wickedness (depravity, malignity) and all deceit and insincerity (pretense, hypocrisy) and grudges (envy, jealousy) and slander and evil speaking of every kind. Like newborn babies you should crave (thirst for, earnestly desire) the pure (unadulterated) spiritual milk, that by it you may be nurtured and grow unto [completed] salvation. (1Peter 2:1-2 AMP)

Identify the Battle: Jesus, what is a "trigger" in my life that results in the awakening of my old nature?

_____

_____

_____

Lord, take me back to those feelings. Why do I respond this way? Show me what desire or goal is being blocked.

_____

_____

_____

Help me understand why this is so important to me. Reveal to me the need I am trying to meet in my flesh. Am I trying to get others around me to meet my needs and wants?

_____

_____

_____

Jesus, show me what lies I am believing about myself. Do I have a false understanding of who You are? What is the Scripture that counters the lie?

_____

_____

_____

As I grab hold of the truth, what are some Spiritual Weapons that will help me fight this battle when that "trigger" shows up again?

_____

_____

_____

Fleshly Motives

For whenever there is jealousy (envy) and contention (rivalry and selfish ambition), there will also be confusion (unrest, disharmony, rebellion) and all sorts of evil and vile practices. (James 3:16 AMP)

[Or] you do ask [God for them] and yet fail to receive, because you ask with wrong purpose and evil, selfish motives. Your intention is [when you get what you desire] to spend it in sensual pleasure. (James 4:3 AMP)

Identify the Battle: Lord, what is one thing in my life right now that I am doing or even asking for that is rooted in a fleshly, selfish motive? Show me so that I may confess it and be set free to do and desire what is good. _Write down whatever He brings to your mind and examine it together. Ask questions._

_____

_____

_____

Jesus, show me truth. As a new creation in Christ, what is my old nature fighting for that has already been settled because of my position as a child of God?

_____

_____

_____

What Spiritual Weapons do I need to employ that will help me every time I am tempted to meet the needs of my flesh in this area?

_____

_____

_____

Generational Strongholds

"'The Lord is slow to anger and abounding in steadfast love, forgiving iniquity and transgression, but he will by no means clear the guilty, visiting the iniquity of the fathers on the children, to the third and the fourth generation.' Please pardon the iniquity of this people, according to the greatness of your steadfast love, just as you have forgiven this people, from Egypt until now." (Numbers 14:18-19)

Identify the Battle: Jesus, show me any evil spirits that have influence on my family line because of the sins of my forefathers. *Allow Him to bring to mind any recurring behaviors or attitudes that could possibly be a generational stronghold. Write them down.*

_____

_____

_____

Lord, help me identify the specific ways in which I have been deceived and have been taken captive by the evil one as a result of the sin I have committed.

_____

_____

_____

Now use the Spiritual Weapon of repentance and pray the
following prayer **out loud:**

**Dear Father,I choose to confess and repent of the sin of
_____ (name the sin) that I and my
forefathers have committed against you. This sin has been in
my family for too long. I accept and receive Your forgiveness
for _____ (name the sin) in regard to me
and my family members. I trust You to cleanse me from all
unrighteousness as You have promised in 1 John 1:9. Because I
have submitted myself to You, I take my authority in Christ
and command this evil presence to be removed from my life
and the lives of my descendants. Jesus, I ask that You take all
of the demonic influence that has gained access to me through
this sin and do with them whatever You please. You have said
in Your Word that vengeance is Yours and that You will repay
the evil those demonic forces have caused me. Lord, I ask that
You come in to heal and fill up all the empty places in my life
so that I may be deeply rooted in You.
In Jesus' name, Amen.**

Lord, now that You have cleansed me from this sin and expelled
the enemy from my life, help me to stand firm and continually
resist him. Show me the best Spiritual Weapons I will need to
maintain my freedom.

_____

_____

_____

_____

_____

_____

Territorial Strongholds

The man saw Jesus at a distance. So he ran to Jesus, bowed down in front of him, and shouted, "Why are you bothering me now, Jesus, Son of the Most High God? Swear to God that you won't torture me." He shouted this because Jesus said, "You evil spirit, come out of the man." Jesus asked him, "What is your name?" He told Jesus, "My name is Legion [Six Thousand], because there are many of us." He begged Jesus not to send them out of the territory. (Mark 5:6-10)

But the end and culmination of all things has now come near; keep sound minded and self-restrained and alert therefore for [the practice] of prayer. (1 Peter 4:7 AMP)

So Jesus called them over to him and began to speak to them in parables: "How can Satan drive out Satan? If a kingdom is divided against itself, that kingdom cannot stand. If a house is divided against itself, that house cannot stand. And if Satan opposes himself and is divided, he cannot stand; his end has come. In fact, no one can enter a strong man's house without first tying him up. Then he can plunder the strong man's house. (Mark 3:23-27 NIV)

Identify the Battle: Lord, show me any ruling territorial strongholds that reside over the places where I go, in order that I may be aware and pray. *Pay attention to any conversations, situations or themes that He is reminding you of right now. Write it down and ask Him questions, waiting for Him to make it clear to you.*

Jesus, is there a sin theme here in my home or neighbor-hood that I need to become aware of?

_____

_____

_____

What about my workplace?

_____

_____

_____

What about my school?

_____

_____

_____

What about my city?

_____

_____

_____

What about my church/ministry?

_____

_____

_____

What about my nation?

_____

_____

_____

*The Lord may or may not show you these things right now, but pay attention to His voice when you are interacting in these places. He will guide You and show you what you need to know.

The Spirit of Truth tells us these things so that we may not be taken captive by the devil and remain unaware of his schemes. He also shows us these things so that we may pray for others walking around in the darkness. Turn each of these answers into a prayer of protection for you and others.

Dear Father,I thank You for Your wisdom to me. I praise You that the darkness is not dark to You and You see clearly when I cannot see. Father, please command Your angelic spirits to come and set up a perimeter around the property lines of _____ (home, workplace, school, city, church,

ministry, or nation). I repent of and renounce the sins _____ (name any the Lord brings to mind) that we have committed against You, Lord, and cut off the power of those lies by the blood of Jesus. I ask that You send angels of far greater strength and rank to fight and defeat the demonic spirits residing over this place. I pray that You will confuse the efforts of the territorial stronghold in this area and transform it into a place of salvation. Lord, teach me how to pray and stand firm against the enemy forces in the heavenly realms. I pray Your shield of protection over my mind and thoughts as I enter into the places I work and travel. Help me to usher in the kingdom of heaven and be a light in the darkness through my prayers and my actions.

In Jesus' name, Amen.

Lord, what are some Spiritual Weapons that I need to have ready before I walk into these territories where sinful strongholds are present?

_____

_____

_____

_____

_____

_____

_____

References

Bright, Bill. *The Four Spritual Laws*. Campus Crusade for
    Christ, 1956. Print.

Freedom in Christ Ministries. n.d. Web. 2015. <https://
    www.ficm.org/>.

Lavigne, Avril. "Girlfriend." *The Best Damn Thing*. RCA,
    2007.

Ramsey, Dave. *Complete Guide to Money: The Handbook of
    Financial Peace University*. Brentwood, TN: Ramsey
    Press, The Lampo Group, Inc., 2011. Print.

"Truth Statements." n.d. *Freedom in Christ Ministries*. 2015.
    <https://www.ficm.org/wp-content/uploads/
    2013/04/Truth-Statements1.pdf>.

Acknowledgments

Craig—What an adventure the Lord has allowed us to go on together! You are a great man of God and I love to see Jesus in you. Thanks for being my best friend throughout it all.

Annika—Thanks for recognizing I was in a battle even before I realized it myself, and re-teaching me what I have taught you. You are a true joy to have as my daughter.

Ella—Thanks for still wanting to hang out with me. I love to go on dates with you and hear your heart. You are beautiful inside and out.

Darci—Thanks for believing in me and for all your delightful encouragement. You are so very understanding and speak words of great wisdom for one so young. I love you, sweetie.

Kyle—Thanks for all your prayers for me and promising to read my book . . . someday. You truly are a Mighty Warrior.

The Trierweiler family (from left to right)
Kyle Darci Kori Craig Ella Annika
[Photo credit: Dan and Melissa Clark]

Mom and Dad—Thanks for all your encouragement and support my entire life—especially all those times I called you crying because I wanted to quit. You listened, reminded me of the truth and prayed me through.

Vic and Donna Trierweiler—Thanks for all your love and the hours and hours of investment into my life. Thanks for opening up and sharing your relationship with Jesus with me. You both have taught me so much. And thanks for raising an amazing son.

Monday Gathering Ladies and Friends—What would I do without my friends? Thanks for listening, believing, praying, and asking about this book. I dearly love you ladies!

Prayer Team—Even though it took two years instead of the six months I wanted it to take, you kept faithfully praying me through the writing of this book. God's blessing back 100-fold on you for your persistent, relentless prayers. (That includes the Prayer Warriors in Medicine Lodge, KS too!)

Editors—You ought to know that I don't think of this book as "my book" but rather "our book." God knew I needed five editors and I am so grateful for every one of you.

Gayle—You came along at the perfect time, offering your services as an editor before I even knew I needed one. You were an answer to a prayer I had yet to pray. I love the way God made you and how much attention you gave to the details of this book. Thanks so much.

Anne—I am so humbled by your dedication, prayers, servant heart and hours of time spent to help me edit this book. Truly your race had not yet been run. May God give you many more years of investment into the kingdom of heaven . . . and please help on my next book!

Lisa—Your constant, steady support of encouragement, editing and prayers have been invaluable to me. You want to see this book get into the hands of spiritual warriors as much as I do. A simple "Thank you, friend," doesn't seem enough, but knowing you, it is!

Brenda—You did what I could not. You helped shaped this book, challenge my thinking, and clarify the message—everything I needed at just the right time. You are an excellent editor and I always thank God every time I think of you.

Sharilyn—I was neck-deep in a battle with discouragement when you came along and told me that the finish line was just up ahead. You reminded me that this book is needed and worth the effort. Thanks for cheering me on and running with me the last few miles of the journey.

Joe and Traci—I am so thankful that you got "out of the boat" and started Overboard Ministries. Your faith and desire to walk on the water with Jesus gave me the courage to step out of the boat too. I am so very thankful for your faith and friendship . . . and coffee. Thanks for taking a chance on a new author.

What is Overboard Books?

Overboard Books publishes quality books that are designed to assist in getting Christians overboard — out of the boat. It's the publishing arm of Overboard Ministries, whose mission is based on Matthew 14. In that chapter we find the familiar story of Jesus walking on water while His disciples were in a boat. It was the middle of the night, the water was choppy and Jesus freaked out His followers who thought He was a ghost. When they realized it was Him, Peter asked to come out to Him on the water, and he actually walked on top of the water like Jesus.

But what truly captivates me is thought of the other eleven disciples who remained in the boat. I've often wondered how many of them questioned that move in the years to come? How many of them wished they hadn't stayed in the boat but had instead gone overboard with Peter? Overboard Ministries aims to help Christians get out of boat and live life for Christ out on the water where He is. We hope and pray that each book published by Overboard Ministries will stir believers to jump overboard and live life all-out for God, full of joy and free from the regret of "I wish I had…"

What we do
Overboard Ministries emerged in the Spring of 2011 as an umbrella ministry for several concepts my wife and I were developing. One of those concepts was a book ministry that would help other Christian authors get published. I experienced a lot of frustration while passing my first manuscript around. I kept getting rejection letters that were kindly written, but each echoed the same sentiment: "We love this book. If you were already a published author, we would love to publish it." They were nice letters, but that didn't make the rejection any easier or the logic less frustrating.

Out of that came the audacious idea to start our own "publishing company." I put that in quotes because I want people to know a couple of things. First of all, we're not a traditional publishing company like most people envision when they hear the name. We don't have a printing press in our garage, and we don't have a marketing team. Basically, we're a middle-man who absorbs most of the cost of publishing in order to help you get published, while making sure the majority of profits end up in your pocket, not ours.

Our desire is to keep costs to a bare minimum for each author. (As of this writing, there is only a minimal contract fee when your manuscript is accepted.) We provide resources and ideas to help authors work on marketing, while also providing the editor and graphic design artist at our expense. We subcontract out the printing, which speeds up the time it takes to move from final draft to bound book. Since we don't have much overhead we can keep our expenses low, allowing seasoned authors, or first-time authors like me, the opportunity to profit from their writing. This makes it possible for authors to publish more books while continuing in their current jobs or ministries.

Contact us
If you are interested in other books or learning about other authors from Overboard Books, please visit our website at www.overboardministries.com and click on the "Overboard Books" link. If you are an author interested in publishing with us, please visit our site and check out the "Authors" tab. There you will find a wealth of information that will help you understand the publishing process and how we might be a good fit for you. If we're not a fit for you, we'll gladly share anything we've learned that might be helpful to you as you pursue publishing through other means.

Thank you
Thanks for supporting our work and ministry. If you believe this book was helpful to you, tell someone about it! Or better yet, buy them a copy of their own! We completely depend on word-of-mouth grassroots marketing to help spread the word about Overboard Ministries and its publications. Please share our

website with others and encourage them to purchase the materials that will help them live "overboard" lives for Christ.

May God bless you as you grab the side of boat, take a deep breath...and jump onto the sea!

Joe Castaneda
Founder, Overboard Ministries

ABOUT THE AUTHOR

Kori Trierweiler is a wife, mother, and Bible teacher who resides in Traverse City, Michigan. She attended Moody Bible Institute, where she met and married her husband, Craig, who is a pastor. She loves to teach about the love of her Lord and Savior, Jesus Christ. She felt a calling by God and, quite unwillingly, began to write. She is a mighty prayer warrior in the kingdom of heaven, and prays that this book would draw you closer to Christ. Kori is donating 100% of the profits of this book to reinvest in Kingdom work.

Made in the USA
Middletown, DE
24 May 2016